CROATIAN

PHRASEBOOK

Compiled by

LEXUS

www.roughguides.com

Credits

Compiled by Lexus with Zlatan Mir, Željka Levačić-Koren and
Ivana Peranić
Lexus Series Editor: Peter Terrell
Rough Guides Reference Director: Andrew Lockett
Rough Guides Series Editor: Mark Ellingham

This first edition published in 2006 by
Rough Guides Ltd,
80 Strand, London WC2R 0RL
345 Hudson St, 4th Floor, New York 10014, USA
Email: mail@roughguides.co.uk.

Distributed by the Penguin Group.

Penguin Books Ltd, 80 Strand, London WC2R 0RL
Penguin Putnam, Inc., 375 Hudson Street, NY 10014, USA
Penguin Group (Australia), 250 Camberwell Road, Camberwell,
Victoria 3124, Australia
Penguin Books Canada Ltd, 10 Alcorn Avenue, Toronto,
Ontario, Canada M4V 1E4
Penguin Group (New Zealand), Cnr Rosedale and Airborne Roads,
Albany, Auckland, New Zealand

Typeset in Bembo and Helvetica to an original design by Henry Iles.
Printed in Italy by LegoPrint S.p.A

British Library Cataloguing in Publication Data
A catalogue for this book is available from the British Library.

ISBN 13: 978-1-84353-645-1
ISBN 10: 1-84353-645-5

1 3 5 7 9 8 6 4 2

The publishers and authors have done their best to ensure the
accuracy and currency of all information in The Rough Guide
Croatian Phrasebook however, they can accept no responsibility
for any loss or inconvenience sustained by any reader using the
book.

Online information about Rough Guides can be
found at our website www.roughguides.com

CONTENTS

Introduction

The Rough Guide Croatian phrasebook is a highly practical introduction to the contemporary language. Laid out in clear A-Z style, it uses key-word referencing to lead you straight to the words and phrases you want – so if you need to book a room, just look up 'room'. The Rough Guide gets straight to the point in every situation, in bars and shops, on trains and buses, and in hotels and banks.

The main part of the Rough Guide is a double dictionary: English-Croatian then Croatian-English. Before that, there's a section called **Basic Phrases** and to get you involved in two-way communication, the Rough Guide includes a set of **Scenario** dialogues illustrating questions and responses in key situations such as renting a car and asking directions. You can hear these and then download them free from **www.rough-guides.com/phrasebooks** for use on your computer or MP3 player.

Forming the heart of the guide, the **English-Croatian** section gives easy-to-use transliterations of the Croatian words wherever pronunciation might be a problem. Throughout this section, cross-references enable you to pinpoint key facts and phrases, while asterisked words indicate where further information can be found in a section at the end of the book called **How the Language Works**. This section sets out the fundamental rules of the language, with plenty of practical examples. You'll also find here other essentials like numbers, dates, telling the time and basic phrases. In the **Croatian-English** dictionary, we've given you not just the phrases you'll be likely to hear (starting with a selection of slang and colloquialisms) but also many of the signs, labels, instructions and other basic words you may come across in print or in public places.

Near the back of the book too the Rough Guide offers an extensive **Menu Reader**. Consisting of food and drink sections (each starting with a list of essential terms), it's indispensable whether you're eating out, stopping for a quick drink, or browsing through a local food market.

sretan put!
have a good trip!

Basic
Phrases

yes
da

no
ne
[neh]

OK
u redu
[oo redoo]

hello
zdravo!
(on telephone)
halo

goodbye
zbogom

good evening
dobra večer
[vecher]

good morning
dobro jutro
[yootro]

good night
laku noć
[lakoo noch]

hi!
zdravo!

cheerio!
doviđenja!
[doveejenya]

please
molim
[moleem]

yes please
da, molim

thanks, thank you
hvala
[Hvala]

thank you very much
hvala lijepo
[l-yepo]

no thanks
ne, hvala
[neh]

that's OK, don't mention it
molim
[moleem]

how are you?
kako ste?
[steh]

fine, thanks, and you?
hvala, dobro, a vi?
[Hvala ...vee]

how do you do?
kako ste
[steh]

nice to meet you
drago mi je
[mee yeh]

8

excuse me
oprostite
[oprosteeteh]
(pardon?)
molim?
[moleem]

(I'm) sorry
oprostite!
[oprosteeteh]

sorry?
molim?
[moleem]

what?
što?
[shto]

I see
vidim
[veedeem]

I understand
razumijem
[razoomeeyem]

I don't understand
ne razumijem
[neh]

do you speak English?
govorite li engleski?
[govoreeteh lee engleskee]

I don't speak Croatian
ne govorim Hrvatskee
[neh govoreem Hervatskee]

could you say it slowly?
da li biste to mogli reći
sporiije?
[lee beesteh to moglee rechee
sporeeyeh]

could you repeat that?
da li biste mogli to ponoviti?
[lee beesteh moglee]

could you write it down?
možete li to zapisati?
[moJeteh lee to zapeesatee]

I'd like a ... (said by man/woman)
želio/željela bih ...
[Jeleeo/Jel-yela beeH]

I'd like to ...
želio/željela bih ...

can I have ...?
mogu li dobiti ...?
[mogoo lee dobeetee]

do you have ...?
imate li ...?
[eemateh lee]

how much is it?
koliko je to?
[koleeko yeh]

cheers!
živjeli!
[Jeev-yelee]

it is ...
to je
[yeh]

where is it?
gdje je to?
[gd-yeh]

where is the ...?
gdje je ...?

is it far from here?
je li to daleko?
[yeh lee]

what's the time?
koliko je sati?
[koleeko yeh satee]

Scenarios

1. Accommodation

is there an inexpensive hotel you can recommend?
▶ možete li mi preporučiti neki jeftin hotel?
[mo**J**eteh lee mee prepor**oo**cheetee n**e**kee y**e**fteen h**o**tel]

žao mi je, izgleda da su svi puni ◀
[**J**ao mee yeh **ee**zgleda da soo svee p**oo**nee]
I'm sorry, they all seem to be fully booked

can you give me the name of a good middle-range hotel?
▶ možete li mi reći za neki hotel srednje klase?
[mo**J**eteh lee mee r**e**chee za n**e**kee h**o**tel sr**e**dn-yeh kl**a**seh]

pogledat ću; želite li biti u središtu? ◀
[p**o**gledat choo **J**eleeteh lee b**ee**tee oo sr**e**deeshtoo]
let me have a look; do you want to be in the centre?

if possible
▶ ako je to moguće
[**a**ko yeh to mog**oo**cheh]

smeta li vam da budete malo izvan grada? ◀
[sm**e**ta lee vam da b**oo**deteh m**a**lo **ee**zvan gr**a**da]
do you mind being a little way out of town?

not too far out
▶ ne baš predaleko
[neh bash pred**a**leko]

where is it on the map?
▶ gdje je to na planu grada?
[gd-yeh yeh to na pl**a**noo gr**a**da]

can you write the name and address down?
▶ možete li zapisati ime i adresu?
[mo**J**eteh lee zap**ee**satee **ee**meh ee adr**e**soo]

I'm looking for a room in a private house
▶ tražim sobu u privatnoj kući
[tra**J**eem s**o**boo oo pr**ee**vatnoy k**oo**chee]

2. Banks

bank account	bankovni račun	[**bankovnee** r**achoon**]
to change money	promijeniti novac	[promee**ye**neetee **no**vats]
cheque	ček	[chek]
to deposit	položiti	[po**lo**Jeetee]
kuna	kuna	[**koo**na]
pin number	pin	[peen]
pound	funta	[**foon**ta]
to withdraw	podići	[**po**deechee]

can you change this into kunas?
▶ možete li mi ovo promijeniti u kune?
[mo**Je**teh lee mee **o**vo promee**ye**neetee oo **koo**neh]

kakve novčanice želite? ◀
[**ka**kveh novch**a**neetseh **Je**leeteh]
how would you like the money?

small notes | **big notes**
▶ male novčanice | ▶ velike novčanice
[**ma**leh novch**a**neetseh] | [**ve**leekeh novch**a**neetseh]

do you have information in English about opening an account?
▶ imate li informacije o otvaranju računa na engleskom?
[**ee**mateh lee eenform**a**tseeyeh o **o**tvaranyoo rach**oo**na na **e**ngleskom]

da, koju vrstu računa želite? ◀
[da **ko**-yoo **ve**rstoo rach**oo**na **Je**leeteh]
yes, what sort of account do you want?

I'd like a current account | vašu putovnicu, molim ◀
▶ želim tekući račun | [**va**shoo p**oo**tovneetsoo **mo**leem]
[**Je**leem te**koo**chee r**a**choon] | **your passport, please**

can I use this card to draw some cash?
▶ mogu li ovom karticom podići gotovinu?
[**mo**goo lee **o**vom kart**ee**tsom **po**deechee got**o**veenoo]

morate otići na blagajnu ◀
[**mo**rateh **o**teechee na blag**aj**noo]
you have to go to the cashier's desk

I want to transfer this to my account at Privredna banka
▶ želim to prebaciti na moj račun u Privrednoj banci
[**Je**leem to prebatseetee na moy r**a**choon oo pr**ee**vrednoy bantsee]

dobro, ali morat ćemo vam naplatiti poziv ◀
[**do**bro **a**lee **mo**rat chemo vam napl**a**teetee p**o**zeev]
OK, but we'll have to charge you for the phonecall

download these scenarios as MP3s from:

3. Booking a room

shower	tuš	[toosh]
telephone in the room	telefon u sobi	[telefon oo sobee]
payphone in the lobby	telefon u predvorju	[telefon oo predvor-yoo]

do you have any rooms?
▶ imate li slobodnu sobu?
[eemateh lee slobodnoo soboo]

za koliko osoba? ◀
[za koleeko osoba]
for how many people?

for one/for two
▶ za jednu osobu/za dvije osobe
[za yednoo osoboo/za dveeyeh osobeh]

da, imamo slobodnu sobu ◀
[da eemamo slobodnoo soboo]
yes, we have rooms free

▶ za koliko noći?
[za koleeko nochee]
for how many nights?

just for one night
samo za jednu noć ◀
[samo za yednoo noch]

how much is it?
▶ koliko je noćenje?
[koleeko yeh nochen-yeh]

šesto kuna s kupaonicom, petsto kuna bez kupaonice ◀
[shesto koona s koopaoneetsom petsto koona bez koopaoneetseh]
600 kunas with bathroom and 500 kunas without bathroom

does that include breakfast?
▶ je li doručak uključen?
[yeh lee doroochak ookl-yoochen]

can I see a room with bathroom?
▶ mogu li vidjeti sobu s kupaonicom?
[mogoo lee veed-yetee soboo s koopa-oneetsom]

ok, I'll take it
▶ uzet ću je
[oozet choo yeh]

when do I have to check out?
▶ kada se moram odjaviti?
[kada seh moram od-yaveetee]

is there anywhere I can leave luggage?
▶ mogu li negdje ostaviti prtljagu?
[mogoo lee negd-yeh ostaveetee prtlyagoo]

4. Car hire

automatic	automatik	[aootomateek]
full tank	pun spremnik	[poon spremneek]
manual (transmission)	ručni mjenjač	[roochnee m-yenyach]
rented car	unajmljeni auto	[oonīm-lyenee aooto]

I'd like to rent a car
▶ želio bih unajmiti auto
[Jeleeo beeH oonīmeetee aooto]

na koliko dugo? ◀
[na koleeko doogo]
for how long?

---

two days
▶ dva dana
[dva dana]

I'll take the ...
▶ uzet ću ...
[oozet choo]

---

is that with unlimited mileage?
▶ je li kilometraža neograničena?
[yeh lee keelometraJa neograneechena]

da ◀
[da]
it is

---

mogu li vidjeti vašu vozačku dozvolu, molim? ◀
[mogoo lee veed-yetee vashoo vozachkoo dozvoloo moleem]
can I see your driving licence, please?

---

i vašu putovnicu ◀
[ee vashoo pootovneetsoo]
and your passport

---

is insurance included?
▶ je li osiguranje uključeno?
[yeh lee oseegooran-yeh ooklyoocheno]

---

da, ali morate platiti prvih sedamsto kuna ◀
[da alee morateh plateetee perveeH sedamsto koona]
yes, but you have to pay the first 700 kunas

---

možete li ostaviti sedamsto kuna kao polog? ◀
[moJeteh lee ostaveetee sedamsto koona kao polog]
can you leave a deposit of 700 kunas?

---

and if this office is closed, where do I leave the keys?
▶ ako je ova poslovnica zatvorena, gdje ću ostaviti ključeve?
[ako yeh ova poslovneetsa zatvorena gd-yeh choo ostaveetee klyoocheveh]

---

ubacite ih u onu kutiju ◀
[oobatseeteh eeH oo onoo kooteeyoo]
you drop them in that box

5. Communications

ADSL modem	ADSL-modem	[a-deh-es-el-mdem]
at (sign)	monkey	[monkey]
dial-up modem	analogni modem	[analognee modem]
dot	točka	[tochka]
Internet	Internet	[internet]
mobile (phone)	mobitel	[mobitel]
password	lozinka	[lozeenka]
telephone socket adaptor	adapter telefonskog priključka	[adapter telefonskog preekljoochka]
wireless hotspot	bežični hotspot	[beJeechnee hotspot]

is there an Internet café around here?
▶ ima li u blizini Internetcafé?
[eema lee oo bleezeenee internetcafé]

can I send email from here?
▶ mogu li odavde poslati email?
[mogoo lee odavdeh poslatee email]

where's the at sign on the keyboard?
▶ gdje se na tipkovnici nalazi monkey?
[gd-yeh seh na teepkovneetsee nalazee monkey]

zero	nula	[noola]
one	jedan	[yedan]
two	dva	[dva]
three	tri	[tree]
four	četiri	[cheteeree]
five	pet	[pet]
six	šest	[shest]
seven	sedam	[sedam]
eight	osam	[osam]
nine	devet	[devet]

can you switch this to a UK keyboard?
▶ mogu li se prebaciti na britansku tipkovnicu?
[mogoo lee seh prebatseetee na breetanskoo teepkovneetsoo]

can you help me log on?
▶ možete li mi pomoći da pristupim Internetu?
[moJeteh lee mee pomochee da preestoopeem eenternetoo]

I'm not getting a connection, can you help?
▶ ne dobivam vezu, možete li mi pomoći?
[neh dobeevam vezoo moJeteh lee mee pomochee]

where can I get a top-up card for my mobile?
▶ gdje mogu kupiti doplatni bon za mobitel?
[gd-yeh mogoo koopeetee doplatnee bon za mobeetel]

can you put me through to ...?
▶ možete li me spojiti s ...?
[moJeteh lee meh spo-yeetee s]

6. Directions

hi, I'm looking for Ilica
▶ oprostite, tražim Ilicu
[oprosteeteh traJeem eeleetsoo]

hi, Ilica, do you know where it is?
oprostite, znate li gdje je Ilica?
[oprosteeteh znateh lee gd-yeh yeh eeleetsa]

žao mi je, nisam čuo za to ◀
[Jao mee yeh neesam choo-o za to]
sorry, never heard of it

hi, can you tell me where Ilica is?
▶ oprostite, možete li mi reći gdje je Ilica?
[oprosteeteh moJeteh lee mee rechee gd-yeh yeh eeleetsa]

i ja sam stranac ◀
[ee yasam stranats]
I'm a stranger here too

where?
gdje?
[gd-yeh]

which direction?
kojim putem?
[ko-yeem pootem]

▶ iza ugla
[eeza oogla]
around the corner

▶ na drugom semaforu lijevo
[na droogom semaforoo leeyevo]
left at the second traffic lights

▶ zatim prva nadesno
[zateem perva nadesno]
then it's the first street on the right

blizu [bleezoo] near	na lijevoj strani [na leeyevoy stranee] on the left	prođite … [projeeteh] past the …	sljedeći [sl-yedechee] next
dalje [dal-yeh] further	nasuprot [nasooprot] opposite	ravno naprijed [ravno napreeyed] straight ahead	tamo prijeko [tamo preeyeko] over there
ispred [eespred] in front of	natrag [natrag] back	skretanje [skretan-yeh] turn off	ulica [ooleetsa] street
na desnoj strani [na desnoy stranee] on the right	odmah nakon [odmaH nakon] just after		

7. Emergencies

accident	nesreća	[nesrecha]
ambulance	kola hitne pomoći	[kola heetneh pomochee]
consul	konzul	[konzool]
embassy	veleposlanstvo	[veleposlanstvo]
fire brigade	vatrogasci	[vatrogastsee]
police	policija	[poleetseeya]

help!
▶ upomoć!
[oopomoch]

can you help me?
▶ možete li mi pomoći?
[moJeteh lee mee pomochee]

please come with me! it's really very urgent
▶ molim pođite sa mnom! doista je hitno
[moleem poJeeteh sa mnom do-eesta yeh heetno]

I've lost (my keys)
▶ izgubila sam (ključeve)
[eezgoobeela sam klyoocheveh]

(my car) is not working
▶ (moj auto) ne radi
[(moy aooto) neh radee]

(my purse) has been stolen
▶ (moj novčanik) je ukraden
[(moy novchaneek) yeh ookraden]

I've been mugged
▶ opljačkana sam
[oplyachkana sam]

---

kako se zovete? ◀
[kako seh zoveteh]
what's your name?

mogu li vidjeti vašu putovnicu? ◀
[mogoo lee veed-yeteh vashoo pootovneetsoo]
I need to see your passport

I'm sorry, all my papers have been stolen
▶ žao mi je, ukrali su mi sve dokumente
[Jao mee yeh ookralee soo mee sveh dokoomenteh]

8. Friends

hi, how're you doing?
▶ bog, kako si?
[bog kako see]

dobro, a ti? ◀
[dobro a tee]
OK, and you?

---

yeah, fine
▶ da, dobro
[da dobro]

not bad
▶ nije loše
[neeyeh losheh]

---

d'you know Mark?
▶ poznaješ Marka?
[pozna-yesh marka]

---

and this is Ana
▶ a ovo je Ana
[a ovo yeh ana]

da, poznajemo se ◀
[da pozna-yemo seh]
yeah, we know each other

---

where do you know each other from?
▶ odakle se znate?
[odakleh seh znateh]

---

sreli smo se kod Luke ◀
[srelee smo seh kod lookeh]
we met at Luka's place

---

that was some party, eh?
▶ bio je to dobar tulum?
[beeo yeh to dobar tooloom]

super ◀
[sooper]
the best

---

are you guys coming for a beer?
▶ idemo na pivo?
[eedemo na peevo]

guba, idemo ◀
[gooba eedemo]
cool, let's go

---

ne mogu, dogovorio sam se s Vesnom ◀
[neh mogoo dogovoreeo sam seh s vesnom]
no, I'm meeting Vesna

---

see you at Luka's place tonight
▶ vidimo se večeras kod Luke
[veedeemo seh vecheras kod lookeh]

---

vidimo se ◀
[veedeemo seh]
see you

---

9. Health

I'm not feeling very well
▶ ne osjećam se baš dobro
[neh **o**s-yecham seh bash d**o**bro]

---

can you get a doctor?
▶ možete li pozvati liječnika?
[m**o**žeteh lee p**o**zvatee leeye**e**chneeka]

gdje vas boli? ◀
[gd-yeh vas b**o**lee]
where does it hurt?

---

it hurts here
▶ ovdje me boli
[**o**vd-yeh meh b**o**lee]

boli li vas stalno? ◀
[b**o**lee lee vas st**a**lno]
is the pain constant?

---

it's not a constant pain
▶ ne boli me stalno
[neh b**o**lee meh st**a**lno]

can I make an appointment?
▶ možete li me naručiti za pregled?
[m**o**žeteh lee meh nar**oo**cheetee za pr**e**gled]

can you give me something for ...?
▶ možete li mi dati nešto za …?
[m**o**žeteh lee mee d**a**tee n**e**shto za]

yes, I have insurance
▶ da, osigurana sam
[da oseeg**oo**rana sam]

antibiotics	antibiotici	[anteebee**o**teetsee]
antiseptic ointment	antiseptična krema	[antees**e**pteechna kr**e**ma]
cystitis	cistitis	[tseest**ee**tees]
dentist	zubar	[z**oo**bar]
diarrhoea	proljev	[pr**o**l-yev]
doctor	liječnik	[leeye**e**chneek]
hospital	bolnica	[b**o**lneetsa]
ill	bolestan	[b**o**lestan]
medicine	lijek	[l**ee**yek]
painkillers	sredstva protiv bolova	[sredstva pr**o**teev b**o**lova]
pharmacy	ljekarna	[l-y**e**karna]
to prescribe	prepisati	[prep**ee**satee]
rash	osip	[**o**seep]

10. Language difficulties

a few words	nekoliko riječi	[nekoleeko ree-yechee]
interpreter	tumač	[toomach]
to translate	prevesti	[prevestee]

vaša kreditna kartica je odbijena ◀
[vasha kredeetna karteetsa yeh odbeeyena]
your credit card has been refused

what, I don't understand; do you speak English?
▶ što, ne razumijem vas; govorite li engleski?
[shto neh razoomeeyem vas govoreeteh lee engleskee]

ovo ne važi ◀
[ovo neh vaJee]
this isn't valid

could you say that again?
▶ možete li to ponoviti?
[moJeteh lee to ponoveetee]

slowly
▶ polako
[polako]

I understand very little Croatian
▶ vrlo slabo razumijem Hrvatski
[verlo slabo razoomeeyem Hervatskee]

I speak Croatian very badly
▶ loše govorim Hrvatski
[losheh govoreem Hervatskee]

ne možete platiti ovom karticom ◀
[nemoJeteh plateetee ovom karteetsom]
you can't use this card to pay

razumijete li? ◀
[razoomeeyeteh lee]
do you understand?

sorry, no
▶ ne, nažalost
[neh naJalost]

is there someone who speaks English?
▶ govori li ovdje netko engleski?
[govoree lee ovd-yeh netko engleskee]

oh, now I understand
▶ ah, sada razumijem
[ah sada razoomeeyem]

is that ok now?
▶ je li sada u redu?
[yeh lee sada oo redoo]

11. Meeting people

hello
▶ zdravo
[zdravo]

bog, zovem se Mira ◀
[bog zovem seh meera]
hello, my name's Mira

Graham, from England, Thirsk
▶ ja sam Graham; iz Thirska u Engleskoj
[ya sam graham eez thirska oo engleskoy]

nisam čula za to mjesto, gdje se nalazi? ◀
[neesam choola za to m-yesto gd-yeh seh nalazee]
don't know that, where is it?

not far from York, in the North; and you?
▶ nije daleko od Yorka, na sjeveru, a vi?
[neeyeh daleko od Yorka na s-yeveroo a vee]

ja sam iz Zagreba, sami ste ovdje? ◀
[ya sam eez zagreba samee steh ovd-yeh]
I'm from Zagreb; here by yourself?

no, I'm with my wife and two kids
▶ ne, tu sam sa ženom i dvoje djece
[neh too sam sa Jenom ee dvo-yeh d-yetseh]

what do you do?
▶ što ste po zanimanju?
[shto steh po zaneemanyoo]

bavim se računalima ◀
[baveem seh rachoonaleema]
I'm in computers

me too
▶ i ja
[ee ya]

here's my wife now
▶ evo moje žene
[evo mo-yeh Jeneh]

drago mi je ◀
[drago mee yeh]
nice to meet you

12. Post offices

airmail	zrakoplovom	[zrakoplovom]
post card	razglednica	[razgledneetsa]
post office	pošta	[poshta]
stamp	marka	[marka]

what time does the post office close?
▶ kada se zatvara pošta?
[kada seh zatvara poshta]

radnim danom u pet ◀
[radneem danom oo pet]
five o'clock weekdays

is the post office open on Saturdays?
▶ je li pošta otvorena subotom?
[yeh lee poshta otvorena soobotom]

prije podne ◀
[preeyeh podneh]
until midday

I'd like to send this registered to England
▶ želio bih to poslati u englesku preporučenom poštom
[Jeleeo beeн to poslatee oo engleskoo preporoochenom poshtom]

dobro, to je sto kuna ◀
[dobro to yeh sto koona]
certainly, that will be 100 kunas

and also two stamps for England, please
▶ i dvije marke za englesku, molim
[ee dveeyeh markeh za engleskoo moleem]

do you have some airmail stickers?
▶ imate li naljepnice za slanje zrakoplovom?
[eemateh lee nal-yepneetseh za slan-yeh zrakoplovom]

do you have any mail for me?
▶ imate li za mene pošte?
[eemateh lee zameneh poshteh]

inozemstvo	international
pisma	letters
tuzemstvo	domestic
paketi	parcels
poste restante	poste restante

13. Restaurants

bill	račun	[rachoon]
menu	jelovnik	[yelovneek]
table	stol	[stol]

can we have a non-smoking table?
▶ možemo li dobiti stol za nepušače?
[mojemo lee dobeetee stol za nepooshacheh]

there are two of us	**there are four of us**
▶ ima nas dvoje	▶ ima nas četvero
[eema nas dvo-yeh]	[eema nas chetvero]

what's this?
▶ što je to?
[shto yeh to]

to je vrsta ribe ◀
[to yeh versta reebeh]
it's a type of fish

to je lokalni specijalitet ◀
[to yeh lokalnee spetsee-yaleetet]
it's a local speciality

uđite i pokazat ću vam ◀
[oojeeteh ee pokazat choo vam]
come inside and I'll show you

we would like two of these, one of these, and one of those
▶ dajte nam dvije od ovih, jednu od ovih i jednu ovu
[dīteh nam dveeyeh od oveeH yednoo od oveeH ee yednoo ovoo]

▶ a za piće?	**red wine**	**white wine**
[a za peecheh]	▶ crno vino	▶ bijelo vino
and to drink?	[tserno veeno]	[beeyelo veeno]

a beer and two orange juices
▶ pivo i dva soka od naranče
[peevo ee dva soka od narancheh]

some more bread please
▶ još malo kruha, molim
[yosh malo krooha moleem]

▶ je li vam je prijalo?
[yeh lee vam yeh preeyalo]
how was your meal?

excellent!, very nice!
izvrsno!, vrlo dobro! ◀
[eezversno verlo dobro]

▶ još nešto?
[yosh neshto]
anything else?

just the bill thanks
samo račun, molim ◀
[samo rachoon moleem]

14. Shopping

mogu li vam pomoći? ◄
[**mo**goo lee vam **po**mochee]
can I help you?

can I just have a look around?
▶ mogu li samo malo pogledati?
[**mo**goo lee **sa**mo **ma**lo **po**gledatee]

yes, I'm looking for ...
da, tražim ... ◄
[da tra**J**eem]

how much is this?
▶ koliko je ovo?
[**ko**leeko yeh **o**vo]

dvijesto kuna ◄
[dv-**ye**sto **koo**na]
200 kunas

OK, I think I'll have to leave it; it's a little too expensive for me
▶ neću to uzeti; malo mi je preskupo
[**ne**choo to **oo**zetee **ma**lo mee yeh pre**skoo**po]

a ovo? ◄
[a **o**vo]
how about this?

can I pay by credit card?
▶ mogu li platiti kreditnom karticom?
[**mo**goo lee pla**tee**tee kre**dee**tnom kar**tee**tsom]

it's too big
▶ preveliko je
[pre**ve**leeko yeh]

it's too small
▶ premalo je
[**pre**malo yeh]

it's for my son – he's about this high
▶ to je za mojega sina – ovolik je
[to yeh za mo-**ye**ga **see**na – o**vo**leek yeh]

▶ želite li još nešto?
[**J**eleeteh lee yosh **ne**shto]
will there be anything else?

that's all thanks
ne, hvala, to je sve ◄
[neh **Hva**la to yeh sveh]

make it 150 kunas and I'll take it
▶ uzet ću ga za stopedeset kuna
[**oo**zet choo ga za sto**pe**deset **koo**na]

fine, I'll take it
▶ dobro, uzimam to
[**do**bro **oo**zeemam to]

akcija	**sale**	zamijeniti	**to exchange**
blagajna	**cash desk**	zatvoreno	**closed**
otvoreno	**open**		

15. Sightseeing

art gallery	umjetnička galerija	[**oo**m-yetneechka ga**l**ereeya]
bus tour	obilazak autobusom	[**o**beelazak **a**ootoboosom]
city centre	središte grada	[sr**e**deeshteh gr**a**da]
closed	zatvoreno	[z**a**tvoreno]
guide	vodič	[v**o**deech]
museum	muzej	[m**oo**zay]
open	otvoreno	[**o**tvoreno]

I'm interested in seeing the old town
▶ želim vidjeti stari grad
[**J**eleem v**ee**d-yetee st**a**ree grad]

are there guided tours?
▶ nudi li se obilazak s vodičem?
[n**oo**dee lee seh **o**beelazak s v**o**deechem]

žao mi je, popunjeno je ◀
[Jao mee yeh pop**oo**n-yeno yeh]
I'm sorry, it's fully booked

how much would you charge to drive us around for four hours?
▶ koliko biste nam naplatili kružnu vožnju u trajanju od četiri sata?
[k**o**leeko b**ee**steh nam napl**a**teelee kr**oo**Jnoo v**o**Jnyoo oo tr**ī**-anyoo od ch**e**teeree sata]

can we book tickets for the concert here?
▶ možemo li ovdje kupiti karte za taj koncert?
[m**o**Jemo lee **o**vd-yeh k**oo**peetee k**a**rteh za t**ī** k**o**ntsert]

▶ da, na čije ime?   ▶ koja kreditna kartica?
[da na ch**ee**yeh **ee**meh]   [k**o**-ya kr**e**deetna k**a**rteetsa]
yes, in what name?   **which credit card?**

where do we get the tickets?
▶ gdje ćemo dobiti karte?
[gd-yeh ch**e**mo d**o**beetee k**a**rteh]

podignite ih na ulazu ◀
[p**o**deegneeteh eeH na **oo**lazoo]
just pick them up at the entrance

is it open on Sundays?
▶ je li otvoreno nedjeljom?
[yeh lee **o**tvoreno n**e**d-yelyom]

how much is it to get in?
koliko je ulaznica? ◀
[k**o**leeko yeh **oo**lazneetsa]

are there reductions for groups of 6?
▶ ima li popusta za grupu od šest osoba?
[**ee**ma lee p**o**poosta za gr**oo**poo od shest **o**soba]

that was really impressive!
▶ to je bilo doista dojmljivo!
[to yeh b**ee**lo d**o**-eesta d**o**ym-lyeevo]

16. Trains

to change trains	presjesti	[pres-yestee]
platform	peron	[peron]
return	povratna karta	[povratna karta]
single	jednosmjerna karta	[yednos-myerna karta]
station	kolodvor	[kolodvor]
stop	postaja	[posta-ya]
ticket	vozna karta	[vozna karta]

how much is ...?
▶ koliko je ...?
[koleeko yeh]

a single, second class to ...
▶ jednosmjerna karta drugog razreda za ...
[yednos-myerna karta droogog razreda za]

two returns, second class to ...
▶ dvije povratne karte drugog razreda za ...
[dveeyeh povratneh karteh droogog razreda za]

for today	**for tomorrow**	**for next Tuesday**
▶ za danas	▶ za sutra	▶ za idući utorak
[za danas]	[za sootra]	[za eedoochee ootorak]

morate nadoplatiti za ekspres ◀
[morateh nadoplateetee za ekspres]
there's a supplement for the express

želite li rezervirati sjedalo? ◀
[Jeleeteh lee rezerveeratee s-yedalo]
do you want to make a seat reservation?

morate presjesti u Zaboku ◀
[morateh pres-yestee oo zabokoo]
you have to change at Zabok

is this seat free?
▶ je li ovo sjedalo slobodno?
[yeh lee ovo s-yedalo slobodno]

excuse me, which station are we at?
▶ oprostite, koja je ovo postaja?
[oprosteeteh ko-ya yeh ovo posta-ya]

is this where I change for Krapina?
▶ moram li ovdje presjesti za Krapinu?
[moram lee ovd-yeh pres-yestee za krapeenoo]

English

→

Croatian

(For words with *, see **How the Language Works**, p. 211 onwards)

A

a, an*

about: about 20 oko dvadeset
  it's about 5 o'clock oko pet
  sati [satee]
  a film about Croatia film o
  Hrvatskoj [feelm o Hervatskoy]

above iznad [eeznad]
  above … iznad …

abroad u inozemstvu [oo
  eenozemstvoo]

absolutely apsolutno
  [apsolootno]

accelerator pedala gasa

accept prihvatiti
  [preeHvateetee]

accident nesreća [nesrecha]
  there's been an accident
  dogodila se nesreća [dogodeela
  seh]

accommodation smještaj [sm-
  yeshtī]

accurate točan [tochan]

ache bol
  my back aches bole me leđa
  [boleh meh leja]

across: across the road preko
  ceste [tsesteh]

adapter ispravljač [eespravl-
  yach]

address adresa
  what's your address? koja je
  vaša adresa? [ko-ya yeh vasha]

address book adresar

admission charge cijena
  ulaznice [tseeyena oolaznitseh]

Adriatic Jadransko more

[yadransko moreh]

adult (adj) odrastao
  (noun) odrasla osoba

advance: in advance
  unaprijed [oonapreeyed]

aeroplane zrakoplov

after poslije [posleeyeh]
  after you poslije vas
  after lunch poslije ručka
  [roochka]

afternoon poslije podne
  [posleeyeh podneh]
  in the afternoon poslije
  podne
  this afternoon danas poslije
  podne

aftershave losion poslije
  brijanja [loseeon posleeyeh
  breeyanya]

aftersun cream krema poslije
  sunčanja [posleeyeh soonchanya]

afterwards kasnije
  [kasneeyeh]

again opet

against protiv [proteev]

age dob

ago: a week ago prije tjedan
  dana [preeyeh t-yedan]
  an hour ago prije sat
  vremena

agree: I agree slažem se
  [slaJem seh]

AIDS AIDS [eH-eeds]

air zrak
  by air zrakoplovom

air-conditioning klimatizacija
  [kleemateezatseeya]

airmail: by airmail
  zrakoplovom

airmail envelope avionska koverta

airport zračna luka [zrachna looka]

to the airport, please u zračnu luku, molim [oo zrachnoo lookoo, moleem]

airport bus autobus za zračnu luku [aootobus za zrachnoo lookoo]

aisle seat sjedalo uz prolaz [s-yedalo ooz]

alarm clock budilica [boodeeleetsa]

Albania Albanija [albaneeya]

Albanian (adj) albanski [albanskee]

(man) Albanac [albanats]

(woman) Albanka [albanka]

alcohol alkohol

alcoholic (adj) alkoholno

all: all the boys svi dečki [svee dechkee]

all the girls sve cure [sveh tsooreh]

all of it sve to

all of them svi oni [onee]

that's all, thanks to je sve, hvala [yeh – Hvala]

allergic: I'm allergic to ... alergičan sam na ... [alergeechan]

allowed: is it allowed? je li to dopušteno? [yeh lee to dopooshteno]

all right dobro

I'm all right dobro sam

are you all right? jeste li dobro? [yesteh]

almond badem

almost gotovo

alone sam

alphabet abeceda [abetseda]

a	ah	o	o
b	buh	p	puh
c	tsuh	q	kvuh (not in
č	chuh		Croatian alphabet)
ć	chuh	r	ruh
d	duh	s	suh
dž	juh	š	shuh
đ	juh	t	tuh
e	eh	u	oo
f	fuh	v	vuh
g	guh	w	doobuhl-veh (not
h	Huh		in Croatian
i	ee		alphabet)
j	yuh	x	eeks (not in
k	kuh		Croatian
l	luh		alphabet)
lj	luh-yuh	y	eepseelon (not in
m	muh		Croatian alphabet)
n	nuh	z	zuh
nj	nuh-yuh	ž	Juh

already već [vech]

also također [takojer]

although mada

altogether sasvim [sasveem]

always uvijek [ooveeyek]

am*: I am ja sam [ya]

a.m.: at seven a.m. u sedam ujutro [ooyootro]

amazing nevjerojatan [nev-yero-yatan]

ambulance vozilo hitne pomoći [vozeelo Heetneh pomochee]

call an ambulance! pozovite hitnu pomoć! [**po**zo**vee**teh **H**eet**noo po**moch]

America Amerika [a**mer**eeka]

American (adj) američki [ame**reech**kee]

I'm American (said by man/woman) ja sam Amerikanac/Amerikanka [ya sam amereek**a**nats/amereek**a**nka]

among među [**me**joo]

amount iznos [**eez**nos]

amp: a 13 amp fuse osigurač od trinaest ampera [oseeg**oo**rach od **tree**na-est ampera]

amphitheatre amfiteatar [amfeete**a**tar]

ancient drevan

and i [ee]

angry ljut [lyoot]

animal životinja [Jeev**o**teenya]

ankle gležanj [gle**J**an]

anniversary godišnjica [g**o**deesh-nyeetsa]

annoy: this man's annoying me ovaj čovjek mi dosađuje [**o**vi chov-yek mee dos**a**jooyeh]

annoying dosadno

another drugi [**droo**gee]

can we have another room? možemo li promijeniti sobu? [m**o**Jemo lee promeey**e**neetee s**o**boo]

another beer, please još jedno pivo, molim [yosh **y**edno **pee**vo, m**o**leem]

antibiotics antibiotici [anteebee**o**teetsee]

antifreeze antifriz [anteefreez]

antihistamine antihistaminik [anteeheestam**ee**neek]

antique: is it an antique? je li to antikvitet? [yeh lee to anteekv**ee**tet]

antique shop antikvarnica [anteekv**a**rneetsa]

antiseptic (adj) antiseptičan [antees**e**pteechan]

any: have you got any bread/tomatoes? imate li kruha/rajčica? [**ee**mateh lee kr**oo**ha/r**ī**cheetsa]

do you have any change? imate li sitnoga? [**ee**mateh lee s**ee**tnoga]

sorry, I don't have any nažalost, nemam [n**a**Jalost]

anybody itko [**ee**tko]

does anybody speak English? govori li itko engleski? [g**o**voree lee **ee**tko **e**ngleskee]

there wasn't anybody there tamo nije bilo nikoga [**t**amo n**ee**yeh **b**eelo n**ee**koga]

anything išta [**ee**shta]

dialogues

anything else? još nešto? [yosh n**e**shto]
nothing else, thanks ništa drugo, hvala [**nee**shta dr**oo**go, H**va**la]

would you like anything to drink? želite li nešto

popiti? [Jeleeteh lee neshto popeetee]
I don't want anything, thanks ništa, hvala

apart from osim [oseem]
apartment stan
aperitif aperitiv [apereeteev]
apology isprika [eespreeka]
appendicitis upala slijepog crijeva [oopala sleeyepog tsreeyeva]
appetizer pikantno predjelo [peekantno pred-yelo]
apple jabuka [yabooka]
appointment sastanak

dialogue

good morning, how can I help you? dobro jutro, mogu li vam pomoći? [yootro mogoo lee vam pomochee]
I'd like to make an appointment (said by man/woman) želio/željela bih dogovoriti sastanak [Jeleeo/Jel-yela beeн dogovoreetee]
what time would you like? u koje vrijeme? [oo ko-yeh vreeyemeh]
three o'clock u tri [tree]
I'm afraid that's not possible; is four o'clock all right? bojim se da to nije moguće; odgovara li vam u četiri? [bo-yeem seh da to

neeyeh mogoocheh; odgovara lee vam oo cheteeree]
yes, that will be fine da, to je u redu [oo redoo]
the name was …? zovete se? [zoveteh seh]

apricot marelica [mareleetsa]
April travanj [travan]
are*: we are mi smo [mee]
you are vi ste [vee steh]
they are oni/one/ona su [onee/oneh – soo]
area područje [podrooch-yeh]
area code poštanski broj [poshtanskee broy]
arm ruka [rooka]
arrange: will you arrange it for us? možete li nam to organizirati? [moJeteh lee nam to organeezeeratee]
arrival dolazak
arrive stići [steechee]
when do we arrive? kada stižemo? [steeJemo]
has my fax arrived yet? je li stigao moj faks? [yeh lee steegao moy]
we arrived today danas smo stigli [steeglee]
art umjetnost [oom-yetnost]
art gallery umjetnička galerija [oom-yetneechka galereeya]
artist umjetnik [oom-yetneek] (woman) umjetnica [oom-yetneetsa]
as: as big as velik kao [veleek]
as soon as possible čim

prije moguće [cheem **pree**yeh mog**oo**cheh]

ashtray pepeljara [pepelyara]

ask pitati [**pee**tatee]

I didn't ask for this nisam to tražio [**nee**sam to tra**J**eeo]

could you ask him to ...? možete li ga zamoliti da ...? [mo**J**eteh lee ga zamoleetee da]

asleep: she's asleep ona spava

aspirin aspirin [as**pee**reen]

asthma astma

astonishing zapanjujući [zapan-yoo**yoo**chee]

at: at the hotel u hotelu [oo ho**te**loo]

at the station na postaji [na posta-yee]

at six o'clock u šest sati [oo shest satee]

at Heruc kod Heruca

athletics atletika [at**lee**teeka]

attractive privlačan [**pree**vlachan]

aubergine patlidžan [pat**lee**jan]

August kolovoz

aunt teta

Australia Australija [aoostra**lee**ya]

Australian (adj) australski [aoos**tral**skee]

I'm Australian (said by man/woman) ja sam Australac/Australka [ya sam aoos**tra**lats/aoos**tral**ka]

Austria Austrija [**a**oostreeya]

Austrian (adj) austrijski [aoos**tree**skee]

(man) Austrijanac [aoostreey**a**nats]

(woman) Austrijanka [aoostree**yan**ka]

automatic automatski [aoo**to**matskee]

automatic teller bankomat

autumn jesen [**ye**sen]

in the autumn ujesen [**oo**yesen]

avenue avenija [ave**nee**ya]

average prosječan [pros-yechan]

on average u prosjeku [oo pros-yekoo]

awake: is he awake? je li budan? [yeh lee b**oo**dan]

away: go away! odlazi! [**o**dlazee]

is it far away? je li daleko? [yeh lee da**le**ko]

awful grozan

axle osovina [os**o**veena]

B

baby beba

baby food dječja hrana [d-yechya н**ra**na]

baby's bottle bočica [bo**cheet**sa]

baby-sitter osoba koja čuva djecu [ko-ya ch**oo**va d-yetsoo]

back (of body) leđa [**le**ja]

at the back straga

can I have my money back? možete li mi vratiti novac? [mo**J**eteh lee mee v**ra**teetee novats] to come/go back vratiti se [seh]

backache bol u leđima [bol oo lejeema]

bacon slanina [slaneena]

bad loš [losh]

a bad headache jaka glavobolja [yaka glavobolya]

badly teško [teshko]

bag torba

baggage prtljaga [pertl-yaga]

baggage check predaja prtljage [preda-ya pertl-yageh]

baggage claim podizanje prtljage [podeezan-yeh pertl-yageh]

bakery pekara

balcony balkon

a room with a balcony soba s balkonom

bald ćelav [chelav]

ball lopta

ballet balet

banana banana

band (music) orkestar

bandage povez

Bandaids® flaster

bank (for money) banka

bank account bankovni račun [bankovnee rachoon]

bar (for drinks etc) kafić [kafeech]

a bar of chocolate tabla čokolade [chokoladeh]

barber's brijačnica [breejachneetsa]

basket košara [koshara]

bath kupanje [koopan-yeh]

can I have a bath? mogu

li se okupati? [mogoo lee seh okoopatee]

bathroom kupaonica [koopaoneetsa]

with a private bathroom s kupaonicom [s koopaoneetsom]

bath towel ručnik za kupanje [roochneek za koopan-yeh]

bathtub kada

battery baterija [batereeya] (for car) akumulator [akoomoolator]

bay zaljev [zal-yev]

be* biti [beetee]

beach plaža [plaJa]

beach mat prostirka za plažu [prosteerka za plaJoo]

beach umbrella suncobran [soontsobran]

beans grah [graн]

French beans mahune [mahooneh]

broad beans konjski grah [konyskee]

beard brada

beautiful lijep [leeyep]

because jer [yer]

because of ... zbog ...

bed krevet

I'm going to bed idem spavati [eedem spavatee]

bed and breakfast noćenje s doručkom [nochen-yeh s doroochkom]

bedroom spavaća soba [spavacha]

beef govedina [govedeena]

beer pivo [peevo]

two beers, please dva piva,
molim [**mo**leem]
before prije [**pree**yeh]
begin početi [**po**chetee]
  when does it begin? kad
  počinje? [**po**cheen-yeh]
beginner početnik [**po**chetneek]
  (woman) početnica
  [**po**chetneetsa]
beginning: at the beginning na
  početku [**po**chetkoo]
behind iza [**ee**za]
  behind me iza mene [**me**neh]
beige bež [beʒ]
believe vjerovati [v-**ye**rovatee]
bell zvono
below ispod [**ee**spod]
belt remen
bend (in road) zavoj [**za**voy]
berth ležaj [le**ʒ**i]
beside: beside the ...
  pokraj ... [**po**krī]
best najbolji [**nī**bol-yee]
better bolji [**bol**-yee]
  are you feeling better?
  osjećate li se bolje? [**os**-
  yechateh lee seh **bol**-yeh]
between između [**eez**mejoo]
beyond iza [**ee**za]
bicycle bicikl [**beet**seekl]
big velik [**ve**leek]
  too big prevelik [**pre**veleek]
  it's not big enough nije
  dovoljno veliko [**nee**yeh
  dovolyno]
bike bicikl [**beet**seekl]
bikini bikini
bill račun [**ra**chun]
  (US: banknote) novčanica

[**nov**chaneetsa]
  could I have the bill, please?
  račun, molim! [**mo**leem]
bin kanta
bin liners vreće za smeće
  [**vre**cheh za **sme**cheh]
binding (for ski) vez
bird ptica [**ptee**tsa]
biro® kemijska olovka
  [**ke**meeyska]
birthday rođendan [**ro**jendan]
  happy birthday! sretan
  rođendan! [**ro**jendan!]
biscuit keks
bit: a little bit malo
  a big bit velik komad [**ve**leek]
  a bit of ... malo ...
  a bit expensive prilično
  skupo [**pree**leechno **sko**opo]
bite (by insect) ugriz [**oo**greez]
bitter gorak
black crn [tsern]
blanket deka
blast! prokletstvo!
bleach izbjeljivač
  [**eezb**-yely**ee**vach]
bless you! (after sneeze)
  nazdravlje! [**nazdravl**-yeh]
blind (cannot see) slijep [**slee**yep]
blinds rolete [**ro**leteh]
blister plik [pleek]
blocked blokiran [**blo**keeran]
block of apartments stambena
  zgrada
blond plav
blood krv [kerv]
  high blood pressure visok
  krvni pritisak [**vee**sok **kerv**nee
  preeteesak]

blouse bluza [**bloo**za]

blow-dry sušenje kose
[**soo**shen-yeh **ko**seh]

I'd like a cut and blow-dry
šišanje i sušenje kose, molim
[**shee**shan-yeh – **mo**leem]

blue plav

blusher rumenilo za obraze
[**roo**meneelo za **o**brazeh]

boarding house pansion
[pan**see**on]

boarding pass bording karta
[**bo**rdeeng karta]

boat čamac [**cha**mats]
(large) brod

body tijelo [**tee**yelo]

boil ključati [**klyoo**chatee]

boiled egg kuhano jaje
[**koo**hano **yī**yeh]

boiler bojler [**boy**ler]

bone kost

bonnet (of car) hauba [**ha**ooba]

book knjiga [k-n**yee**ga]
(verb) rezervirati
[rezer**vee**ratee]

can I book a seat? mogu li
rezervirati sjedalo? [**mo**goo
lee – s-**ye**dalo]

dialogue

I'd like to book a table
for two (said by man/
woman) želio/željela
bih rezervirati stol za
dvoje [**J**eleeo/**J**elyela beeн
rezer**vee**ratee stol za d**vo**-yeh]
what time would you like
it booked for? za kada ga

želite rezervirati
half past seven pola osam
that's fine dobro
and your name? vaše ime?
[**vasheh ee**meh]

bookshop, bookstore knjižara
[k-n**yee**Jara]

boot (footwear) čizma [**chee**zma]
(of car) prtljažnik [**pert**l-
ya**J**neek]

border (of country) granica
[**gra**neetsa]

bored: I'm bored dosadno mi
je [mee yeh]

boring dosadan

born: I was born in
Manchester (said by man/
woman) rođen/rođena sam
u Manchesteru [**ro**jen/**ro**jena
sam oo]

I was born in 1960 (said by
man/woman) rođen/rođena
sam tisuću devetsto
šezdesete [**tee**soochoo d**e**vetsto
shezd**e**seteh]

borrow posuditi [pos**oo**deetee]
may I borrow ...? mogu li
posuditi ...? [**mo**goo lee]

Bosnia Bosna

Bosnia-Herzegovina
Bosna i Hercegovina [ee
hertsego**vee**na]

Bosnian (adj) bosanski
[bo**sa**nskee]
(man) Bosanac [**bo**sanats]
(woman) Bosanka

both oba

bother: sorry to bother you

oprostite što vam smetam
[oprosteeteh shto]
bottle boca [botsa]
  a bottle of house red boca
  točenog crnog vina [tochenog
  tsernog veena]
bottle-opener otvarač za boce
  [otvarach za botseh]
bottom dno
  (of person) stražnica [straJn-
  yeetsa]
  at the bottom of ... (hill etc) u
  podnožju ... [oo podnoJyoo]
box kutija [kooteeya]
box office blagajna [blagīna]
boy dječak [d-yechak]
boyfriend dečko [dechko]
bra grudnjak [groodnyak]
bracelet narukvica
  [narookveetsa]
brake (noun) kočnica
  [kochneetsa]
brandy konjak [konyak]
  (local variety) rakija [rakeeya]
bread kruh [krooH]
  white bread bijeli kruh
  [beeyelee]
  brown bread crni kruh
  [tsernee]
  wholemeal bread kruh od
  cijelog zrna [tseeyelog zerna]
break (verb) slomiti [slomeetee]
  I've broken the ... (said by
  man/woman) slomio/slomila
  sam ... [slomeeo/slomeela]
  I think I've broken my wrist
  (said by man/woman) mislim da
  sam slomio/slomila ručni
  zglob [meesleem – roochnee]

break down pokvariti se
  [pokvareetee seh]
  I've broken down pokvario
  mi se auto [pokvareeo mee seh
  aooto]
breakdown kvar
breakdown service služba
  pomoći na cesti [slooJba
  pomochee na tsestee]
breakfast doručak [doroochak]
break-in: I've had a break-in
  netko mi je provalio [mee yeh
  provaleeo]
breast prsa [persa]
breathe disati [deesatee]
breeze povjetarac
  [pov-yetarats]
bridge (over river etc) most
brief kratak
briefcase aktovka
bright (colour, light) svijetao
  [sveeyetao]
bright red jarkocrven
  [yarkotserven]
brilliant sjajan [sya-yan]
bring donijeti [doneeyetee]
  I'll bring it back later vratit
  ću to kasnije [vrateechoo to
  kasneeyeh]
Britain Britanija [breetaneeya]
British (adj) britanski
  [breetanskee]
  I'm British (said by man/woman)
  ja sam Britanac/Britanka [ya
  sam breetanats/breetanka]
brochure brošura [broshoora]
broken slomljen [sloml-yen]
bronchitis bronhitis
  [bronheetees]

brooch broš [brosh]
broom metla
brother brat
brother-in-law šurjak
[shooryak]
brown smeđ [smej]
  brown eyes smeđe oči
  [smejeh ochee]
bruise modrica [modreetsa]
brush četka [chetka]
  (artist's) kist [keest]
bucket kablica [kableetsa]
buffet car vagon restoran
buggy (for child) kolica
[koleetsa]
building zgrada
bulb (for light) žarulja [Jaroolya]
bumper odbojnik [odboyneek]
bunk ležaj [leji]
bureau de change
  mjenjačnica [m-yenyachneetsa]
burglary provala
burn (verb) spaliti [spaleetee]
burnt: this is burnt ovo je
  spaljeno [yeh spal-yeno]
burst: a burst pipe puknuta
  cijev [pook-noota tseeyev]

bus autobus [aootoboos]
  what number bus is it to ...?
  koji autobus vozi za ...?
  [ko-yee – vozee]
  when is the next bus to ...?
  kada kreće sljedeći autobus
  za...? [krecheh sl-yedechee]
  what time is the last bus?
  kada kreće posljednji
  autobus? [posl-yedn-yee]
  could you let me know when
  we get there? možete li mi

reći kada stignemo?
[moJeteh lee mee rechee kada
steegnemo]

dialogue

does this bus go to ...?
vozi li ovaj autobus za...?
[vozee lee ovī aootoboos]
no, you need a number ...
ne, trebate broj... [trebateh
broy]

business posao
bus station autobusni
  kolodvor [aootoboosnee]
bus stop autobusna postaja
  [posta-ya]
bust poprsje [popers-yeh]
busy (street, restaurant)
  prometan
I'm busy tomorrow sutra sam
  zauzet [sootra sam zaoozet]
but ali [alee]
butcher's mesnica
  [mesneetsa]
butter maslac [maslats]
button dugme [doogmeh]
buy kupiti [koopeetee]
  where can I buy ...? gdje
  mogu kupiti ...? [gd-yeh
  mogoo]
by: by bus/car autobusom/
  autom [aootoboosom /aootom]
  written by ... napisao ...
  [napeesao]
  by the window do prozora
  by the sea uz more [ooz
  moreh]

by Thursday do četvrtka [chetvertka]

bye doviđenja [doveejenya]

C

cabbage kupus [koopoos]

cabin kabina [kabeena]

cable car žičara [Jeechara]

café kavana

cagoule baloner

cake kolač [kolach]

cake shop slastičarnica [slasteecharneetsa]

call (verb) zvati [zvatee]

(on phone) nazvati [nazvatee]

what's it called? kako se ovo zove? [seh – zoveh]

he/she/it is called ... on/ona/ono se zove ... [sheh zoveh]

please call the doctor zovite liječnika [zoveeteh leeyechneeka]

please give me a call at 7.30 a.m. tomorrow nazovite me sutra ujutro u pola osam [nazoveeteh meh sootra ooyootro oo]

please ask him to call me molim vas, recite mu da me nazove [moleem vas retsiteh moo da meh nazoveh]

call back: I'll call back later vratit ću se kasnije [vrateechoo seh kasneeyeh]

(phone back) nazvat ću vas kasnije [nazvachoo]

call round: I'll call round

tomorrow doći ću sutra [dochee choo sootra]

camcorder kamera

camera fotoaparat

camera shop trgovina tehničkom robom [tergoveena teHneechkom]

camp kampirati [kampeeratee]

can we camp here? možemo li ovdje kampirati? [moJemo lee ovd-yeh]

camping gas plinska boca [pleenska botsa]

campsite kamp

can (tin) limenka [leemenka]

a can of beer limenka piva [peeva]

can*: can you ...? možete li ...? [moJeteh lee]

can I have ...? mogu li dobiti ... [mogoo lee dobeetee]

I can't ... ne mogu ... [nemogoo –]

Canada Kanada

Canadian (adj) kanadski [kanadski]

I'm Canadian (said by man/woman) ja sam Kanađanin/Kanađanka [ya sam kanajaneen/kanajanka]

canal kanal

cancel otkazati [otkazatee]

candies bomboni [bombonee]

candle svijeća [sveeyecha]

canoe kanu [kanoo]

canoeing vožnja kanuom [voJnya kanoo-om]

can opener otvarač za limenke [otvarach za leemenkeh]

cap (headwear) kapa

car auto (m) [aooto]

by car autom

carafe boca [botsa]

a carafe of house white, please bocu točenog bijelog vina, molim [botsoo tochenog beeyelog veena moleem]

caravan kamp prikolica [preekoleetsa]

caravan site kamp

carburettor karburator [karboorator]

card karta

my (business) card moja vizitka [mo-ya veezeetka]

cardigan vesta na kopčanje [kopchan-yeh]

cardphone telefonska govornica [govorneetsa]

careful oprezno

be careful! oprezno!

caretaker pazikuća [pazeekoocha]

car ferry trajekt [tra-yekt]

car hire rentakar

carnival karneval

car park parkiralište [parkeeraleeshteh]

carpet tepih [tepeeн]

carriage (of train) vagon

carrier bag vrećica [vrecheetsa]

carrot mrkva [merkva]

carry nositi [noseetee]

carry-cot nosiljka za bebu [noseelyka za beboo]

carton kutija [kooteeya]

carwash pranje auta [pran-yeh aoota]

case (suitcase) kovčeg [kovcheg]

cash gotovina [gotoveena]

will you cash this cheque for me? molim vas unovčite mi ovaj ček [moleem vas oonovcheeteh mee ovi chek]

cash desk blagajna [blagīna]

cash dispenser bankomat

cashier blagajnik [blagīneek]

(woman) blagajnica [blagīneetsa]

cassette kazeta

cassette recorder kazetofon

castle dvorac [dvorats]

casualty department stanica za hitnu pomoć [staneetsa za heetnoo pomoch]

cat mačka [machka]

catch (verb) uhvatiti [ooнvateetee]

where do we catch the bus to ...? gdje možemo uhvatiti autobus ...? [gd-yeh moJemo – aootoboos]

cathedral katedrala

Catholic katolik [katoleek]

cauliflower cvjetača [tsv-yetacha]

cave špilja [shpeelya]

ceiling plafon

celery celer [tseler]

cellar podrum [podroom]

cellphone mobitel

cemetery groblje [grobl-yeh]

Centigrade* Celzij [tselzee]

centimetre* centimetar [tsenteemetar]

central središnji [sredeeshn-yee]

central heating centralno grijanje [tsentralno greeyan-yeh]

centre središte [sredeeshteh]
how do we get to the city centre? kako ćemo stići u središte grada? [chemo steechee oo sredeeshteh]
cereal pahuljice [pahool-yeetseh]
certainly naravno
certainly not naravno da ne [neh]
chair stolac [stolats]
chair lift sjedečnica [s-yedechneetsa]
change (verb) zamijeniti [zameeyeneetee]
can I change this for ...? mogu li ovo zamijeniti za ...? [mogoo lee]
I don't have any change nemam ništa sitno [neeshta seetno]
can you give me change for a 50 kuna note? možete li mi razmijeniti pedeset kuna [moJeteh lee mee razmee-yeneetee – koona]

dialogue

do we have to change (trains)? moramo li presjesti? [lee pres-yestee]
yes, change at Zabok/ no, it's a direct train da, presjednite u Zaboku/ne, to je direktni vlak [pres-yedneeteh oo zabokoo/neh to yeh deerektnee]

changed: to get changed presvući se [presvoochee seh]
chapel kapela
charge: what is the charge per night? koliko je noćenje? [koleeko yeh nochen-yeh]
cheap jeftin [yefteen]
do you have anything cheaper? imate li nešto jeftinije? [eemateh lee neshto jefteeneeyeh]
check (verb) provjeriti [provyereetee]
could you check the ..., please? možete li provjeriti [moJeteh lee]
check (US: cheque) ček [chek]
(US: bill) račun [rachun]
check book čekovna knjižica [chekovna k-nyeeJeetsa]
check-in prijava [preeyava]
(at airport) check-in
check in (at hotel) prijaviti se [preeyaveetee seh]
(at airport) čekirati [chekeeratee]
where do we have to check in? gdje je check-in? [gd-yeh yeh]
cheek obraz
cheerio! doviđenja! [doveejenya]
cheers! živjeli! [Jeev-yelee]
cheese sir [seer]
chemist's ljekarna [l-yekarna]
cheque ček [chek]
do you take cheques? primate li čekove? [preemateh lee chekoveh]
cheque book čekovna

knjižica [chekovna k-n-yeeJeetsa]

cheque card čekovna kartica [chekovna karteetsa]

cherry trešnja [treshnya]

chess šah [shaH]

chest grudi [groodee]

chewing gum žvakaća guma [Jvakacha gooma]

chicken piletina [peeleteena]

chickenpox male boginje [maleh bogeen-yeh]

child dijete [deeyeteh]

child minder osoba koja čuva djecu [ko-ya choova d-yetsoo]

children's pool dječji bazen [d-yech-yee]

children's portion dječja porcija [portseeya]

chin brada

china porculan [portsoolan]

chips pomfrit [pomfreet]

chocolate čokolada [chokolada]

milk chocolate mliječna čokolada [mleeyechna]

plain chocolate obična čokolada [obeechna]

a hot chocolate vruća čokolada [vroocha]

choose birati [beeratee]

Christian name ime [eemeh]

Christmas Božić [boJeech]

merry Christmas! Sretan Božić [boJeech]

Christmas Eve Badnjak [badnyak]

church crkva [tserkva]

cider jabukovača [yabookovacha]

cigar cigara [tseegara]

cigarette cigareta [tseegareta]

cigarette lighter upaljač [oopalyach]

cinema kino [keeno]

circle krug [kroog]

upper circle balkon

city grad

city centre središte grada [sredeeshteh]

clean (adj) čist [cheest]

can you clean these for me? možete li ovo očistiti? [moJeteh lee ovo ocheesteetee]

cleaning solution sredstvo za čišćenje [cheesh-chen-yeh]

cleansing lotion tekućina za čišćenje [tekoocheena]

clear jasan [yasan]

clever pametan

cliff litica [leeteetsa]

climbing penjanje [penyan-yeh]

cling film plastična folija [plasteechna foleeya]

clinic klinika [kleeneeka]

cloakroom garderoba

(toilet) WC [vetseh]

clock sat

close (near) blizu [bleezoo]

dialogue

what time do you close?
kada zatvarate? [zatvarateh]
we close at 8 pm
zatvaramo u osam navečer [navecher]
do you close for lunch?
zatvarate li za vrijeme

ručka? [lee za vreeyemeh **roo**chka]

yes, between 1 and 3.30 pm da, između jedan i pola četiri [**ee**zmejoo **ye**dan ee **po**la che**tee**ree]

closed zatvoreno

cloth (material) tkanina [tka**nee**na]

(rag) krpa [**ker**pa]

clothes odjeća [od-**ye**cha]

clothes line konop za sušenje rublja [**soo**shen-yeh **roo**blya]

clothes peg štipaljka [sht**ee**palyka]

cloud oblak

cloudy oblačan [**o**blachan]

clutch kvačilo [kva**chee**lo]

coach autobus [**a**ootoboos]

coach station autobusni kolodvor [**a**ootoboosnee]

coach trip izlet autobusom [**ee**zlet]

coast obala

on the coast na obali

coat (overcoat etc) kaput [ka**poot**]

(jacket) jakna [**ya**kna]

coathanger vješalica [v-**ye**shaleetsa]

cockroach žohar [**Jo**har]

cocoa kakao

code kod

what's the (dialling) code for Dubrovnik? koji je pozivni broj za Dubrovnik? [**ko**-yee yeh po**zee**vnee broy za doo**bro**vneek]

coffee kava

two coffees, please dvije kave, molim [**dvee**yeh **ka**veh **mo**leem]

coin kovanica [kova**nee**tsa]

Coke® koka-kola

cold (adj) hladan [**Hla**dan]

I'm cold hladno mee yeh [**Hla**dno mee yeh]

I have a cold (said by man/woman) prehlađen/prehlađena sam [pre**Hla**jen]

collapse: he's collapsed on se srušio [seh sroo**shee**o]

collar ovratnik [**o**vratneek]

collect: I've come to collect ... (said by man/woman) došao/došla sam po ... [**do**shao]

collect call razgovor na račun primatelja poziva [**ra**choon pree**ma**telya po**zee**va]

college koledž [**ko**lej]

colour boja [**bo**-ya]

do you have this in other colours? imate li ovo u drugim bojama? [**ee**mateh lee **o**vo oo **droo**geem **bo**-yama]

colour film film u boji [feelm oo **bo**-yee]

comb češalj [**che**shal]

come doći [**do**chee]

dialogue

where do you come from? odakle ste? [**o**dakleh steh]
I come from Edinburgh iz Edinburga [eez ehdeen**boor**ga]

come back vratiti se [**vr**ateetee seh]

I'll come back tomorrow vratit ću se sutra [choo seh **soo**tra]

come in uđite [**oo**jeeteh]

comfortable udoban [**oo**doban]

compact disc CD [tsedeh]

company (firm) tvrtka [**tvertka**]

compartment (train) kupe [**koo**peh]

compass kompas

complain žaliti se [**J**aleetee seh]

complaint pritužba [**preet**ooJba]

I have a complaint imam pritužbu [**ee**mam **preet**ooJboo]

completely potpuno [**pot**poono]

computer računalo [**rach**oonalo]

concert koncert [**kont**sert]

concussion potres

conditioner (for hair) regenerator

condom kondom

conference konferencija [konfer**ents**eeya]

confirm potvrditi [potver**deetee**]

congratulations! čestitam! [**ch**esteetam]

connecting flight nastavak leta

connection veza

conscious svjestan [sv-**y**estan]

constipation tvrda stolica [**tver**da stol**eetsa**]

consulate konzulat [konz**oo**lat]

contact (verb) kontaktirati [kontak**eer**atee]

contact lenses kontaktne leće [**k**ontaktneh **l**echeh]

contraceptive kontracepcijsko

sredstvo [kontrats**ept**seeysko **sr**etstvo]

convenient pogodno

that's not convenient to nije pogodno [**n**eeyeh]

cook kuhati [**koo**hatee]

it's not cooked to nije kuhano [**n**eeyeh **koo**hano]

cooker štednjak [**sht**ednyak]

cookie keks

cooking utensils kuhinjska pomagala [**koo**heenyska]

cool hladan [**H**ladan]

cork čep [chep]

corkscrew vadičep [**va**deechep]

corner: on the corner na uglu [**oo**gloo]

in the corner u kutu [oo **koo**too]

cornflakes kukuruzne pahuljice [**koo**kooroozneh pah**ool**-yeetseh]

correct ispravan [**ee**spravan]

corridor hodnik [**hod**neek]

cosmetics kozmetika [kozmet**eek**a]

cost: how much does it cost? koliko košta? [**kol**eeko **ko**shta]

cot dječji krevetić [d-**y**ech-yee krev**eteech**]

cotton pamuk [**pa**mook]

cotton wool vata

couch kauč [**ka**ooch]

couchette kušet [**koo**shet]

cough (noun) kašalj [**ka**shal]

cough medicine sirup za kašalj [**seer**oop za **ka**shal]

could: could you ...? možete

li ...? [moJeteh lee]
could I have ...? mogu li
dobiti ...? [mogoo lee dobeetee]
I couldn't ... (said by man/
woman) nisam mogao/
mogla ... [neesam]
country zemlja [zemlya]
  in the country(side) na selu
  [seloo]
couple par
  a couple of ... par ...
courgette bučica
  [boocheetsa]
courier vodič [vodeech]
course (of meal) jelo [yelo]
  of course naravno
  of course not naravno da ne
  [neh]
cousin rođak [roJak]
  (female) rođakinja
  [roJakeenya]
cow krava
crab rak
cracker kreker
craft shop narodna radinost
  [radeenost]
crash (noun) sudar [soodar]
  I've had a crash (said by
  man/woman) imao/imala sam
  sudar [eemao/eemala sam
  soodar]
crazy lud [lood]
cream vrhnje [verHn-yeh]
  (for skin) krema
  (colour) žučkasta [Joochkasta]
crèche (for kids) jaslice
  [jasleetseh]
credit card kreditna kartica
  [kredeetna karteetsa]

do you take credit cards?
primate li kreditne kartice?
[preemateh lee]

dialogue

can I pay by credit card?
mogu li platiti kreditnom
karticom? [mogoo lee
plateetee kredeetnom
karteetsom]
which card do you want
to use? koju karticu
želite upotrijebiti?
[ko-yoo karteetsoo Jeleeteh
oopotreeyebeetee]
Access/Visa
yes, sir da, gospodine
[gospodeeneh]
what's the number? koji
je broj kartice? [ko-yee yeh
broy karteetseh]
and the expiry date? kada
prestaje važiti? [presta-yeh
vaJeetee]

crisps čips [cheeps]
Croatia Hrvatska [Hervatska]
Croatian (adj) hrvatski
  [Hervatskee]
  (man) Hrvat [Hervat]
  (woman) Hrvatica [Hervateetsa]
crockery posuđe [posooJeh]
crossing (by sea) prijelaz
  [preeyelaz]
crossroads križanje [kreeJan-
  yeh]
crowd mnoštvo [mnoshtvo]
crowded prepun [prepoon]

crown (on tooth) kruna [kroona]
cruise (noun) krstarenje
[kerstaren-yeh]
crutches štake [shtakeh]
cry plakati [plakatee]
cucumber krastavac
[krastavats]
cup šalica [shaleetsa]
a cup of ..., please šalicu ...
molim [moleem]
cupboard ormar
cure (noun) lijek [leeyek]
curly kovrčav [koverchav]
current (elec, in water) struja
[strooya]
curtains zavjese [zav-yeseh]
cushion jastuk [yastook]
custom običaj [obeechī]
Customs carina [tsareena]
cut (verb) sjeći [s-yechee]
I've cut myself (said by man/
woman) posjekao/posjekla
sam se [pos-yekao/ pos-yekla sam
seh]
cutlery pribor za jelo [preebor
za yelo]
cycling vožnja biciklom
[vojnya beetseeklom]
cyclist biciklist [beetseekleest]
(female) biciklistica
[beetseekleesteetsa]

D

dad tata
daily dnevno
damage (noun) šteta [shteta]
damaged oštećen [oshtechen]

I'm sorry, I've damaged this
(said by man/woman) žao mi je,
ovo sam oštetio/oštetila [Jao
mee yeh – oshteteeo/oshteteela]
damn! dovraga!
damp vlažan [vlaJan]
dance (verb) plesati [plesatee]
(noun) ples
would you like to dance?
želite li plesati? [Jeleeteh lee]
dangerous opasan
Danish danski [danskee]
dark mračan [mrachan]
(colour, hair) taman
it's getting dark smrkava se
[smerkava seh]
date*: what's the date today?
koji je danas datum? [ko-yee
yeh – datoom]
let's make a date for next
Monday ugovorimo sastanak
za iduči ponedjeljak
[oogovoreemo – eedoochee poned-
yelyak]
dates datulje [datool-yeh]
daughter kći [kechee]
daughter-in-law snaha [snaHa]
dawn zora
at dawn u zoru [oo]
day dan
the day after dan kasnije
[kasneeyeh]
the day after tomorrow
prekosutra [prekosootra]
the day before dan ranije
[raneeyeh]
the day before yesterday
prekjučer [prekyoocher]
every day svaki dan [svakee]

all day? cijeli dan? [tseeyelee]

in two days' time za dva
dana

have a nice day! ugodan
vam dan! [oogodan]

day trip jednodnevni izlet
[yednodnevnee eezlet]

dead mrtav [mertav]

deaf gluh [glooн]

deal (business) dogovor

it's a deal dogovoreno!

death smrt (f) [smert]

decaffeinated coffee kava bez
kofeina [kofe-eena]

December prosinac
[proseenats]

decide odlučiti [odloocheetee]

we haven't decided yet
nismo još odlučili [neesmo
yosh odloocheelee]

decision odluka [odlooka]

deck paluba [palooba]

deckchair ležaljka [leжalyka]

deep dubok [doobok]

definitely definitivno
[defeeneeteevno]

definitely not ni u kom
slučaju [nee oo kom sloocha-yoo]

degree (from university) diploma
[deeploma]

(temperature) stupanj [stoopan]

delay kašnjenje [kashn-yen-yeh]

deliberately namjerno [nam-
yerno]

delicatessen delikatesni
dućan [deleekatesnee doochan]

delicious ukusan [ookoosan]

deliver dostaviti [dostaveetee]

delivery dostava

Denmark Danska

dental floss konac za čišćenje
zuba [konats za cheeshen-yeh
zooba]

dentist zubar [zoobar]
(woman) zubarica
[zoobareetsa]

dialogue

it's this one here to je ovaj
[yeh ovi]
this one? ovaj?
no that one ne, onaj [neh
oni]
here? ovdje? [ovd-yeh]
yes da

dentures umjetno zubalo
[oom-yetno zoobalo]

deodorant deodorant

department odjel [od-yel]

department store robna kuća
[koocha]

departure odlazak

departure lounge čekaonica
za odlaske [chekaoneetsa za
odlaskeh]

depend: it depends ovisi
[oveesee]

it depends on ... ovisi
o ...

deposit (downpayment)
predujam [predooyam]

description opis [opees]

dessert desert

destination odredište
[odredeeshteh]

develop razviti [razveetee]

dialogue

could you develop these
films? možete li razviti
ove filmove? [**mo**Jehten lee
razveetee **o**veh feelmoveh]
yes certainly naravno
when will they be ready?
kada će biti gotovi? [cheh
beetee gotovee]
tomorrow afternoon sutra
popodne [**soo**tra pop**o**dneh]
how much is the 24-hour
service? koliko stoji
usluga za dvadesetčetiri
sata? [**koleeko sto**-yee **oo**slooga
za dvadeset-cheteeree]

diabetic dijabetičar
[deeyab**e**teechar]
diabetic foods dijetetska
hrana [deeyet**e**tska нrana]
dial birati [b**ee**ratee]
dialling code pozivni broj
[p**o**zeevnee broy]
diamond dijamant [deey**a**mant]
diarrhoea proljev [pr**o**l-yev]
diary dnevnik [dn**e**vneek]
dictionary rječnik [r-y**e**chneek]
didn't*
see not
die umrijeti [**oo**mreeyetee]
diesel dizel [d**ee**zel]
diet dijeta [d**ee**yeta]
I'm on a diet ja sam na dijeti
[ya – d**ee**yetee]
I have to follow a special
diet moram se pridržavati
posebne dijete [seh

preederJ**a**vatee p**o**sebneh dee**y**eteh]
difference razlika [r**a**zleeka]
what's the difference? u
čemu je razlika? [oo ch**e**moo
yeh r**a**zleeka]
different različit [razl**ee**cheet]
this one is different ovaj je
različit [**o**vī yeh]
a different table drugi stol
[dr**oo**gee]
difficult težak [t**e**Jak]
difficulty teškoća [teshk**o**cha]
dinghy gumeni čamac
[g**oo**menee ch**a**mats]
dining room blagovaonica
[blagova-**o**neetsa]
dinner večera [v**e**chera]
to have dinner večerati
[v**e**cheratee]
direct (adj) direktan [deer**e**ktan]
is there a direct train? je li
ovo direktni vlak? [yeh lee
– deer**e**ktnee]
direction smjer [sm-y**e**r]
which direction is it? u kojem
je smjeru? [oo k**o**-yem yeh
sm-y**e**roo]
is it in this direction? je li u
ovom smjeru? [yeh lee oo
ovom sm-y**e**roo]
directory enquiries telefonske
informacije [telef**o**nskeh
eenform**a**tseeyeh]
dirt prljavština [perly**a**vshteena]
dirty prljav [p**e**rlyav]
disabled invalid [**ee**nvaleed]
is there access for the
disabled? postoji li pristup
za invalide? [p**o**sto-yee lee
pr**ee**stoop za eenval**ee**edeh]

disappear nestati [nestatee]

it's disappeared nestalo je [nestalo yeh]

disappointed razočaran [razocharan]

disappointing razočaravajući [razocharava-yoochee]

disaster katastrofa

disco diskoteka [deeskoteka]

discount popust [popoost]

is there a discount? postoji li popust [posto-yee lee]

disease bolest

disgusting odvratan

dish posuda [posooda]

(meal) jelo [yelo]

dishes posuđe [posoojeh]

dishcloth kuhinjska krpa [kooheenyska kerpa]

disinfectant dezinfekcijsko sredstvo [dezeenfekt-seeysko sretstvo]

disk ploča [plocha]

disposable diapers/nappies pelene za jednokratnu uporabu [peleneh za yednokratnoo ooporaboo]

distance udaljenost [oodal-yenost]

in the distance u daljini [oo dalyeenee]

distilled water destilirana voda [desteeleerana]

district područje [podrooch-yeh]

disturb uznemiriti [ooznemeereetee]

diversion obilaznica [obeelazneetsa]

diving board daska za skokove u vodu [skokoveh oo vodoo]

divorced razveden

dizzy: I feel dizzy vrti mi se [vertee mee seh]

do raditi [radeetee]

what shall we do? što ćemo učiniti? [shto chemo ucheeneetee]

how do you do it? kako to radite? [radeeteh]

will you do it for me? hoćete li mi to učiniti? [hocheteh lee mee]

dialogues

how do you do? kako ste [steh]

nice to meet you drago mi je [mee yeh]

what do you do? (work) čime se bavite? [cheemeh seh baveeteh]

I'm a teacher, and you? ja sam učitelj, a vi? [ya sam oocheetel a vee]

I'm a student ja sam student [stoodent]

what are you doing this evening? što radite večeras? [shto radeeteh vecheras]

we're going out for a drink; do you want to join us? idemo na piće: želite li nam se pridružiti? [eedehmo na peecheh Jehleeteh lee nam seh preedrooJeetee] do you want cream? želite li vrhnje? [Jehleeteh lee verHn-yeh]

I do, but she doesn't ja da, ali ona ne [ya da alee ona neh]

doctor liječnik [leeyechneek]
(woman) liječnica [leeyechneetsa]

we need a doctor trebamo liječnika [leeyechneeka]

please call a doctor molim zovite liječnika [moleem zoveeteh leeyechneeka]

dialogue

where does it hurt? gdje vas boli? [gd-yeh vas bolee]

right here točno ovdje [tochno ovd-yeh]

does that hurt more? boli li vas ovo jače? [bolee lee vas ovo yacheh]

yes da

take this to a chemist pođite s ovim u ljekarnu [pojeeteh soveem oo el-yekarnoo]

document dokument [dokooment]
dog pas
doll lutka [lootka]
domestic flight let na domaćoj liniji [domachoy leeneeyee]
donkey magarac [magarats]

don't: don't do that! ne činite to! [neh cheeneeteh]
see not

door vrata
doorman vratar
double dvostruk [dvostrook]
double bed bračni krevet [brachnee]
double room dvokrevetna soba
doughnut uštipak [ooshteepak]
down dolje [dol-yeh]

down here ovdje dolje [ovd-yeh]

put it down over there spustite to tamo [spoosteeteh]

it's down there on the right tamo je dolje desno

it's further down the road to je niže ulicom [yeh neeJeh ooleetsom]

downhill skiing spust [spoost]
downmarket jeftin [yefteen]
downstairs dolje [dol-yeh]
dozen tucet [tootset]

half a dozen pola tuceta [tootseta]

drain odvodna cijev [tseeyev]
draught beer točeno pivo [tocheno peevo]
draughty: it's draughty propuh je [propooH yeh]
drawer ladica [ladeetsa]
drawing crtež [tserteJ]
dreadful užasan [ooJasan]
dream san
dress haljina [hal-yeena]
dressed: to get dressed obući se [oboochee seh]

dressing (for wound, cut) povoj [**po**voy]

salad dressing umak za salatu [**oo**mak za sa**la**too]

dressing gown kućni ogrtač [**koo**chnee o**ger**tach]

drink (noun) piće [**pee**cheh]
(verb) piti [**pee**tee]

a cold drink hladno piće [**H**ladno **pee**cheh]

can I get you a drink? mogu li vas počastiti pićem? [**mo**goo lee vas po**chas**teetee **pee**chem]

what would you like (to drink)? što ćete popiti? [shto cheteh po**pee**tee]

no thanks, I don't drink hvala, ne pijem [**H**vala neh **pee**yem]

I'll just have a drink of water popit ću samo malo vode [choo – **vo**deh]

drinking water pitka voda [**peet**ka]

is this drinking water? je li to pitka voda? [yeh lee]

drive voziti [**vo**zeetee]

can you drive? vozite li vi? [lee vee]

we drove here ovdje smo dovezli [**ov**d-yeh smo seh do**vez**lee]

I'll drive you home odvest ću vas kući [**o**dvest choo vas **koo**chee]

driver vozač [**vo**zach]
(woman) vozačica [**vo**zacheetsa]

driving licence vozačka dozvola [**vo**zachka]

drop: just a drop, please samo kap, molim [**mo**leem]

drug (medical) lijek [**lee**yek]
(narcotic) droga

drugs droge [**dro**geh]

drunk pijan [**pee**yan]

drunken driving vožnja u pripitom stanju [**vo**znya oo pree**pee**tom **stan**yoo]

dry suh [**soo**H]

dry-cleaner kemijska čistionica [**ke**meeyska cheeste**o**neetsa]

duck patka

due: he was due to arrive yesterday trebao je jučer stići [trebao yeh **yoo**cher **stee**chee]

when is the train due? kada stiže vlak? [**stee**Jeh]

dull (pain) tup [**too**p]
(weather) loše [**lo**sheh]

dummy (for baby) duda [**doo**da]

during tijekom [**tee**yekom]

dust prašina [pra**shee**na]

dusty prašnjav [**prash**nyav]

dustbin kanta za smeće [**sme**cheh]

duty-free (goods) bescarinski [bestsa**reen**skee]

duty-free shop bescarinski dućan [**doo**chan]

duvet poplun [**po**ploon]

E

each svaki [**sva**kee]

how much are they each? pošto je svaki? [**posh**to yeh]

ear uho [ooHo]
earache: I have earache boli me uho [bolee meh]
early rano
early in the morning rano ujutro [ooyootro]
I called by earlier svratio sam ranije [svrateeo sam raneeyeh]
earrings naušnice [naooshneetseh]
east istok [eestok]
in the east na istoku [eestokoo]
Easter Uskrs [ooskers]
easy lako
eat jesti [yestee]
we've already eaten, thanks već smo jeli, hvala [vech smo yelee]
eau de toilette kolonjska voda [kolonyska]
EC (European Community) EZ [eh zeh]
economy class ekonomska klasa
Edinburgh Edinburg [edeenboorg]
egg jaje [yīyeh]
eggplant patlidžan [patleejan]
Eire Irska [eerska]
either: either ... or ... ili ... ili ... [eelee]
either of them bilo koji od njih [beelo ko-yee od n-yeeH]
elastic elastika [elasteeka]
elastic band gumica [goomeetsa]
elbow lakat
electric električni [elektreechnee]

electrical appliances elektični uređaji [ooreja-yee]
electric fire električna grijalica [elektreechna greeyaleetsa]
electrician električar [elektreechar]
electricity struja [strooya]
elevator dizalo [deezalo]
else: something else nešto drugo [neshto droogo]
somewhere else negdje drugdje [negd-yeh droogd-yeh]

dialogue

> would you like anything else? želite li još nešto? [Jeleeteh lee yosh neshto]
> no, nothing else, thanks ništa drugo, hvala [neeshta droogo Hvala]

email (noun) email
embassy veleposlanstvo
emergency uzbuna [oozboona]
this is an emergency! ovo je uzbuna! [yeh]
emergency exit izlaz u nuždi [eezlaz oo nooJdee]
empty prazan
end kraj [krī]
at the end of the street na drugom kraju ulice [droogom kraioo ooleetseh]
when does it end? kada završava? [zavershava]
engaged (to be married) zaručen [zaroochen]
(toilet) zauzet [zaoozet]

engine motor
England engleska
English (adj, language) engleski
 [engleskee]
I'm English (said by man/woman)
 ja sam Englez/ Engleskinja
 [ya sam Engleskeenya]
do you speak English?
 govorite li engleski
 [govoreeteh lee engleskee]
enjoy: to enjoy oneself
 zabavljati se [zabavlyatee seh]

dialogue

> how did you like the film?
> kako vam se sviđa film?
> [seh sveeja feelm]
> I enjoyed it very much; did
> you enjoy it? jako mi se
> sviđa, a vama? [yako mee]

enjoyable ugodan [oogodan]
enlargement (of photo)
 povećanje [povechan-yeh]
enormous ogroman
enough dovoljno [dovolyno]
 there's not enough … nema
 dovoljno
 it's not big enough nije
 dovoljno velik [neeyeh
 – veleek]
 that's enough dosta je [yeh]
entrance ulaz [oolaz]
envelope koverta
epileptic epileptičar
 [epeelepteechar]
equipment oprema
error pogreška [pogreshka]

especially naročito [narocheeto]
essential: it is essential that …
 bitno je da … [beetno yeh da]
EU EU [eh oo]
euro euro [eh-ooro]
Europe Europa [ehooropa]
European (adj) europski
 [eHooropskee]
even čak [chak]
 even if … čak ako
evening večer [vecher]
 this evening večeras [vecheras]
 in the evening navečer
 [navecher]
evening meal večera [vechera]
eventually konačno [konachno]
ever uvijek [ooveeyek]

dialogue

> have you ever been to
> Osijek? jeste li ikad bili u
> Osijeku? [yesteh lee eekad
> beelee oo oseeyekoo]
> yes, I was there two years
> ago da, prije dvije godine
> [preeyeh dveeyeh godeeneh]

every svaki [svakee]
 every day svaki dan
everyone svatko
everything sve
everywhere svuda [svooda]
exactly! točno! [tochno]
exam ispit [eespeet]
example primjer [preem-yer]
 for example na primjer
excellent odličan [odleechan]
 excellent! odlično!

EX

except osim [**o**seem]

excess baggage višak prtljage [**vee**shak pertl-yageh]

exchange rate kurs [koors]

exciting uzbudljiv [oozb**oo**dl-yeev]

excuse me oprostite [opr**o**steeteh]
 (pardon?) molim? [**mo**leem]
 (annoyed) pazite malo! [p**a**zeeteh **ma**lo]

exhaust (pipe) ispušna cijev [**ee**spooshna ts**ee**yev]

exhausted iscrpljen [**ee**stserpl-yen]

exhibition izložba [**ee**zlo**J**ba]

exit izlaz [**ee**zlaz]
 where's the nearest exit? gdje je najbliži izlaz? [gd-yeh yeh n**a**ibleeJee]

expect očekivati [och**e**keevatee]

expensive skup [skoop]

experienced iskusan [**ee**skoosan]

explain objasniti [oby**a**sneetee]
 can you explain that? možete li to objasniti? [m**o**Jeteh lee]

express (mail, train) ekspres

extension kućni broj [k**oo**chne broy]
 extension 221, please kućni 221, molim [dvadva-y**e**dan m**o**leem]

extension lead produžni kabel [prod**oo**Jnee]

extra: can we have an extra one? možemo li dobiti još jedan? [m**o**Jemo lee d**o**beetee yosh y**e**dan]

do you charge extra for that? naplaćujete li to posebno? [napla**choo**yeteh]

extraordinary neobičan [neob**ee**chan]

extremely krajnje [kr**ī**n-yeh]

eye oko
 will you keep an eye on my suitcase for me? možete li pripaziti na moj kofer [m**o**Jeteh lee pre**e**pazeetee na moy k**o**fer]

eyebrow pencil olovka za obrve [**o**berveh]

eye drops kapi za oči [k**a**pee za **o**chee]

eyeglasses naočale [n**a**ochaleh]

eyeliner eyeliner

eye makeup remover skidač šminke [sk**ee**dach shm**ee**nkeh]

eye shadow sjenilo za oči [s-y**e**neelo za **o**chee]

F

face lice [**lee**tseh]

factory tvornica [tv**o**rneetsa]

Fahrenheit* Farenheitov stupanj [f**a**renhītov st**oo**pan]

faint onesvijestiti se [onesve**e**yesteetee seh]
 she's fainted onesvijestila se [onesve**e**yesteela seh]
 I feel faint osjećam vrtoglavicu [**o**s-yecham vert**o**glaveetsoo]

fair (funfair) lunapark [**loo**napark]
 (commercial) sajam [s**a**-yam]
 (adj: just) pravedan

fairly prilično [**pree**leechno]

fake krivotvorina [kreevot**vo**reena]

fall pasti [**pas**tee]

she's had a fall ona je pala [yeh]

(US: season) jesen [**ye**sen]

false lažan [**la**Jan]

family obitelj [**o**beetel]

famous slavan

fan ventilator [ven**tee**lator]

(sport) navijač [na**vee**yach]

(woman) navijačica [naveey**a**cheetsa]

fan belt remen ventilatora [ven**tee**latora]

fantastic fantastičan [fan**ta**steechan]

far dalek

dialogue

is it far from here? je li to daleko? [yeh lee]

no, not very far ne, nije daleko [neh **nee**yeh]

well how far? koliko daleko? [**ko**leeko]

it's about 20 kilometres oko dvadeset kilometara [**kee**lometara]

fare vozarina [voz**a**reena]

farm farma

fashionable u modi [oo **mo**dee]

fast brz [berz]

fat (person) debeo

(on meat) masno meso

father otac [**o**tats]

father-in-law (husband's father) svekar

(wife's father) tast

faucet slavina [sl**a**veena]

fault greška [**gre**shka]

sorry, it was my fault oprostite, ja sam kriv [opr**o**steeteh ya sam kreev]

it's not my fault nisam ja kriv [**nee**sam ya kreev]

faulty neispravan [ne**hee**spravan]

favourite omiljen [**o**meel-yen]

fax faks

February veljača [**ve**lyacha]

feel osjećati [**os**-yeh-chatee]

I feel hot vruće mi je [**vroo**cheh meh yeh]

I feel unwell nije mi dobro [**nee**yeh mee **do**bro]

I feel like going for a walk rado bih prošetao [beeн pr**o**shetao]

how are you feeling? kako se osjećate? [seh **os**-yechateh]

I'm feeling better bolje mi je [**bol**-yeh mee yeh]

felt-tip (pen) flomaster

fence ograda

fender (US: of car) branik [br**a**neek]

ferry trajekt [tra-**yekt**]

festival festival [**fe**steeval]

fetch poći (po) [**po**chee]

I'll fetch him ja ću ga povesti [ya choo ga p**o**vestee]

will you come and fetch me later? možete li kasnije doći po mene? [m**o**Jeteh lee kasneey**e**h d**o**chee]

feverish grozničav [grozneechav]
few: a few nekoliko [nekoleeko]
  a few days nekoliko dana
fiancé zaručnik [zaroochneek]
fiancée zaručnica [zaroochneetsa]
field polje [pol-yeh]
fight tuča [toocha]
figs smokve [smokveh]
fill puniti [pooneetee]
fill in ispuniti [eespooneetee]
  do I have to fill this in?
  moram li to ispuniti [lee]
fill up napuniti [napooneetee]
  fill it up, please napunite ga,
  molim [napooneeteh ga
  moleem]
filling plomba
film film [feelm]

dialogue

> do you have this kind of
> film? imate li ovu vrstu
> filma? [eemateh lee ovoo
> verstoo feelma]
> yes, how many exposures?
> da, koliko ekspozicija?
> [koleeko ekspozeetseeya]
> 36 tridesetšest
> [treedesetshest]

film processing razvijanje
  filma [razveeyan-yeh]
filthy prljav [perlyav]
find naći [nachee]
  I can't find it ne mogu to
  naći [nemogoo]

I've found it (said by man/
  woman) našao/našla sam
  [nashao/nashla]
find out saznati [saznatee]
  could you find out for me?
  možete li to saznati? [mojeteh
  lee]
fine (adj: good) dobro
  (punishment) globa

dialogues

> how are you? kako ste?
> [steh]
> I'm fine, thanks hvala,
> dobro [Hvala]
> is that OK? je li to u redu?
> [yeh lee to oo redoo]
> that's fine, thanks u redu
> je, hvala

finger prst [perst]
finish završiti [zaversheetee]
  I haven't finished yet (said
  by man/woman) nisam još
  završio/završila [neesam yosh
  zaversheeo/ zaversheela]
  when does it finish? kada
  završava? [zavershava]
fire: fire! požar! [pojar]
  can we light a fire here?
  možemo li ovdje upaliti
  vatru? [mojemo lee ovd-yeh
  zapaleetee vatroo]
  it's on fire gori [goree]
fire alarm požarna uzbuna
  [pojarna oozboona]
fire brigade vatrogasci
  [vatrogastsee]

fire escape požarni izlaz
[po**J**arnee **ee**zlaz]
fire extinguisher aparat za
gašenje požara [**g**ashen-yeh]
first prvi [**per**vee]
I was first (said by man/woman)
bio/bila sam prvi/prva [**bee**o/
beela]
at first isprva [**ee**sperva]
the first time prvi put [poot]
first on the left prva nalijevo
[**per**va na**lee**yevo]
first aid prva pomoć [**po**moch]
first aid kit komplet za prvu
pomoć [**per**voo]
first floor prvi kat
(US) prizemlje [**pree**zem-lyeh]
first name ime [**ee**meh]
fish riba [**ree**ba]
fishing village ribarsko selo
[**ree**barsko]
fishmonger's ribarnica
[**ree**barneetsa]
fit pristajati [**pree**sta-yatee]
it doesn't fit me ne pristaje
mi [**pree**sta-yeh mee]
fitting room soba za
presvlačenje [**pre**svlachen-yeh]
fix (repair) popraviti [**po**praveetee]
can you fix this? možete li to
popraviti [mo**J**eteh lee]
fizzy gaziran [**g**azeeran]
flag zastava [**z**astava]
flannel krpica za pranje lica
[**ker**peetsa za pran-yeh **lee**tsa]
flash (for camera) svjetlucati
[sv-yetl**oo**tsatee]

flat (noun: apartment) stan
(adj) ravan
I've got a flat tyre imam
praznu gumu [**ee**mam pr**a**znoo
goomoo]
flavour okus [**o**koos]
flea buha [**boo**Ha]
flight let
flight number broj leta [broy]
flippers peraje [**per**a-yeh]
flood poplava
floor pod
(storey) kat
on the floor na podu [**po**doo]
florist cvjećarna [tsv**ee**ye**cha**rna]
flour brašno [**bra**shno]
flower cvijet [**tsvee**yet]
flu gripa [**gree**pa]
fluent: he speaks fluent
Croatian on tečno govori
hrvatski [**te**chno **g**ovoree
Hervatskee]
fly (verb) letjeti [**let**-yetee]
(noun: insect) muha [**moo**ha]
fly in doletjeti [**dolet**-yetee]
fly out odletjeti [**odlet**-yetee]
fog magla
foggy: it's foggy magla je
[yeh]
folk dancing narodni ples
[**naro**dnee]
folk music narodna glazba
[**naro**dna]
follow slijediti [**slee**ye**dee**tee]
follow me slijedite me
[**slee**ye**dee**teh]
food hrana [**Hra**na]
food poisoning trovanje
hranom [**tro**van-yeh]

food shop/store
samoposluživanje
[samposloo**j**eevan-yeh]
foot* st**o**palo
on foot pje**š**ice [p-y**e**sheetseh]
football n**o**gomet
(ball) l**o**pta
football match nogometna
utakmica [**oo**takmeetsa]
for za
do you have something
for ...? imate li nešto za ...?
[**ee**mateh lee n**e**shto]

dialogues

who's the ice cream for?
za k**o**ga je sladoled? [yeh]
that's for me za mene
[m**e**neh]
and this one? a **o**vo?
that's for her to je za nju
[n-y**oo**]

where do I get the bus for
stari grad? **o**dakle kre**ć**e
autobus za stari grad?
[**o**dakleh kr**e**cheh **a**ootoboos za
star**ee**]
the bus for stari grad
leaves from the bus
station autobus za stari
grad kr**e**će s autobusnog
k**o**lodvora [sa**oo**toboosnog]

how long have you been
here for? koliko ste ve**ć**
ovdje? [k**o**leeko steh vech
ovd-yeh]

I've been here for two
days, how about you? dva
dana, a vi? [vee]
I've been here for a week
ovdje sam već tjedan dana
[t-y**e**dan]

forehead **č**elo [ch**e**lo]
foreign stran
foreigner stranac [str**a**nats]
(woman) strankinja [strank**ee**nya]
forest šuma [sh**oo**ma]
forget zaboraviti [zabor**a**veetee]
I forget zaboravljam
[zabor**a**vlyam]
I've forgotten (said by man/
woman) zaboravio/zaboravila
sam [zabor**a**veeo/ zabor**a**veela]
fork vilica [v**ee**leetsa]
(in road) ra**č**vanje [r**a**chvan-yeh]
form (paper) formular [form**oo**lar]
formal slu**ž**ben [sl**oo**ben]
fortnight dva tjedna [t-y**e**dna]
fortunately sre**ć**om [sr**e**chom]
forward: could you forward
my mail? mo**ž**ete li mi
poslati moju poštu? [m**o**jeteh
lee mee p**o**slatee mo-yoo p**o**shtoo]
forwarding address adresa za
slanje pošte [slan-yeh p**o**shteh]
foundation cream p**o**dloga
fountain fontana
(drinking) **č**esma [ch**e**sma]
foyer predvorje [predvor-yeh]
fracture (noun) lom
France Francuska [frants**oo**ska]
free (at liberty) slobodan
is it free (of charge)? je li to
besplatno [yeh lee]

freeway autocesta [a**oo**totseta]

freezer zamrzivač [zamerz**ee**vach]

French (adj, language) francuski [frants**oo**skee]

French fries pomfrit [p**o**mfreet]

frequent često [ch**e**sto]

how frequent is the bus to Pula? koliko često vozi autobus za Pulu? [kol**ee**ko ch**e**sto v**o**zee a**oo**toboos za p**oo**loo]

fresh svjež [sv-y**e**J]

fresh orange juice svjež sok od naranče [n**a**rancheh]

Friday petak

fridge hladnjak [Hl**a**dnyak]

fried pržen [p**e**rJen]

fried egg prženo jaje [y**ī**yeh]

friend prijatelj [pr**ee**yatel]
 (female) prijateljica [-tel-yeetsa]

friendly prijateljski [pr**ee**yatelyskee]

from
 when does the next train from Zadar arrive? kada stiže sljedeći vlak iz Zadra? [st**ee**Jeh sleey**e**dechee]
 from Monday to Friday od ponedjeljka do petka
 from next Thursday od sljedećeg četvrtka [sleey**e**decheg ch**e**tvertka]

front (adj) prednji [pr**e**dn-yee]
 in front ispred [**ee**spred]
 in front of the hotel ispred hotela
 at the front na čelu [ch**e**loo]

frost mraz

frozen smrznut [sm**e**rznoot]

frozen food zamrznuta hrana [z**a**merznoota Hr**a**na]

fruit voće [v**o**cheh]

fruit juice voćni sok [v**o**chnee]

fry pržiti [p**e**rJeetee]

frying pan tava

full pun [poon]
 it's full of ... pun je ... [yeh]
 I'm full sit sam [seet]

full board puni pansion [p**oo**nee pans**ee**on]

fun: it was fun bilo je zabavno [b**ee**lo]

funeral pogreb

funny (peculiar) čudan [ch**oo**dan]
 (amusing) smiješan [smeey**e**shan]

furniture namještaj [nam-y**e**shtī]

further dalje [d**a**l-yeh]
 it's further down the road to je niže cestom [yeh n**ee**Jeh ts**e**stom]

fuse osigurač [oseegoorach]
  the lights have fused
  pregorio je osigurač
  [pregoreeo yeh]
fuse box kutija s osiguračima
  [kooteeya soseegooracheema]
fuse wire žica za osigurač
  [Jeetsa]
future budućnost
  [boodoochnost]
  in future ubuduće
  [ooboodoocheh]

G

gallon* galon
game igra [eegra]
garage (petrol) benzinska
  pumpa [benzeenska poompa]
  (repair) autoservis
  [aootoservees]
  (parking) garaža [garaJa]
garden vrt [vert]
garlic češnjak [cheshnyak]
gas plin [pleen]
  (US: petrol) benzin [benzeen]
gas cylinder plinska boca
  [pleenska botsa]
gasoline benzin [benzeen]
gas permeable lenses
  porozne leće [porozneh lecheh]
gas station benzinska pumpa
  [benzeenska poompa]
gate vrata
  (at airport) izlaz [eezlaz]
gay gay
gay bar gay bar
gear brzina [berzeena]

gearbox mjenjač [m-yenyach]
gear lever ručica mjenjača
  [roocheetsa m-yenyacha]
general opći [opchee]
gents (toilet) muški [mooshkee]
genuine pravi [pravee]
German (adj) njemački
  [n-yemachkee]
German measles rubeola
  [roobeola]
Germany Njemačka
  [n-yemachka]
get dobiti [dobeetee]
  will you get me another one,
  please? mogu li dobiti još
  jedan, molim? [mogoo lee
  –yosh yedan moleem]
  how do I get to ...? kako ću
  doći do ...? [choo dochee]
  do you know where I can get
  them? znate li gdje ih mogu
  dobiti? [gd-yeh eeH]

dialogue

can I get you a drink?
mogu li vas počastiti
pićem? [mogoo lee vas
pochasteetee peechem]
no, I'll get this one, what
would you like? ne, ja ću,
što ćete popiti? [ya choo
shto cheteh popeetee]
a glass of red wine čašu
crnog vina [chashoo tsernog
veena]

get back (return) vratiti se
  [vrateetee seh]

get in (arrive) stići [**steechee**]

get off sići [**seechee**]

where do I get off? gdje trebam sići? [gd-yeh]

get on (to train etc) ući [**oochee**]

get out (of car etc) izaći [**eezachee**]

get up (in the morning) ustati [**oostatee**]

gift dar

gift shop trgovina darovima [**tergoveena daroveema**]

gin džin [jeen]

a gin and tonic, please džin i tonik, molim [**moleem**]

girl djevojka [d-**yevoyka**]

girlfriend cura [**tsoora**]

give dati [**datee**]

can you give me some change? možete li mi dati sitno? [**mo**Jeteh lee mee – **seetno**]

I gave it to him dao sam mu to [**moo**]

will you give this to ...? možete li to dati ...?

dialogue

how much do you want for this? koliko tražite za to? [**koleeko** traJeeteh za to]
30 kunas trideset kuna
I'll give you 18 dat ću vam osamnaest [**choo**]

give back vratiti [**vrateetee**]

glad zadovoljan [**za**dovolyan]

glass (material) staklo

(drink) čaša [**chasha**]

a glass of wine čaša vina [**veena**]

glasses naočale [**naochaleh**]

gloves rukavice [**rookaveetseh**]

glue ljepilo [l-**yepeelo**]

go ići [**eechee**]

we'd like to go to the Roman Forum željeli bismo vidjeti rimski forum [Jel-**yelee** beesmo veed-yetee reemskee foroom]

where are you going? kamo idete? [**eedeteh**]

where does this bus go? kamo vozi ovaj autobus? [**vo**zee ovī aootoboos]

let's go! idemo! [**eedemo**]

she's gone otišla je [**oteeshla** yeh]

where has he gone? kamo je otišao? [**oteeshao**]

I went there last week bio sam tamo prošli tjedan [**proshlee** t-yedan]

pizza to go pizza za van

go away otići [**oteechee**]

go away! odlazi! [**odlazee**]

go back (return) vratiti se [**vrateetee** seh]

go down (the stairs etc) sići [**seechee**]

go in ući [**oochee**]

go out izaći [**eezachee**]

do you want to go out tonight? želite li večeras izaći? [Jeleeteh lee vecheras]

go through proći kroz [**prochee**]

go up (the stairs etc) ići gore [**ee**chee **go**reh]

goat koza

goats' cheese kozji sir [**koz**-yee seer]

God Bog

goggles naočale za plivanje [na**o**chaleh za plee**van**-yeh]

gold zlato

golf golf

golf course golfsko igralište [**ee**graleeshteh]

good dobro

good! dobro!

it's no good nema smisla [**smee**sla]

goodbye zbogom

good evening dobra večer [**ve**cher]

Good Friday Veliki petak [**ve**leekee]

good morning dobro jutro [**yoo**tro]

good night laku noć [**la**koo noch]

goose guska [**goo**ska]

got: we've got to leave moramo poći [**po**chee]

have you got any ...? imate li ...? [**ee**mateh lee]

government vlada

gradually postupno [**po**stoopno]

grammar gramatika [**grama**teeka]

gram(me) gram

granddaughter unuka [**oo**nooka]

grandfather djed [d-yed]

grandmother baka

grandson unuk [**oo**nook]

grapefruit grejpfrut [**gray**pfroot]

grapefruit juice sok od grejpfruta

grapes grožđe [**gro**Jjeh]

grass trava

grateful zahvalan [**za**Hvalan]

gravy umak [**oo**mak]

great velik [**ve**leek]

that's great! super! [**soo**per]

a great success velik uspjeh [**oo**sp-yeh]

Great Britain Velika Britanija [bree**ta**neeya]

Greece Grčka [**ger**chka]

greedy lakom

Greek (adj, language) grčki [**ger**chkee]

green zelen

green card zelena karta

greengrocer's voćarna [**vo**charna]

grey siv [seev]

grill (noun) roštilj [**rosh**teel]

grilled s roštilja [sroshteel**ya**]

grocer's trgovina mješovitom robom [ter**go**veena m-yesh**o**veetom]

ground tlo

on the ground na tlu [tloo]

ground floor prizemlje [**pree**zem-lyeh]

group skupina [sk**oo**peena]

guarantee jamstvo [**yam**stvo]

is it guaranteed? je li to zajamčeno? [yeh lee to za-**yam**cheno]

guest gost

guesthouse pansion [pan**see**on]

guide vodič [**vo**deech]
guidebook vodič
guided tour obilazak
s vodičem [**o**beelazak s
vod**ee**chem]
guitar gitara [**ge**etara]
gum guma [**goo**ma]
gun puška [**poo**shka]
gym teretana

H

hair kosa
hairbrush četka za kosu
[**che**tka za **ko**soo]
haircut frizura [freez**oo**ra]
hairdresser frizer [**freezer**]
hairdryer sušilo za kosu
[**soo**sheelo]
hair gel gel za kosu
hairgrip kopča za kosu
[**ko**pcha]
hair spray lak za kosu
half pola
  half an hour pola sata
  half a litre pola litre [**lee**treh]
  about half that otprilike pola
  od toga [**ot**preeleekeh]
half board polupansion
[**po**loopanseeon]
half bottle pola boce [**bo**tseh]
half fare pola karte
half price pola cijene
[tse**e**yeneh]
ham šunka [**shoo**nka]
hamburger hamburger
[**ham**boorger]
hammer čekić [**che**keech]

hand ruka [**roo**ka]
handbag ručna torba [**roo**chna]
handbrake ručna kočnica
[**ko**chneetsa]
handkerchief džepna
maramica [**je**pna mar**a**meetsa]
handle (noun) ručica
[**roo**cheetsa]
hand luggage ručna prtljaga
[**roo**chna pertl-yaga]
hang-gliding zmajarstvo [zma-
yarstvo]
hangover mamurluk
[mam**oor**look]
I've got a hangover (said
by man/woman) mamuran/
mamurna sam [**ma**mooran/
mam**oo**rna]
happen dogoditi [dog**o**deetee]
what's happening? što se
događa [shto seh d**o**gaja]
what has happened? što se
dogodilo [dog**o**deelo]
happy sretan
I'm not happy about this
nisam time zadovoljan
[**nee**sam t**ee**meh z**a**dovolyan]
harbour luka [**loo**ka]
hard težak [teh**J**ak]
hardboiled egg tvrdo kuhano
jaje [t**ver**do k**oo**hano y**ī**yeh]
hard lenses tvrde leće [t**ver**deh
lecheh]
hardly teško [**te**shko]
hardly ever gotovo nikad
[**nee**kad]
hardware shop željezarija [Jel-
yezar**ee**ya]
hat šešir [**she**hsheer]

hate mrziti [**mer**zeetee]
have* imati [**ee**matee]
  can I have ...? mogu li
  dobiti ...? [**mo**goo lee **do**beetee]
  do you have ...? imate li ...?
  what'll you have? što ćete?
  [shto **che**teh]
  I have to leave now sad
  moram poći [**po**chee]
  do I have to ...? moram
  li ...?
  can we have some ...?
  možemo li dobiti ...?
  [**mo**Jemo]
hayfever peludna groznica
  [pe**loo**dna gro**zneetsa**]
hazelnuts lješnjaci
  [l-**yesh**nyatsee]
he* on
head glava
headache glavobolja
  [glavo**bolya**]
headlights farovi [**fa**rovee]
headphones slušalice
  [sloo**shaleetseh**]
health food shop trgovina
  zdravom hranom [ter**go**veena
  Hranom]
healthy zdrav
hear čuti [**choo**tee]

dialogue

  can you hear me? čujete li
  me? [**choo**yeteh lee meh]
  I can't hear you, could you
  repeat that? ne čujem vas,
  možete li to ponoviti?
  [**mo**Jeteh lee to po**no**veetee]

hearing aid slušno pomagalo
  [**sloo**shno]
heart srce [**sert**seh]
heart attack infarkt [**een**farkt]
heat vrućina [vroo**cheena**]
heater grijač [**gree**yach]
heating grijanje [**gree**yan-yeh]
heavy težak [**te**Jak]
heel peta
  could you heel these?
  možete li staviti nove pete?
  [**mo**Jeteh lee sta**veetee** noveh
  peteh]
heelbar postolar
height visina [vee**seena**]
helicopter helikopter
hello zdravo, bog
  (on telephone) halo
helmet (for motorcycle) kaciga
  [**kat**seega]
help pomoć (f) [**po**moch]
  help! upomoć! [**oo**pomoch]
  can you help me? možete li
  mi pomoći? [**mo**Jeteh lee mee
  po**mochee**]
  thank you very much for your
  help puno vam hvala na
  pomoći [**poo**no–**H**vala]
helpful koristan [**ko**reestan]
hepatitis hepatitis [hepa**teetees**]
her*: I haven't seen her (said
  by man/woman) nisam je vidio/
  vidjela [**nee**sam yeh **vee**deeo/
  veed-**yela**]
  to her njoj [nyoy]
  with her s njom [snyom]
  for her za nju [za nyoo]
  that's her to je ona [yeh]
  that's her towel to je njen

ručnik [n-yen **roo**chneek]
herbal tea biljni čaj [**bee**lynee
chī]
herbs trave [**trav**eh]
here ovdje [**ov**d-yeh]
 here is/are ... ovdje je/su ...
 [yeh/soo]
 here you are izvolite
 [eez**vo**leeteh]
hers*: that's hers to je njeno
 [n-**ye**no]
hey! ej! [ay]
hi! zdravo!, bog!
hide sakriti [**sa**kreetee]
high visok [**vee**sok]
highchair dječja stolica
 [d-**ye**chya **sto**leetsa]
highway autocesta [**a**oototseta]
hill brdo [**ber**do]
him*: I haven't seen him
 (said by man/woman) nisam
 ga vidio/vidjela [**nee**sam ga
 veedeeo/ **veed**-yela]
 to him njemu [n-**ye**moo]
 with him s njim [sn-yeem]
 for him za njega [zan-**ye**ga]
 that's him to je on [yeh]
hip kuk [kook]
hire unajmiti [oon**ī**meetee]
 for hire u najam [oo na-yam]
 where can I hire a bike? gdje
 mogu unajmiti bicikl?
 [gd-yeh **mo**goo – beet**see**kl]
his*: it's his car to je njegov
 auto [to yeh n-**ye**gov **a**ooto]
 that's his to je njegovo
 [n-**ye**govo]
hit udariti [**oo**dareetee]
hitchhike stopirati [**sto**peeratee]

hobby hobi [**ho**bee]
hockey hokej [**ho**kay]
hold (verb) držati [der**J**atee]
hole rupa [**roo**pa]
holiday odmor
 on holiday na odmoru
 [**od**moroo]
home dom
 at home kod kuće [**koo**cheh]
 (in my country) u domovini [oo
 do**mo**veenee]
 we go home tomorrow sutra
 idemo doma [**soo**tra **ee**demo]
honest pošten [**posh**ten]
honey med
honeymoon medeni mjesec
 [**me**denee m-**ye**sets]
hood hauba [**ha**ooba]
hope nada
 I hope so nadam se da je
 tako [yeh]
 I hope not nadam se da nije
 tako [**nee**yeh]
hopefully nadajmo se [**na**dīmo
 seh]
horn (of car) truba [**troo**ba]
horrible strašan [**strash**an]
horse konj [**ko**nyuh]
horse riding jahanje konja
 [**ya**Han-yeh **ko**nya]
hospital bolnica [**bol**neetsa]
hospitality gostoprimstvo
 [gosto**preem**stvo]
 thank you for your hospitality
 hvala vam na gostoprimstvu
hot vruć [vrooch]
 (spicy) ljut [lyoot]
 I'm hot vruće mi je [**vroo**cheh
 mee yeh]

it's hot today danas je vruće
hotel hotel
hotel room hotelska soba
hour sat
house kuća [koocha]
house wine domaće vino
[domacheh veeno]
hovercraft hoverkraft
how kako
how many? koliko? [koleeko]
how much? koliko?

dialogues

how are you? kako ste?
[steh]
fine, thanks, and you?
hvala, dobro, a vi?
[Hvala – vee]

how much is it? koliko je
to? [koleeko yeh]
... kunas ... kuna [koona]
I'll take it uzet ću to [oozet
choo]

humid vlažan [vlaJan]
humour humor [hoomor]
Hungarian (adj) mađarski
[majarskee]
(man) Mađar [majar]
(woman) Mađarica [majareetsa]
Hungary Mađarska [majarska]
hungry: I'm hungry gladan sam
are you hungry? jeste li
gladni [yesteh lee gladnee]
hurry (verb) žuriti [Jooreetee]
I'm in a hurry žurim se
[Jooreem seh]

there's no hurry nije hitno
[neeyeh heetno]
hurry up! požurite!
[poJooreeteh]
hurt (verb) boljeti [bol-yetee]
it really hurts jako me boli
[yako meh bolee]
husband muž [mooJ]
hydrofoil hidrogliser
[heedrogleeser]
hypermarket hipermarket
[heepermarket]

I
■

I ja [ya]
ice led
with ice s ledom
no ice, thanks bez leda,
molim [moleem]
ice cream sladoled
icecream cone kornet
iced coffee ledena kava
ice lolly sladoled na štapiću
[shtapeechoo]
ice rink klizalište
[kleezaleeshteh]
idea zamisao [zameesao]
idiot idiot [eedeeot]
if ako
ignition paljenje [pal-yen-yeh]
ill bolestan
I feel ill osjećam se bolesno
[os-yecham seh]
illness bolest
imitation imitacija
[eemeetatseeya]
immediately odmah [odmaH]

important važan [va**J**an]
  it's very important to je jako
  važno [yeh **y**ako]
  it's not important to nije
  važno [**nee**yeh]
impossible nemoguć
  [**ne**mogooch]
impressive dojmljiv [d**o**ym-
  lyeev]
improve popraviti [**po**praveetee]
  I want to improve my
  Croatian želim popraviti
  svoj hrvatski [**J**eleem – svoy
  H**e**rvatskee]
in: it's in the centre to je u
  središtu [yeh oo s**re**deeshtoo]
in my car u mom autu
  [**a**ootoo]
in Rijeka u Rijeci [reey**e**tsee]
in two days from now za dva
  dana
in five minutes za pet minuta
  [meen**oo**ta]
in May u svibnju [oo
  sv**ee**bnyoo]
in English na engleskom
in Croatian na hrvatskom
  [H**e**rvatskom]
is he in? je li on unutra? [yeh
  lee on **oo**nootra]
inch* inč [eench]
include uključiti
  [ookly**oo**cheetee]
  does that include meals? je
  li hrana uključena? [yeh lee
  H**ra**na ookly**oo**chena]
  is that included? je li to
  uključeno? [ookly**oo**cheno]
inconvenient neprikladan

[ne**pree**kladan]
incredible nevjerojatan [nev-
  yer**o**yatan]
Indian (adj) indijski
  [**ee**ndeeyskee]
indicator (of car) žmigavac
  [**J**m**ee**gavats]
indigestion loša probava
  [**lo**sha]
indoor pool zatvoreni bazen
  [**za**tvorenee]
indoors unutra [**oo**nootra]
inexpensive jeftin [**y**efteen]
infection infekcija
  [eenf**e**ktseeya]
infectious zarazan
inflammation upala [**oo**pala]
informal neslužben [nesloo**J**ben]
information informacija
  [eenformatseeya]
  do you have any information
  about ...? imate li
  informacije o ...? [**ee**mateh lee
  eenformatseeyeh]
information desk šalter za
  informacije [**sh**alter]
injection injekcija
  [een-y**e**ktseeya]
injured ozlijeđen [**o**zleeyejen]
  she's been injured ona je
  ozlijeđena [yeh **o**zleeyejena]
inlaws (husband's) muževa
  obitelj [**moo**Jeva ob**e**etel]
  (wife's) ženina obitelj
  [**J**eneena]
inner tube zračnica
  [**z**rachneetsa]
innocent nevin [**ne**veen]
insect insekt [**ee**nsekt]

insect bite ubod insekta
[**oo**bod]
do you have anything
for insect bites? imate li
nešto protiv uboda insekta
[**ee**mateh lee n**e**shto pr**o**teev]
insect repellent sredstvo
za zaštitu od insekata
[zashteetoo]
inside unutra [**oo**nootra]
inside the hotel u hotelu [oo
hot**e**loo]
let's sit inside sjednimo
unutra [s-y**e**dneemo]
insist inzistirati
[eenzeest**ee**ratee]
I insist inzistiram
[eenz**ee**steeram]
insomnia nesanica [n**e**saneetsa]
instant coffee instant kava
[**ee**nstant]
instead umjesto [**oo**m-yesto]
give me that one instead
uzet ću radije toga [**oo**zechoo
rad**ee**yeh]
instead of ... umjesto ...
insulin inzulin [eenz**oo**leen]
insurance osiguranje
[oseeg**oo**ran-yeh]
intelligent inteligentan
[eenteleeg**e**ntan]
interested: I'm interested in ...
zanima me ... [z**a**neema meh]
interesting zanimljiv [zaneeml-
yeev]
that's very interesting to je
vrlo zanimljivo [yeh v**e**rlo]
international međunarodni
[mejoonar**o**dnee]

Internet internet
interpret prevoditi
[prev**o**deetee]
interpreter prevoditelj
[prev**o**deetel]
(woman) prevoditeljica
[prevodeet**e**lyeetsa]
intersection raskrižje [rask**ree**J-
yeh]
interval interval [**ee**nterval]
into u [oo]
I'm not into ... nisam ja za ...
[n**ee**sam ya]
introduce predstaviti
[predst**a**veetee]
may I introduce ...? mogu li
predstaviti ...? [m**o**goo lee]
invitation poziv [p**o**zeev]
invite pozvati [p**o**zvatee]
Ireland Irska [**ee**rska]
Irish (adj) irski [**ee**rskee]
I'm Irish (said by man/woman) ja
sam Irac/Irkinja [ya – **ee**rats/
eerkeenya]
iron (metal) željezo [J**e**l-yezo]
(for clothes) glačalo [gl**a**chalo]
can you iron these for me?
možete li mi ovo ispeglati?
[m**o**Jeteh lee mee **o**vo **ee**speglateh]
is* je [yeh]
island otok
it to
it is ... to je [yeh]
is it ...? je li to ...? [lee]
where is it? gdje je to? [gd-
yeh]
it's him to je on
it was ... to je bio [b**ee**o]
Italian (adj, language) talijanski

[**tal**eeyanskee]
Italy Italija [**ee**taleeya]
itch: it itches svrbi [**sver**bee]

J

jack (for car) dizalica
  [deezal**ee**tsa]
jacket jakna [**yak**na]
jar staklenka
jam (food) pekmez
  (traffic) gužva [**goo**Jva]
jammed: it's jammed blokiran
  je [bl**o**keeran yeh]
January siječanj [**see**yechan]
jaw vilica [v**ee**leetsa]
jazz džez [jez]
jealous ljubomoran
  [ly**oo**bomoran]
jeans traperice [trapereetseh]
jellyfish meduza [med**oo**za]
jersey pulover [pool**o**ver]
jetty molo
Jewish židovski [**Jee**dovskee]
jeweller's zlatarna
jewellery nakit [**na**keet]
job posao
jogging trčanje [**ter**chan-yeh]
  to go jogging idem na
  trčanje [**ee**dem]
joke šala [shala]
journey putovanje [poot**o**van-
  yeh]
  have a good journey! sretan
  put! [poot]
jug bokal
  a jug of water bokal vode
  [v**o**deh]

juice sok
July srpanj [**ser**pan]
jump skočiti [sk**o**cheetee]
jumper džemper [**je**mper]
jump leads kabeli za punjenje
  akumulatora [kabelee za p**oo**n-
  yen-yeh akoomool**a**tora]
junction križanje [kree**Jan**-yeh]
June lipanj [**lee**pan]
just (only) samo
  just two samo dva
  just for me samo za mene
  [**me**neh]
  just here baš ovdje [bash **ovd**-
  yeh]
  not just now ne baš sada [neh]
  we've just arrived baš smo
  stigli [**stee**glee]

K

keep držati [**der**Jatee]
  keep the change zadržite
  ostatak [zader**Jee**teh]
  can I keep it? mogu li to
  zadržati? [**mo**goo lee]
  please keep it zadržite to
ketchup kečap [**ke**chap]
kettle kotlić [**ko**tleech]
key ključ [klyooch]
  the key for room 201, please
  ključ za sobu 201, molim
  [**so**boo dva **noo**la **ye**dan, **mo**leem]
key ring privjesak za ključeve
  [preev-yesak za kly**oo**cheveh]
kidneys bubrezi [**boo**brezee]
kill ubiti [**oo**beetee]
kilo* kilogram [**kee**logram]

71

kilometre* kilometar
[keel**o**metar]
how many kilometres is it
to ...? koliko je kilometara
do ...? [k**o**leeko yeh]
kind ljubazan [ly**oo**bazan]
that's very kind of you vrlo
ste ljubazni [v**er**lo steh]

dialogue

which kind do you want?
koju vrstu želite? [k**o**-yoo
v**er**stoo Jel**ee**teh]
I want this/that kind želim
ovu vrstu [J**e**leem **o**voo]

king kralj [kral]
kiosk kiosk
kiss (noun) poljubac [p**o**lyoobats]
(verb) poljubiti [poly**oo**beetee]
kitchen kuhinja [k**oo**Heenya]
kitchenette čajna kuhinja
[ch**ī**na]
Kleenex® papirnate
maramice [p**a**peernateh
maram**ee**tseh]
knee koljeno [k**o**l-yeno]
knickers (ženske) gaće [J**e**nskeh
g**a**cheh]
knife nož [noJ]
knitwear trikotaža [treekot**a**Ja]
knock udariti [**oo**dareetee]
knock down: he's been
knocked down oboren je
[yeh]
knock over oboriti
[ob**o**reetee]
know znati [zn**a**tee]

I don't know ne znam [neh]
I didn't know that nisam to
znao [n**ee**sam]
do you know where I can
find ...? znate li gdje mogu
naći ...? [zn**a**teh lee gd-yeh
m**o**goo n**a**chee]
Kosovo Kosovo
Kosovan (adj) kosovski
[k**o**sovskee]
(man) Kosovljanin, Kosovar
[k**o**sovl-yaneen]
(woman) Kosovljanka,
Kosovarka [kosovl-yanka]

L

label naljepnica [n**a**l-yepneetsa]
ladies' (toilets) ženski [J**e**nskee]
ladies' wear ženska odjeća
[J**e**nska **o**d-yecha]
lady gospođa [g**o**spoja]
lager pivo [p**ee**vo]
lake jezero [y**e**zero]
lamb (animal) janje [y**a**n-yeh]
(meat) janjetina [y**a**n-yeteena]
lamp lampa
lane staza
(on motorway) trak
language jezik [y**e**zeek]
language course jezični tečaj
[y**e**zeechnee t**e**chī]
large velik [v**e**leek]
last posljednji [p**o**sl-yedn-yee]
what time is the last train
to Zagreb? kada kreće
posljednji vlak za Zagreb?
[k**a**da kr**e**cheh]

last week prošli tjedan
[proshlee t-yedan]
last Friday prošli petak
last night sinoć [seenoch]
late kasno
sorry I'm late oprostite
što kasnim [oprosteeteh shto
kasneem]
the train was late vlak je
kasnio [yeh kasneeo]
we must go – we'll be late
moramo krenuti – zakasnit
ćemo [krenootee zakasneet
chemo]
it's getting late vrijeme je
odmaklo [vreeyemeh yeh]
later kasnije [kasneeyeh]
I'll come back later vratit ću
se kasnije [vrateechoo seh]
see you later vidimo se
kasnije [veedeemo]
later on kasnije
latest najkasnije [naikasneeyee]
by Wednesday at the
latest najkasnije do srijede
[sreeyedeh]
laugh smijati se [smeeyatee seh]
launderette, laundromat
praonica rublja [praoneetsa
rooblya]
laundry (clothes) rublje [roobl-yeh]
lavatory zahod [zaHod]
law zakon
lawn travnjak [travnyak]
lawyer pravnik [pravneek]
(woman) pravnica [pravneetsa]
laxative laksativ [laksateev]
lazy lijen [leeyen]
lead (verb) voditi [vodeetee]

where does this lead to?
kamo to vodi? [vodee]
leaf list [leest]
leaflet letak
leak curiti [tsooreetee]
the roof leaks krov
prokišnjava [prokeeshnyava]
learn učiti [oocheetee]
least: not in the least nimalo
[neemalo]
at least najmanje [nīman-yeh]
leather koža [koJa]
leave otići [oteechee]
I am leaving tomorrow sutra
odlazim [sootra odlazeem]
he left yesterday jučer je
otišao [yoocher yeh oteeshao]
may I leave this here? mogu
li to ostaviti ovdje? [mogoo lee
to ostaveetee ovd-yeh]
I left my coat in the bar
(said by man/woman) ostavio/
ostavila sam kaput u baru
[ostaveeo/ostaveela sam kapoot oo
baroo]
when does the bus for Split
leave? kada kreće autobus
za Split [krecheh aootoboos za
spleet]
leek poriluk [poreelook]
left lijevo [leeyevo]
on the left, to the left s lijeve
strane [sleeyeveh straneh]
turn left skrenite lijevo
[skreneeteh leeyevo]
there's none left ništa nema
na lijevo [neeshta]
lefthanded ljevoruk [l-
yevorook]

left luggage (office) garderoba

leg noga

lemon limun [leemoon]

lemonade limunada [leemoonada]

lemon tea čaj s limunom [chai sleemoonom]

lend posuditi

  will you lend me your ...? hoćete li mi posuditi svoj ...? [hocheteh lee mee –svoy]

lens leće [lecheh]

lesbian lezbijka [lezbeeyka]

less manje [man-yeh]

  less than manje od

  less hot manje vruć

  less expensive jeftiniji [yefteeneeyee]

lesson poduka [podooka]

let pustiti [poosteetee]

  will you let me know? možete li me obavijestiti? [moJeteh lee meh obaveeyesteetee]

  I'll let you know obavijestit ću vas [choo]

  let's go for something to eat idemo nešto pojesti [eedemo neshto po-yestee]

  let off: will you let me off at ...? možete li stati da siđem ...? [moJeteh lee statee da seejem]

letter pismo [peesmo]

  do you have any letters for me? ima li pošte za mene? [eema lee poshteh za meneh]

letterbox poštanski sandučić [poshtanskee sandoocheech]

lettuce salata

lever ručica [roocheetsa]

library knjižnica [k-nyeeJneetsa]

licence dozvola

lid poklopac [poklopats]

lie (untruth) laž [laJ]

  (verb: tell untruth) lagati [lagatee]

  (in a position) ležati [leJatee]

  lie down leći [lechee]

life život [Jeevot]

lifebelt pojas za spašavanje [po-yas za spashavan-yeh]

lifeguard spasilac [spaseelats]

life jacket prsluk za spašavanje [perslook]

lift (in building) dizalo [deezalo]

  could you give me a lift? možete li me povesti? [moJeteh lee meh povestee]

  would you like a lift? želite li da vas povezem? [Jeleetee]

lift pass pokazna karta za žičaru [Jeecharoo]

  a daily/weekly lift pass dnevna/tjedna pokazna karta za žičaru [t-yedna]

light (noun) svjetlo [sv-yetlo]

  (not heavy) lak

  (of colour) svijetao [sveeyetao]

  do you have a light? imate li vatre? [eemateh lee vatreh]

light green svijetlozelen [sveeyetlozelen]

light bulb žarulja [Jaroolya]

  I need a new light bulb trebam novu žarulju [novoo Jaroolyoo]

lighter upaljač [oopalyach]

lightning munja [moonya]

like: I like it sviđa mi se [sveeja mee seh]
I like going for walks volim šetati [voleem shetatee]
I like you sviđate mi se [sveejateh mee seh]
I don't like it ne sviđa mi se to
do you like ...? sviđa li vam se ...? [lee]
I'd like a beer (said by man/woman) želio/ željela bih pivo [Jeleeo/Jel-yela beeн peevo]
I'd like to go swimming želio/željela bih na plivanje [pleevan-yeh]
would you like a drink? želite li piće? [Jeleeteh lee peecheh]
would you like to go for a walk? želite li prošetati [proshetatee]
what's it like? kakvo je? [yeh]
like this ovakvo
I want one like this želim ovakav [Jeleem]
lime limeta [leemeta]
line linija [leeneeya]
could you give me an outside line? mogu li dobiti vanjsku liniju? [mogoo lee dobeetee vanyskoo leeneeyoo]
lips usne [oosneh]
lip salve krema za usne
lipstick ruž za usne [rooJ]
liqueur liker [leeker]
listen slušati [slooshatee]
litre* litra [leetra]
a litre of white wine litra bijelog vina [beeyelog veena]

little malo
just a little, thanks samo malo, hvala
a little milk malo mlijeka [mleeyeka]
a little bit more još malo [yosh]
live (verb) živjeti [Jeev-yetee]
we live together mi živimo zajedno [mee Jeevemo za-yedno]

dialogue

where do you live? gdje živite? [gd-yeh Jeeveeteh]
I live in London u Londonu [oo londonoo]

lively živahan [Jeevahan]
liver jetra [yetra]
loaf kruh [krooн]
lobby (in hotel) predvorje [predvor-yeh]
lobster jastog [yastog]
local lokalni [lokalnee]
can you recommend a local wine/restaurant? možete li preporučiti lokalno vino/lokalni restoran [moJeteh lee preporoocheetee – veeno]
lock zaključati [zaklyoochatee]
(noun) brava
it's locked zaključano je [zaklyoochano yeh]
lock in zaključati iznutra [eeznootra]
lock out: I've locked myself out (said by man/woman) ostao/

ostala sam vani bez ključa [vanee bez klyoocha]

locker (for luggage etc) pretinac [preteenats]

lollipop lizaljka [leezalyka]

London London

long dug [doog]

how long will it take to fix it? koliko će trajati popravak? [koleeko cheh tra-yatee]

how long does it take? koliko dugo traje? [doogo tra-yeh]

a long time dugo vremena

one day/two days longer još jedan/dva dana [yosh yedan]

longdistance call međugradski poziv [mejoogradskee pozeev]

look: I'm just looking, thanks samo gledam, hvala [Hvala]

you don't look well ne izgledate dobro [neh eezgledateh]

look out! pazite! [pazeeteh]

can I have a look? mogu li pogledati? [mogoo lee pogledatee]

look after paziti [pazeetee]

look at pogledati [pogledatee]

look for potražite [potraJeetee]

I'm looking for ... tražim ... [traJeem]

look forward to veselim se [veseleem seh]

I'm looking forward to it veselim se tome [tomeh]

loose (handle etc) labav

lorry kamion [kameeon]

lose izgubiti [eezgoobeetee]

I'm lost, I want to get to ... (said by man/woman) izgubio/ izgubila sam se, želim do ... [eezgoobeeo/ eezgoobeela seh Jeleem]

I've lost my bag izgubio/ izgubila sam torbu [torboo]

lost property (office) ured za izgubljene stvari [oored za eezgoobl-yeneh stvaree]

lot: a lot, lots mnogo

not a lot ne mnogo [neh]

a lot of Parmesan puno parmezana [poono parmezana]

a lot of sauce puno umaka [oomaka]

a lot of people mnogo ljudi [lyoodee]

a lot of boys mnogo dječaka [d-yechaka]

a lot of drinks mnogo pića [peecha]

a lot bigger mnogo veći [vechee]

I like it a lot jako mi se sviđa [yako mee seh sveeja]

lotion losion [loseeon]

loud glasan

lounge salon

love ljubav (f) [lyoobav] (verb) voljeti [vol-yetee]

I love Croatia volim Hrvatsku [voleem Hervatskoo]

lovely divan [deevan]

low nizak [neezak]

luck sreća [srecha]

good luck! sretno! [sretno]

luggage prtljaga [pertl-yaga]

luggage trolley kolica za prtljagu [koleetsa za pertl-yagoo]
lump izbočina [eezbocheena]
lunch ručak [roochak]
lungs pluća [ploocha]
luxurious luksuzan [looksoozan]
luxury luksuz [looksooz]

M

machine stroj [stroy]
mad (insane) lud [lood]
(angry) ljut [l-yoot]
magazine časopis [chasopees]
maid (in hotel) sobarica [sobareetsa]
maiden name djevojačko ime [d-yevoyachko eemeh]
mail pošta [poshta]
is there any mail for me? ima li za mene pošte? [eema lee za meneh poshteh]
mailbox poštanski sandučić [poshtanskee sandoocheech]
main glavni [glavnee]
main course glavno jelo [yelo]
main post office glavna pošta [poshta]
main road (in town) glavna ulica [ooleetsa]
(in the country) glavna cesta [tsesta]
mains switch glavni prekidač [prekeedach]
make (brand) marka
(verb) praviti [praveetee]
I make it 50 kunas to je pedeset kuna [yeh – koona]

what is it made of? od čega je to? [chega yeh]
make-up šminka [shmeenka]
man čovjek [chov-yek]
manager direktor [deerektor]
can I see the manager? mogu li razgovarati s direktorom? [mogoo lee razgovaratee razgovaratee]
manageress direktorica [deerektoreetsa]
manual (with manual gears) ručni mjenjač [roochnee m-yenzach]
many mnogi [mnogee]
not many ne mnogi [neh]
map karta
March ožujak [oJooyak]
margarine margarin [margareen]
market (in town) tržnica [terJneetsa]
marmalade marmelada
married: I'm married (said by man/woman) ja sam oženjen/udata [ya sam oJen-yen/oodata]
are you married? (said to man/woman) jeste li oženjeni/udati? [yesteh lee oJen-yenee/oodatee]
mascara maskara
match (football etc) utakmica [ootakmeetsa]
matches šibice [sheebeetseh]
material (cloth) tkanina [tkaneena]
matter: it doesn't matter nije važno [neeyeh vaJno]
what's the matter? u čemu je stvar? [oo chemo yeh]

mattress madrac [**ma**drats]

May svibanj [**s**veeban]

may: may I have another bottle? molim vas još jednu bocu [**mo**leem vas yosh **y**ednoo **bo**tsoo]

may I come in? mogu li ući? [**mo**goo lee **oo**chee]

may I see it? mogu li to vidjeti? [**v**eed-yetee]

may I sit here? mogu li sjesti ovdje? [s-**y**estee **o**vd-yeh]

maybe možda [**mo**Jda]

mayonnaise majoneza [mīy**o**neza]

me*: that's for me za mene je [**m**eneh yeh]

send it to me pošaljite mi to [poshal-yeeteh mee]

me too i ja [ee ya]

meal jelo [**y**elo]

dialogue

did you enjoy your meal? je li jelo bilo dobro? [ye lee **y**elo **b**eelo]

it was excellent, thank you bilo je izvrsno, hvala [**ee**zversno нvala]

mean (verb) misliti [**m**eesleetee]

what do you mean? kako to mislite? [**m**eesleeteh]

dialogue

what does this word mean? što znači ova riječ?

it means ... in English znači ... na engleskom

measles ospice [**o**speetseh]

meat meso

mechanic: is there a mechanic here? imate li ovdje mehaničara? [**ee**mateh lee **o**vd-yeh meн**a**neechara]

medicine (for cold etc) lijek [**l**eeyek]

Mediterranean Mediteran [medeet**e**ran]

medium (adj) srednji [**s**redn-yee]

medium-dry (wine) polusuho [**p**oloos**oo**нo]

medium-rare srednje pečeno [**s**redn-yeh **p**echeno]

medium-sized srednje veličine [vel**ee**ch**ee**neh]

meet sresti [**s**restee]

nice to meet you drago mi je [mee yeh]

where shall I meet you? gdje ćemo se naći? [gd-yeh **ch**emo seh **n**achee]

meeting sastanak

meeting place mjesto sastanka [m-**y**esto]

melon dinja [**d**eenya]

men ljudi [**l**yoodee]

mend popraviti [**p**opraveetee]

could you mend this for me? možete li ovo popraviti? [**mo**Jeteh lee]

menswear muška odjeća [**m**ooshka **o**d-yecha]

mention spomenuti
[spom**e**noo**tee**]
don't mention it nema na
čemu [n**e**ma na ch**e**moo]
menu jelovnik [y**e**lovneek]
**may I see the menu,
please?** molim vas jelovnik
[m**o**leem]
see **Menu Reader** page 186
message poruka [p**o**roo**ka**]
**are there any messages for
me?** ima li poruka za mene?
[**ee**ma lee – m**e**neh]
**I want to leave a message
for ...** (said by man/woman)
želio/željela bih ostaviti
poruku za ... [**J**eleeo/**J**el-yela
bee**H** **o**stav**ee**tee p**o**rookoo]
metal metal
metre* metar
microwave (oven) mikrovalka
[m**ee**krovalka]
midday podne [p**o**dneh]
at midday u podne [oo]
middle: **in the middle** u sredini
[oo sred**ee**neeh]
in the middle of the night
usred noći [**oo**sred n**o**chee]
the middle one srednji [sredn-
yee]
midnight ponoć (f) [p**o**noch]
at midnight u ponoć [oo]
might: **I might (not) go** možda
ću (neću) ići [m**o**Jda choo
(nechoo) **ee**chee]
**I might want to stay another
day** možda poželim ostati
još jedan dan [p**o**Jeleem **o**statee
yosh y**e**dan]

migraine migrena [meegr**e**na]
mild blag
mile* milja [m**ee**lya]
milk mlijeko [ml-y**e**ko]
milkshake frape [frap**e**h]
millimetre* milimetar
[m**ee**leemetar]
minced meat mljeveno meso
[ml-y**e**veno]
mind: **never mind** ništa za to
[n**ee**shta]
I've changed my mind
predomislio sam se
[pred**o**mees**lee**o sam seh]

dialogue

**do you mind if I open the
window?** smeta li vas ako
otvorim prozor?
[**o**tvoreem]
no, I don't mind ne smeta
[n**e**smeta]

mine*: **it's mine** moje je [m**o**-
yeh yeh]
mineral water mineralna voda
[m**ee**neralna]
minibar minibar
mints mentol bonboni
[bonb**o**nee]
minute minuta [meen**oo**ta]
in a minute odmah [**o**dmaH]
just a minute samo trenutak
[tren**oo**tak]
mirror zrcalo [z**e**rtsalo]
miss: **I missed the bus** nisam
uhvatio autobus [n**ee**sam
ooHvateeo **a**ootoboos]

Mi

Miss gospođica [gospojeetsa]
missing nedostajati [nedosta-yatee]
one of my ... is missing jedan moj ... nedostaje [yedan moy nedosta-yeh]
there's a suitcase missing nedostaje jedan kovčeg [kovcheg]
mist magla
mistake pogreška [pogreshka]
I think there's a mistake mislim da je ovo pogreška [meesleem da yeh ovo]
sorry, I've made a mistake oprostite, pogriješio sam [oprosteeteh pogreeyesheeo]
misunderstanding nesporazum [nesporazoom]
mix-up: sorry, there's been a mix-up oprostite, došlo je do zbrke [oprosteeteh doshlo yeh do zberkeh]
mobile phone mobitel [mobeetel]
modern moderan
modern art gallery moderna galerija [galereeya]
moisturizer hidrantna krema [heedrantna]
moment: I won't be a moment odmah se vraćam [odmaH seh vracham]
monastery samostan
Monday ponedjeljak [ponedyelyak]
money novac [novats]
Montenegro Crna Gora [tserna]

Montegran (adj) crnogorski [tsrnogorskee]
(man) Crnogorac [tsrnogorats]
(woman) Crnogorka
month mjesec [m-yesets]
monument spomenik [spomeneek]
moon mjesec [m-yesets]
moped moped
more* više [veesheh]
can I have some more water, please? mogu li dobiti još vode, molim [mogoo lee dobeetee yosh vodeh moleem]
more expensive/interesting skuplji/zanimljiviji [skoopl-yee/zaneeml-yeeveeyee]
more than 50 više od pedeset [veesheh]
more than that više od toga
a lot more puno više [poono]

dialogue

would you like some more? želite li još malo? [Jeleeteh lee yosh]
no, no more for me, thanks ne bih više, hvala [neh beeH veesheh Hvala]
how about you? a vi? [vee]
I don't want any more, thanks ne bih više, hvala

morning jutro [yootro]
this morning jutros
in the morning ujutro [ooyootro]
mosquito komarac [komarats]

mosquito repellent sredstvo protiv komaraca [**pro**teev kom**a**ratsa]

most: I like this one most of all najviše mi se sviđa ovaj [n**ī**veesheh mee seh sv**ee**eja **o**vī]

most of the time najveći dio vremena [n**ī**vechee d**ee**o]

most tourists većina turista [vech**ee**na t**oo**reesta]

mostly uglavnom [**oo**glavnom]

mother majka [m**ī**ka]

motorbike motocikl [mot**o**tseekl]

motorboat motorni čamac [m**o**tornee ch**a**mats]

motorway autocesta [**a**ootsesta]

mountain planina [plan**ee**na]

in the mountains u planinama [oo plan**ee**nama]

mountaineering planinarenje [plan**ee**naren-yeh]

mouse (also for computer) miš [meesh]

moustache brkovi [b**e**rkovee]

mouth usta [**oo**sta]

mouth ulcer rana u ustima [oo **oo**steema]

move (verb) pomaknuti [p**o**maknootee]

he's moved to another room promijenio je sobu [prom-y**e**neeo yeh s**o**boo]

could you move your car? možete li pomaknuti auto? [m**o**Jeteh lee – **a**ooto]

could you move up a little? možete li se malo pomaknuti [seh]

where has it been moved to? gdje je to premješteno [gd-yeh yeh to prem-yeshteno]

movie film [feelm]

movie theater kino [k**ee**no]

Mr gospodin [gosp**o**deen]

Mrs gospođa [g**o**spoja]

Ms gospođica [g**o**spojeetsa]

much mnogo

much better/worse mnogo bolje/lošije [b**o**l-yeh/l**o**sheeyeh]

much hotter mnogo vruće [vr**oo**cheh]

not much ne mnogo [neh]

not very much ne vrlo mnogo [v**e**rlo]

I don't want very much ne želim vrlo mnogo [neh Jeleem]

mud blato

mug (for drinking) krigla [kr**ee**gla]

I've been mugged napali su me i opljačkali [n**a**palee soo meh ee **o**pl-yachkalee]

mum mama

mumps zauške [z**a**ooshkeh]

museum muzej [m**oo**zay]

mushrooms gljive [gl-y**ee**veh]

music muzika [m**oo**zeeka]

musician muzičar [m**oo**zeechar]

Muslim (adj) muslimanski [moosl**ee**manskee]

mussels mušule [m**oo**shooleh]

must*: I must ... moram ...

I mustn't drink alcohol ne smijem piti alkohol [neh sm**ee**eyem p**ee**tee **a**lkohol]

mustard senf
my* moj [moy]
myself: I'll do it myself uradit
ću sam [ooradeechoo]
by myself sam

N

nail (on finger) nokat
(for wood) čavao [chavao]
nail clippers grickalica za
nokte [greetskaleetsa za nokteh]
nail varnish lak za nokte
name ime [eemeh]
my name's John zovem se
John
what's your name? kako se
zovete? [seh zoveteh]
what is the name of this
street? kako se zove ova
ulica? [zoveh ova ooleetsa]
napkin salveta
nappy pelena
narrow uzak [oozak]
nasty gadan
national narodni [narodnee]
nationality državljanstvo
[derJavlyanstvo]
natural prirodan [preerodan]
nausea mučnina [moochneena]
navy (blue) tamnomodra
near blizu [bleezoo]
is it near the city centre? je li
to blizu središta grada? [yeh
lee – sredeeshta]
do you go near ...? prolazite
li blizu ...? [prolazeeteh lee]
where is the nearest ...? gdje

je najbliži ...? [gd-yeh yeh
nibleezJee]
nearby obližnji [obleezJn-yee]
nearly gotovo
necessary potreban
neck vrat
necklace ogrlica [ogerleetsa]
necktie kravata
need: I need ... treba mi ...
[mee]
do I need to pay? moram li
platiti [lee plateetee]
needle (for sewing) igla [eegla]
negative negativ [negateev]
neither: neither (one) of them
nijedan od njih [neeyedan od
n-yeeH]
neither ... nor ... ni ... ni ...
[nee]
nephew nećak [nechak]
net (fishing, sport) mreža [mreJa]
Netherlands Nizozemska
[neezozemska]
never nikad [neekad]

dialogue

have you ever been to
Čakov? jeste li ikad bili u
Čakovcu? [yesteh lee eekad
beelee oo chakovtsoo]
no, never, I've never been
there ne, nikad nisam bio
tamo [neh neekad neesam
beeo]

new nov
New year Nova godina
[godeena]

Happy New year! sretna
Nova godina
New year's Eve Stara godina
New Zealand Novi Zeland
[novee]
New Zealander: I'm a New
Zealander (said by man/woman)
ja sam Novozelanđanin
/Novozelanđanka [ya sam
novozelanJaneen/novozelanJanka]
news vijest (f) [v-yest]
(on TV, radio) vijesti [v-yestee]
newsagent's prodavaonica
novina [prodavaoneetsa
noveena]
newspaper novine [noveeneh]
newspaper kiosk novinski
kiosk [noveenskee keeosk]
next sljedeći [sl-yedechee]
   the next turning/street on the
   left sljedeće skretanje
   [sl-yedecheh skretan-yeh]
   the next street on the left
   sljedeća ulica na lijevo
   [ooleetsa na l-yevo]
   at the next stop na sljedećoj
   postaji [sl-yedechoy postiyee]
next week sljedeći tjedan
   [t-yedan]
next to pokraj [pokrī]
nice (person, town, day) prijatan
   [preeyatan]
   (meal) krasan
niece nećakinja
   [nechakeenya]
night noć (f) [noch]
   at night noću [nochoo]
   good night laku noć
   [lakoo]

dialogue

do you have a single room
for one night? imate li
jednokrevetnu sobu za
jednu noć? [eemateh lee
yedno-krevetnoo soboo za
yednoo noch]
yes, madam da, gospođo
[gospojo]
how much is it per night?
koliko je noćenje? [koleeko
yeh nochen-yeh]
it's 500 kunas for one night
petsto kuna noć [koona
noch]
thank you, I'll take it hvala,
uzet ću je [Hvala oozet choo
yeh]

nightclub noćni lokal [nochnee]
nightdress spavaćica
   [spavacheetsa]
night porter noćni portir
   [nochnee porteer]
no ne [neh]
   I've no change nemam sitno
   there's no ... left nije ostalo
   ništa ... [neeyeh ostalo neeshta]
   no way! ne dolazi u obzir!
   [neh dolazee oo obzeer]
   oh no! (upset) nije valjda!
   [neeyeh val-yda]
nobody nitko [neetko]
   there's nobody there tamo
   nema nikoga [neekoga]
noise buka [booka]
noisy: it's too noisy previše je
   bučno [preveesheh yeh boochno]

non-alcoholic (drink) bezalkoholan
none nijedan [neeyedan]
nonsmoking compartment (train) kupe za nepušače [koope za nepooshacheh]
noon podne [podneh]
no-one nitko [neetko]
nor: nor do I ni ja [nee ya]
normal normalan
north sjever [s-yever]
   in the north na sjeveru [s-yeveroo]
   north of Zadar sjeverno od Zadra [s-yeverno]
northern sjeverni [s-yevernee]
Northern Ireland Sjeverna Irska [s-yeverna eerska]
Norway Norveška [norveshka]
nose nos
nosebleed krvarenje iz nosa [kervaren-yeh eez]
not* ne [neh]
   no, I'm not hungry ne, nisam gladan [neesam]
   I don't want any, thank you neću, hvala [nechoo Hvala]
   it's not necessary nije potrebno [neeyeh]
   I didn't know that (said by man/woman) nisam to znao/znala
   not that one – this one ne taj – ovaj [neh ti ovi]
note (bank note) novčanica [novchaneetsa]
notebook bilježnica [beel-yeJneetsa]
notepaper listovni papir [leestovnee papeer]

nothing ništa [neeshta]
   nothing for me, thanks ništa za mene, hvala [zameneh Hvala]
   nothing else ništa drugo [droogo]
novel roman
November studeni [stoodenee]
now sada
number (figure) broj [broy]
   I've got the wrong number imam krivi broj [eemam kreevee]
   what is your phone number? koji je vaš telefonski broj? [ko-yee yeh vash telefonskee]
number plate registarki broj [regeestarskee]
nurse bolničarka [bolneecharka] (male) bolničar [bolneechar]
nut (for bolt) matica [mateetsa]
nuts (to eat) oraščići [orash-cheechee]

O

occupied zauzeto [zaoozeto]
o'clock*: at 7 o'clock u sedam sati [oo sedam satee]
October listopad [leestopad]
odd (strange) čudan [choodan] (number) neparan
of* od
off (lights) isključeno [eeskl-yoocheno]
   it's just off Korzo odmah uz Korzo [odmaH ooz]
   we're off tomorrow sutra

odlazimo [**soo**tra **o**dlazeemo]

offensive uvredljiv [oovredl-yeev]

(attacking) napadački [**napa**dachkee]

office ured [**oo**red]

officer (to policeman) gospodine [gos**po**deeneh]

often često [chesto]

not often ne često [neh]

how often are the buses? koliko često vozi autobus? [**ko**leeko – **vo**zee **a**ootoboos]

oil (for car, salad) ulje [**ool**-yeh]

ointment mast

OK u redu [oo **re**doo]

are you OK? jeste li u redu? [**ye**steh lee]

is that OK with you? slažete li se s tim? [sla**je**teh lee seh steem]

is it OK to ...? je li u redu ako ...? [yeh]

that's OK thanks u redu, hvala [**H**vala]

I'm OK dobro sam

is this train OK for ...? mogu li ovim vlakom do ...? [**mo**goo lee s**o**veem vlakom]

I'm sorry, OK žao mi je, u redu? [**Ja**o mee yeh]

old star

dialogue

how old are you? koliko vam je godina? [**ko**leeko vam yeh **go**deena]
I'm twenty-five

dvadesetpet
and you? a vama?

old town stari grad [**sta**ree]

in the old town u starom gradu [oo – **gra**doo]

old-fashioned staromodan

olive oil maslinovo ulje [**ma**sleenovo **oo**l-yeh]

olives masline [**ma**sleeneh]

black/green olives crne/zelene masline [**tser**neh/**ze**leneh]

omelette omlet

on* na

on the street/beach na ulici/plaži [**oo**leetsee/pla**Jee**]

is it on this road? to je na ovoj cesti? [yeh na **o**voy ts**e**stee]

on the plane u zrakoplovu [oo zrakoplo**voo**]

on Saturday u subotu [**soo**botoo]

on television na televiziji [televe**ee**zeeyee]

I haven't got it on me nemam kod sebe [sebeh]

this one's on me ovo ja plaćam [ya **pla**cham]

the light wasn't on svjetlo nije bilo uključeno [sv-**ye**tlo **nee**yeh **bee**lo **oo**kl-yoocheno]

what's on tonight? što je večeras? [shto yeh ve**che**ras]

on/off switch prekidač za uključivanje/isključivanje [prek**ee**dach za **oo**kl-yoochee**va**n-yeh/**ee**skl-yoochee**va**n-yeh]

once jednom [**ye**dnom]

at once (immediately) odmah
[odmaн]

the white one onaj bijeli [onaī
beeyelee]

one-way ticket: a one-way
ticket to ... jednosmjerna
karta za [yednosm-yerna]

onion luk [look]

only samo

only one (just one) samo jedan
[yedan]

it's only 6 o'clock tek je šest
sati [yeh shest satee]

I've only just got here (said by
man/woman) tek sam stigao/
stigla [steegao/steegla]

open (adj) otvoren
(verb) otvoriti [otvoreetee]

when do you open? kad
otvarate?

I can't get it open ne mogu
otvoriti [nemogoo]

in the open air vani [vanee]

opening times radno vrijeme
[vr-yemeh]

open ticket otvorena karta

opera opera

operation (surgical) operacija
[operatseeya]

operator (telephone) telefonist
[telefoneest]

(woman) telefonistkinja
[telefoneestkeenya]

opposite: the opposite
direction suprotan smjer
[sooprotan sm-yer]

the bar opposite bar
nasuprot [nasooprot]

opposite my hotel nasuprot
moga hotela

optician optičar [opteechar]

or ili [eelee]

orange (fruit) naranča
[narancha]

(colour) narančast [naranchast]

orange juice sok od naranče
[narancheh]

orchestra orkestar

order: can we order now?
možemo li sada naručiti?
[moJemo lee sada naroocheetee]

I've already ordered, thanks
već sam naručio, hvala [vech
sam naroocheeo, нvala]

I didn't order that nisam to
naručio [neesam]

out of order neispravan [neh-
eespravan]

ordinary običan [obeechan]

other drugi [droogee]

the other one onaj drugi
[onī]

the other day neki dan
[nekee]

I'm waiting for the others
čekam druge [chekam droogeh]

do you have any others?
imate li drugih? [eemateh lee
droogeeн]

otherwise inače [eenacheh]

our* naš [nash]

ours* naš [nash]

out: he's out izišao je
[eezeeshao yeh]

three kilometres out of town
tri kilometra od grada [tree
keelometra]

86

outdoors vani [vanee]

outside vani [vanee]

can we sit outside? možemo
li sjediti vani? [moJemo lee
s-yedeetee]

oven pećnica [pechneetsa]

over: over here ovdje
[ovd-yeh]

over there tamo

over 500 preko petsto

it's over gotovo je [yeh]

**overcharge: you've
overcharged me** previše ste
mi naplatili [preveesheh steh
mee naplateelee]

overcoat ogrtač [ogertach]

**overlook: I'd like a room
overlooking the courtyard**
(said by man/woman) želio/
željela bih sobu s pogledom
na dvorište [Jeleeo/Jel-yela beeн
soboo – dvoreeshteh]

overnight (stay) prekonoć
[prekonoch]

(travel) noćni [nochnee]

overtake preticati
[preteetsatee]

**owe: how much do I owe
you?** koliko vam dugujem?
[koleeko vam doogooyem]

own: my own ... moj
osobni ... [moy osobnee]

are you on your own? da li
ste sami? [lee steh samee]

I'm on my own sam sam

owner (man) vlasnik [vlasneek]
(woman) vlasnica [vlasneetsa]

pack (verb) pakirati [pakeeratee]

a pack of ... paketić ...
[paketeech]

package (at post office) paket

package holiday turistički
aranžman [tooreesteechkee
aranJman]

packed lunch spakakirani
ručak [spakeeranee roochak]

packet: a packet of cigarettes
kutija cigareta [kooteeya
tseegareta]

padlock (noun) lokot

page strana

could you page Mr ...?
da li biste mogli pozvati
gospodina ... preko
razglasa? [lee beesteh moglee
pozvatee gospodeena]

pain bol

I have a pain here ovdje me
boli [ovd-yeh meh bolee]

painful bolan

painkillers sredstvo protiv
bolova [sredstvo proteev
bolova]

paint (noun) boja [bo-ya]

painting (picture) slika [sleeka]

pair: a pair of ... par ...

Pakistani (adj) pakistanski
[pakeestanskee]

palace palača [palacha]

pale blijed [bl-yed]

pale blue svijetlo plav [sv-
yetlo]

pan tava

panties gaćice [gacheetseh]

pants (underwear) gaćice
 (US) hlače [Hlacheh]
pantyhose hulahopke
 [hoolahopkeh]
paper papir [papeer]
 a piece of paper komad
 papira [komad papeera]
paper handkerchiefs
 papirnata maramica
 [papeernata maramitsa]
parcel paket
pardon (me)? (didn't understand)
 molim? [moleem]
parents roditelji [rodeetel-yee]
park (noun) park
 (verb) parkirati [parkeeratee]
 can I park here? mogu li
 ovdje parkirati? [mogoo lee
 ovd-yeh]
parking lot parkiralište
 [parkeeraleeshteh]
part (noun) dio (m) [deeo]
partner (boyfriend, girlfriend etc)
 partner
party (group) grupa [groopa]
 (celebration) zabava
pass (in mountain) klanac
 [klanats]
passenger putnik [pootneek]
 (woman) putnica [pootneetsa]
passport putovnica
 [pootovnitsa]
past: in the past u prošlosti
 [oo proshlostee]
 just past the information
 office odmah nakon
 informacijskog ureda [odmaH
 eenformatseey-skog ooreda]
path staza

pattern uzorak [oozorak]
pavement pločnik [plochneek]
 on the pavement na pločniku
 [plochneekoo]
pavement café kafić na
 otvorenom [kafeech]
pay platiti [plateetee]
 can I pay, please? mogu li
 platiti, molim? [mogoo lee
 – moleem]
 it's already paid for to je već
 plaćeno [yeh vech placheno]

dialogue

> who's paying? tko plaća?
> [placha]
> I'll pay ja ću platiti [ya choo
> plateetee]
> no, you paid last time, I'll
> pay ne, vi ste platili prošli
> put, ja ću [neh vee steh
> plateelee proshlee poot]

pay phone telefonska
 govornica [telefonska
 govorneetsa]
peaceful miran [meeran]
peach breskva
peanuts kikiriki [keekeereekee]
pear kruška [krooshka]
peas grašak [grashak]
peculiar čudan [choodan]
pedestrian crossing pješački
 prijelaz [p-yeshackee pryelaz]
pedestrian precinct pješačka
 zona [p-yeshachka]
peg (for washing) štipaljka
 [shteepalyka]

(for tent) klin [kleen]

pen pero

pencil olovka

penfriend prijatelj za dopisivanje [preeyatel za dopeeseevan-yeh]

penicillin penicilin [peneetseeleen]

penknife džepni nož [jepnee noJ]

pensioner umirovljenik [oomeerovl-yeneek] (woman) umirovljenica [oomeerovl-yeneetsa]

people narod
  the other people in the hotel drugi ljudi u hotelu [droogee l-yoodee oo hoteloo]
  too many people previše ljudi [preveesheh]

pepper biber [beeber]
  green/red pepper zelena/crvena paprika [tservena papreeka]

peppermint pepermint [pepermeent]

per: per night za noć [noch]
  how much per day? koliko po danu [koleeko po danoo]

per cent posto

perfect savršen [savershen]

perfume parfem

perhaps možda [moJda]

perhaps not možda ne [neh]

period (of time) period [pereeod] (menstruation) menstruacija [menstrooatseeya]

perm trajna [trına]

permit (noun) dozvola

person osoba

personal stereo osobni stereo [osobnee]

petrol benzin [benzeen]

petrol can kanta za benzin

petrol station benzinska stanica [benzeenska staneetsa]

pharmacy ljekarna [l-yekarna]

phone (noun) telefon (verb) telefonirati [telefoneeratee]

phone book telefonski imenik [telefonskee eemeneek]

phone box telefonska govornica [telefonska govorneetsa]

phonecard telefonska kartica [karteetsa]

phone number telefonski broj [broy]

photo fotografija [fotografeeya]
  excuse me, could you take a photo of us? možete li nas snimiti? [moJeteh lee nas sneemeetee]

phrasebook rječnik fraza [r-yechneek]

piano klavir [klaveer]

pick up: will you be there to pick me up? hoćete li doći po mene? [Hocheteh lee do-chee pomeneh]

pickpocket džeparoš [jeparosh]

picnic (noun) piknik [peekneek]

picture slika [sleeka]

pie (meat) (mesna) pita [peeta] (fruit) (voćna) pita [vochna]

piece komad
  a piece of ... komad ...

pill pilula [**pee**loola]

I'm on the pill uzimam pilule za kontracepciju [**oo**zeemam **pee**looleh za kontrats**e**ptseeyoo]

pillow jastuk [**ya**stook]

pillow case jastučnica [**ya**stoochneetsa]

pin (noun) pribadača [preeb**a**dacha]

pineapple ananas

pineapple juice sok od ananasa

pink ružičast [roo**ee**chast]

pipe (to smoke) lula [**loo**la]

(for water) cijev [ts-yev]

pity: it's a pity šteta [**sht**eta]

pizza pizza

place mjesto [m-**ye**sto]

is this place taken? je li ovo mjesto zauzeto? [yeh lee **o**vo – za**oo**zeto]

at your place kod vas

at his place kod njega [n-**ye**ga]

plain (not patterned) jednobojan [yedn**o**boyan]

plane zrakoplov

by plane zrakoplovom

plant biljka [**bee**lyka]

plaster cast gips [geeps]

plaster žbuka [**Jbo**oka]

plastic plastičan [plast**ee**chan]

plastic bag plastična vrećica [pl**a**steechna vr**e**cheetsa]

plate tanjur [tan-**yoor**]

platform peron

which platform is it for Split, please? na kojem peronu je

za Split? [ko-yem per**o**noo yeh za spleet]

play (verb) igrati se [**ee**gratee seh]

(noun: in theatre) kazališni komad [kazal**ee**shnee]

playground igralište [**ee**graleeshteh]

pleasant prijatan [pr**ee**yatan]

please molim [m**o**leem]

yes please da, molim

could you please ...? možete li ...? [m**o**Jeteh lee]

please don't ... molim, nemojte [n**e**moyteh]

pleased to meet you drago mi je da smo se sreli [mee yeh da smo seh sr**e**lee]

pleasure: my pleasure drago mi je

plenty: plenty of ... mnogo ...

there's plenty of time ima mnogo vremena [**ee**ma]

that's plenty, thanks dosta je, hvala [**do**sta yeh нv**a**la]

pliers kliješta [kl-**ye**shta]

plug (electrical) utikač [oot**ee**kach]

(in sink) čep [chep]

(for car) svjećica [sv-ye**chee**tsa]

plumber vodoinstalater [vodoeenstal**a**ter]

plum brandy šljivovica [shl-yeev**o**veetsa]

p.m.*: 1 p.m. 1 poslije podne [yedan posl-yeh p**o**dneh]

7 p.m. 7 uvečer [sedam **oo**vecher]

poached egg pošírano jaje [posheerano yīyeh]

pocket džep [jep]

point: two point five dva zarez pet

there's no point nema svrhe [sverнeh]

points (in car) platine [plateeneh]

poisonous otrovan

police policija [poleetseeya]

call the police! zovite policiju! [zoveeteh poleetseeyoo]

policeman policajac [poleetsīyats]

police station policijska postaja [poleetseeyska postīya]

policewoman policajaka [poleetsīyaka]

polish (noun) laštilo [lashteelo]

polite uljudan [ool-yoodan]

polluted zagađen [zagajen]

pony poni [ponee]

pool (swimming) bazen

poor (not rich) siromašan [seeromashan]

(quality) loš [losh]

pop music pop glazba

pop singer pop pjevač [p-yevach]

(woman) pop pjevačica [p-yevacheetsa]

population stanovništvo [stanovneeshtvo]

pork svinjetina [sveen-yeteena]

port (for boats) luka [looka]

(drink) porto

porter (in hotel) portir [porteer]

portrait portret

posh (hotel etc) otmjen [otm-yen]

possible moguć [mogooch]

is it possible to ...? je li moguće ...? [yeh lee mogoocheh]

as soon as possible čim prije moguće [cheem preeyeh mogoocheh]

post pošta [poshta]

could you post this for me? možete li ovo predati na poštu? [moJeteh lee ovo predatee na poshtoo]

postbox (on street) poštanski sandučić [poshtanskee sandoocheech]

postcard razglednica [razgledneetsa]

postcode poštanski broj [poshtanskee broy]

poste restante poste restante [post restant]

poster (for room, on street) plakat

post office pošta [poshta]

potato krumpir [kroompeer]

potato chips čips [cheeps]

pots and pans lonci i tave [lontsee ee taveh]

pottery (objects) keramika [kerameeka]

pound* (weight, money) funta [foonta]

power cut prekid struje [prekeed strooyeh]

power point utičnica [ooteechneetsa]

practise: I want to practise my Croatian želim vježbati hrvatski [Jeleem v-yeJbatee Hervatskee]

prawns račići [racheechee]

prefer: I prefer ... više volim [veesheh voleem]

pregnant trudna [troodna]

prescription recept [retsept]

present (gift) dar

president (of country) predsjednik [preds-yedneek] (woman) predsjednica [preds-yedneetsa]

pretty zgodan it's pretty expensive prilično je skupo [preeleechno yeh skoopo]

price cijena [ts-yena]

priest svećenik [svecheneek]

prime minister premijer [premeeyer] (woman) premijerka [premeeyerka]

printed matter tiskanica [teeskaneetsa]

priority (in driving) prednost

prison zatvor

private privatan [preevatan]

private bathroom privatna kupaonica [preevatna koopaoneetsa]

probably vjerojatno [v-yero-yatno]

problem problem no problem! nema problema!

program(me) (noun) program

promise: I promise obećavam [obechavam]

pronounce: how is this

pronounced? kako ovo izgovarate? [eezgovarateh]

properly (repaired, locked etc) dobro

protection factor faktor zaštite [zashteeteh]

Protestant protestant (woman) protestantica [protestanteetsa]

public convenience javni zahod [yavnee]

public holiday državni praznik [derJavnee prazneek]

pudding (dessert) desert

pull vući [voochee]

pullover pulover [poolover]

puncture probušena guma [prabooshena gooma]

purple ljubičast [l-yoobeechast]

purse novčanik [novchaneek]

push gurati [gooratee]

pushchair dječja kolica [d-yechya koleetsa]

put staviti [staveetee] where can I put ...? gdje mogu staviti ...? [gd-yeh mogoo staveetee] could you put us up for the night? da li bismo mogli kod vas prenoćiti? [lee beesmo moglee kod vas prenocheetee]

pyjamas pidžama [peejama]

Q

quality kvaliteta [kvaleeteta]

quarantine karantena

quarter četvrt [chetvert]

quayside: on the quayside u pristaništu [oo preestaneeshtoo]
question pitanje [peetan-yeh]
queue (noun) red
quick brz [berz]
   that was quick to je bilo brzo [yeh beelo berzo]
   what's the quickest way there? kako se tamo najbrže stiže? [nīberjeh steejeh]
   fancy a quick drink? može li na brzinu piće? [mojeh lee na berzeenoo peecheh]
quickly brzo [berzo]
quiet (person, street) tih [teeH]
quite (fairly) prilično [preeleechno]
   (very) vrlo [verlo]
   that's quite right to je točno [yeh tochno]
   quite a lot prilično mnogo

R

rabbit kunić [kooneech]
race (for runners, cars) trka [terka]
racket (tennis) reket
radiator radijator [radeeyator]
   (in car) hladnjak [Hladn-yak]
radio radio (m) [radeeo]
   on the radio na radiju [radeeyoo]
rail: by rail željeznicom [Jel-yezneetsom]
railway željeznica [Jel-yezneetsa]

rain kiša [keesha]
   in the rain na kiši [keeshee]
   it's raining pada kiša
raincoat baloner
randy pohotan
rape (noun) silovanje [seelovan-yeh]
rare (uncommon) rijedak [r-yedak]
   (steak) manje pečen [man-yeh pechen]
rash (on skin) osip [oseep]
raspberry malina [maleena]
rat štakor [shtakor]
rate (for changing money) kurs [koors]
rather: it's rather good prilično je dobro [preeleechno yeh]
   I'd rather … radije bih … [radeeyeh beeH]
razor (dry) britva [breetva]
   (electric) aparat za brijanje [breeyan-yeh]
razor blades žileti [Jeeletee]
read čitati [cheetatee]
ready gotov
   are you ready? jeste li spremni? [yesteh lee spremnee]
   I'm not ready yet (said by man/woman) nisam još spreman/spremna [neesam yosh]

dialogue

when will it be ready? kada će biti gotovo? [cheh beetee]
it should be ready in a

couple of days bit će gotovo za dva dana [beet]

real stvaran

really stvarno

I'm really sorry stvarno mi je žao [mee yeh Jao]

that's really great to je stvarno super [sooper]

really? doista? [doeesta]

rearview mirror retrovizor [retroveezor]

reasonable (prices) umjeren [oom-yeren]

receipt priznanica [preeznaneetsa]

recently nedavno

reception desk recepcija [retseptseeya]

reception (for guests) prijem [preeyem]

reception (in hotel) recepcija [retseptseeya]

at reception na recepciji

receptionist recepcioner [retseptseeoner]
(woman) recepcionerka

recognize prepoznati [prepoznatee]

recommend: could you recommend ...? da li biste mogli preporučiti ...? [lee beesteh moglee preporoocheetee]

red crven [tserven]

red wine crno vino [tserno veeno]

refund vraćanje novca [vrachan-yeh novtsa]

can I have a refund? možete

li mi vratiti novac? [moJeteh lee mee vrateetee novats]

region kraj [krī]

registered: by registered mail preporučeno [preporoocheno]

registration number registarski broj [regeestarskee broy]

relative (noun) rođak [roJak]
(female) rođakinja [roJakeenya]

religion religija [releegeeya]

remember: I don't remember ne sjećam se [neh s-yecham seh]

I remember sjećam se

do you remember? sjećate li se? [s-yechateh lee seh]

rent (noun) najamnina [nīyamneena]
(for apartment) stanarina [stanareena]
(verb) unajmiti [oonīmeetee]

for rent za najam [na-yam]

rented car unajmljeni auto (m) [oonīml-yenee aooto]

repair (verb) popraviti [popraveetee]

can you repair it? možete li popraviti? [moJeteh lee]

repeat ponoviti [ponoveetee]

could you repeat that? da li biste mogli to ponoviti? [lee beesteh moglee]

reservation rezervacija [rezervatseeya]

I'd like to make a reservation (said by man/woman) želio/željela bih izvršiti rezervaciju [Jeleeo/Jel-yela beeH eezversheetee rezervatseeyoo]

dialogue

I have a reservation
imam rezervaciju [**ee**mam
rezerv**a**tseeyoo]
yes sir, what name please?
da gospodine, na koje
ime? [**go**spodeeneh na **ko**-yeh
eemeh]

reserve (verb) rezervirati
[rezerv**ee**ratee]

dialogue

**can I reserve a table
for tonight?** mogu li
rezervirati stol za večeras
[**mo**goo lee rezerv**ee**ratee stol za
ve**che**ras]
**yes madam, for how many
people?** da, gospođo, za
koliko osoba? [**go**spojo za
k**o**leeko]
for two za dvoje [za dv**o**-
yeh]
and for what time? u
koliko sati? [oo k**o**leeko
satee]
for eight o'clock u osam
**and could I have your
name please?** vaše ime,
molim? [v**a**sheh **ee**meh
m**o**leem]
see alphabet for spelling

rest: I need a rest potreban
mi je odmor [p**o**treban mee yeh]
the rest of the group ostatak

grupe [gr**oo**peh]
restaurant rest**o**ran
restaurant car vagon rest**o**ran
rest room zahod
retired: I'm retired u mirovini
sam [oo meer**o**veenee]
return: a return to ... povratnu
(kartu) za ... [**po**vratnoo
(k**a**rtoo)]
reverse charge call telefonski
razgovor na račun primatelja
poziva [tel**e**fonskee r**a**choon
preem**a**tel-ya p**o**zeeva]
reverse gear brzina za vožnju
unazad [berz**ee**na za v**o**Jn-yoo
oon**a**zad]
revolting **o**dvratan
rib rebro
rice riža [r**ee**Ja]
rich (person) b**o**gat
(food) kal**o**ričan [kal**o**reechan]
ridiculous smiješan
[sm-y**e**shan]
right (correct) ispravan
[**ee**spravan]
(not left) desno
you were right bili ste u
pravu [b**ee**lee steh oo pr**a**voo]
that's right točno [t**o**chno]
that can't be right to ne
može biti točno [neh m**o**Jeh
b**ee**tee]
right! dobro!
is this the right road for ...?
je li ovo cesta za ...? [yeh lee
ovo ts**e**sta]
on the right desno
turn right skrenite desno
[skr**e**neeteh]

right-hand drive vozilo s volanom na desnoj strani [**vo**zeelo s – **des**noy str**a**nee]

ring (on finger) prsten [**per**sten]

I'll ring you nazvat ću vas [choo]

ring back nazvati [**naz**vatee]

ripe (fruit) zreo

rip-off: it's a rip-off to je prijevara [yeh pr-y**e**vara]

rip-off prices previsoke cijene [pr**e**veesokeh ts-**ye**neh]

risky riskantan [r**ee**skantan]

river rijeka [r-**ye**ka]

road cesta [**tse**sta]

is this the road for …? je li ovo cesta za …? [yeh lee **o**vo]

down the road u blizini [oo bleez**ee**nee]

road accident prometna nesreća [**ne**srecha]

road map autokarta [**a**ootokarta]

roadsign prometni znak [pr**o**metnee]

rob: I've been robbed (said by man/woman) pokraden/ pokradena sam

rock (stone) stijena [st-**ye**na] (music) rock

on the rocks (with ice) s ledom

roll (bread) pecivo [p**e**tseevo]

Romania Rumunjska [r**oo**moon-yuh-ska]

roof krov

roof rack krovni prtljažnik [kr**o**vnee pertl-ya**J**neek]

room (in hotel etc) soba

in my room u mojoj sobi [oo

mo-yoy s**o**bee]

room service posluga u sobi [posl**oo**ga]

rope uže [**oo**Jeh]

rosé ruža [r**oo**Ja]

roughly (approximately) otprilike [otpr**ee**leekeh]

round: it's my round ja plaćam ovu rundu [ya pl**a**cham **o**voo r**oo**ndoo]

roundabout (on road) kružni tok [kr**oo**Jnee]

round trip ticket povratna karta

route ruta [r**oo**ta]

what's the best route? koja je najbolja ruta? [**ko**-ya yeh n**ī**bol-ya]

rubber (material) guma [g**oo**ma] (eraser) gumica za brisanje [g**oo**meetsa za br**ee**san-yeh]

rubber band gumena pasica [g**oo**mena pas**ee**tsa]

rubbish (waste, poor quality) smeće [sm**e**cheh]

rubbish! to je glupost! [yeh gl**oo**post]

rucksack ruksak [r**oo**ksak]

rude neuljudan [n**e**ool-yoodan]

ruins ruševine [r**oo**sheveeneh]

rum rum [room]

rum and coke rum i koka-kola [ee]

run (verb: person) trčati [t**e**rchatee]

how often do the buses run? kako su česti autobusi? [soo ch**e**stee **a**ootoboosee]

I've run out of money (said by

man/woman) ostao/ostala sam
bez novca [novtsa]
rush hour prometna gužva
[gooJva]
Russia Rusija [roseeya]

S

sad tužan [tooJan]
saddle (for bike, horse) sedlo
safe siguran [seegooran]
safety pin ziherica
[zeehereetsa]
sail (noun) jedro [yedro]
sailboard daska za jedrenje
[yedren-yeh]
sailboarding jedrenje na dasci
[dastsee]
salad salata
salad dressing začin za salatu
[zacheen za salatoo]
sale: for sale za prodaju
[prodiyoo]
salmon losos
salt sol (f)
same: the same isti [eestee]
the same as this isto kao ovo
[eesto]
the same again, please opet
isto, molim [moleem]
it's all the same to me
meni je svejedno [menee yeh
sveyedno]
sand pijesak [p-yesak]
sandals sandale [sandaleh]
sandwich sendvič [sendveech]
sanitary napkins/towels
higijenski uložak

[heegeeyenskee ooloJak]
sardines sardine [sardeeneh]
Saturday subota [soobota]
sauce umak [oomak]
saucepan lonac [lonats]
saucer tanjurić [tanyooreech]
sauna sauna [saoona]
sausage kobasica [kobaseetsa]
say: how do you say ...
in Croatian? kako se na
hrvatskom kaže ...?
[Hervatskom kaJeh]
what did he/she say? što je
rekao? [shto yeh]
I said ... (said by man/woman)
rekao/rekla sam ...
he/she said ... rekao/rekla
je ...
could you say that again?
možete li to ponoviti?
[moJeteh lee to ponoveetee]
scarf (for neck) šal [shal]
(for head) marama
scenery krajolik [kra-yoleek]
schedule raspored
scheduled flight redovan let
school škola [shkola]
scissors: a pair of scissors
škare [shkareh]
scooter skuter [skooter]
Scotch (whisky) škotski viski
[shkotskee veeskee]
Scotch tape® selotejp
[selotayp]
Scotland Škotska [shkotska]
Scottish škotski [shkotskee]
I'm Scottish (said by man/
woman) ja sam Škot/Škotkinja
[ya sam shkot/shkotkeenya]

scrambled eggs pržena jaja
[perJena yĪya]

scratch (noun) ogrebotina
[ogreboteena]

screw vijak [veeyak]

screwdriver odvijač
[odveeyach]

scrubbing brush (for hands)
četka za ruke [chetka za
rookeh]
(for floors) četka za ribanje
[reeban-yeh]

sea more
by the sea kraj mora [krĪ]

seafood morski specijaliteti
[morskee spetseeyaleetetee]

seafront morska obala
on the seafront na morskoj
obali [morskoy obalee]

seagull galeb

search tražiti [traJeetee]

seashell morska školjka
[shkolyka]

seasick: I feel seasick imam
morsku bolest [eemam
morskoo]
I get seasick dobijem
morsku bolest [dobeeyem]

seaside: by the seaside kraj
mora [krĪ]

seat sjedalo [s-yedalo]
is this anyone's seat? je li
to nečije sjedalo [yeh lee to
necheeyeh]

seat belt sigurnosni pojas
[seegoornosnee po-yas]

sea urchin morski jež [morskee
yeJ]

seaweed morska trava

secluded osamljen [osaml-yen]

second drugi [droogee]
just a second! samo
trenutak! [trenootak]

second class drugi razred
[droogee]

second floor drugi kat

second-hand polovan

see vidjeti [veed-yetee]
can I see? mogu li vidjeti?
have you seen ...? jeste li
vidjeli ...? [yesteh lee veed-
yelee]
I see vidim [veedeem]
I saw him this morning (said
by man/woman) vidio/vidjela
sam ga jutros [veedeeo/ veed-
yela sam ga yootroos]

self-catering apartment stan

self-service samoposluživanje
[samoposlooJeevan-yeh]

sell prodavati [prodavatee]
do you sell ...? prodajete
li ...? [prodĪ-yeteh lee]

Sellotape® selotejp [selotayp]

send poslati [poslatee]
I want to send this to
England želim ovo poslati
u Englesku [Jeleem ovo – oo
engleskoo]

senior citizen umirovljenik
[oomeerovl-yeneek]
(woman) umirovljenica
[oomeerovl-yeneetsa]

separate odvojen [odvo-yen]

separated: I'm separated (said
by man/woman) rastavljen/
rastavljena sam [rastavl-yen]

separately odvojeno [odvoyeno]

September rujan [**roo**yan]

septic septičan [**sep**teechan]

Serb Srbin [**ser**been]

(woman) Srpkinja [**serp**keenya]

Serbia Srbija [**ser**beeya]

Serbian (adj) srpski [**ser**pskee]

(man) Srbin [**ser**been]

(woman) Srpkinja [**serp**keenya]

a **Serb from Serbia** Srbijanac

[srbeeyanats]

(woman) Srbijanka [srbeeyanka]

serious ozbiljan [**oz**beelyan]

service charge servis [**ser**vees]

service station benzinska

pumpa [benzeenska **poo**mpa]

serviette salveta

set menu meni

several nekoliko [**ne**koleeko]

sew šiti [**shee**tee]

could you **sew** this back

on? da li biste mogli ovo

zašiti? [lee **bee**steh mogle **o**vo

zasheetee]

sex seks

sexy seksi [**sek**see]

shade: in the shade u hladu

[oo **H**ladoo]

shake: to shake hands

rukovati se [**roo**kovatee seh]

shallow plitak [**plee**tak]

shame: what a shame! šteta!

[**sht**eta]

shampoo šampon [**sham**pon]

shampoo and set pranje kose

i frizura [**pran**-yeh **ko**seh ee

free**zoo**ra]

share (room, table) dijeliti

[d-**ye**leetee]

sharp oštar [**o**shtar]

shattered (very tired) iscrpljen

[ees-tserpl-yen]

shaver aparat za brijanje

[**bree**yan-yeh]

shaving foam pjena za

brijanje [p-**ye**na]

shaving point utičnica za

brijanje [**oo**teechneetsa]

she* ona

sheet plahta [**pla**Hta]

shelf polica [**po**leetsa]

shellfish školjke [**shk**olykeh]

sherry šeri [**she**ree]

ship brod

by **ship** br**o**dom

shirt košulja [**ko**shoolya]

shit! sranje! [**sran**-yeh]

shock šok [shok]

I got an **electric shock** from

the ... udarila me struja

na ... [**oo**dareela meh st**roo**ya]

shock-absorber amortizer

[amor**tee**zer]

shocking skandalozan

shoe cipela [**tsee**pela]

a **pair of shoes** par cipela

shoelaces vezice [**vee**zeetseh]

shoe polish pasta za cipele

[**tsee**peleh] ₊

shoe repairer postolar

shop prodavaonica

[prodava**o**neetsa]

shopping: I'm going shopping

idem u kupovinu [**ee**dem oo

koo**po**veenoo]

shopping centre trgovački

centar [**ter**govachkee **tse**ntar]

shop window izlog [**ee**zlog]

shore (of see, lake) obala
short kratak
shortcut prečica [precheetsa]
shorts kratke hlače [Hlacheh]
should: what should I do? što
da radim? [shto da radeem]
he shouldn't be long ne bi
mu trebalo dugo [neh bee moo
trebalo doogo]
you should have told me
trebali ste mi reći [trebalee
steh mee rechee]
shoulder rame [rameh]
shout vikati [veekateh]
show: could you show me?
možete li mi pokazati?
[moJeteh lee mee pokazateh]
shower gel gel za tuširanje
[toosheeran-yeh]
shower (in bathroom) tuš [toosh]
with shower s tušem
shut (verb) zatvarati [zatvarateh]
when do you shut? kad
zatvarate? [zatvarateh]
when do they shut? kad
zatvaraju? [zatvarīyoo]
they're shut zatvoreno je
[yeh]
I've shut myself out (said by
man/woman) zalupio/zalupila
sam vrata, a ključ je ostao
unutra [zaloopeeo/ zaloopeela
sam vrata a kl-yooch yeh ostao
oonootra]
shut up! zaveži! [zaveJee]
shutter (camera) blenda
(window) kapak
shy stidljiv [steedl-yeev]
sick bolestan

I'm going to be sick slabo mi
je [slabo mee yeh]
side strana
the other side of town druga
strana grada [drooga]
side lights poziciona svjetla
[pozeetseeona sv-yetla]
side salad salata
side street sporedna ulica
[ooleetsa]
sidewalk pločnik [plochneek]
sight: the sights of ...
znamenitosti ...
[znameneetostee]
sightseeing: we're going
sightseeing idemo u
razgledavanje [eedemo oo
razgledavan-yeh]
sightseeing tour razgledanje
sign (roadsign etc) prometni
znak [prometnee]
signal: he didn't give a signal
nije dao znak [neeyeh dao]
signature potpis [potpees]
signpost putokaz [pootokaz]
silence tišina [teesheena]
silk svila [sveela]
silly glup [gloop]
silver srebro
silver foil aluminijska folija
[aloomeeneeyska foleeya]
similar sličan [sleechan]
simple jednostavan
[yednostavan]
since od
since I got here (said by man/
woman) otkad sam stigao/
stigla ovdje [steegao/steegla
ovd-yeh]

sing pjevati [pyevatee]
singer pjevač [p-yevach]
(woman) pjevačica
[p-yevacheetsa]
single: a single to ... kartu
za ... [kartoo]
I'm single (said by man/woman)
ja sam neoženjen/neudata
[ya – neoJen-yen/neoodata]
single bed normalan krevet
single room jednokrevetna
soba [yednokrevetna]
sink (in kitchen) sudoper
[soodoper]
sister sestra
sister-in-law (brother's wife)
snaha
(husband's sister) zaova
(wife's sister) šogorica
[shogoreetsa]
(wife of husband's brother) jetrva
[yeturva]
sit: can I sit here? mogu li
ovdje sjesti? [mogoo lee ovd-yeh
s-yesteh]
is anyone sitting here? sjedi
li netko ovdje? [s-yedee lee]
sit down sjesti [s-yestee]
size veličina [veleecheena]
ski (noun) skija [skeeya]
(verb) skijati se [skeeyatee seh]
a pair of skis skije [skeeyeh]
ski boots skijaške cipele
[skeeyashkeh tseepeleh]
skiing skijanje [skeeyan-yeh]
we're going skiing idemo na
skijanje [eedemo]
ski instructor instruktor
skijanja [eenstrooktor skeeyanya]

ski-lift skijaška žičara
[skeeyashka Jeechara]
skin koža [koJa]
skin-diving ronjenje [ron-yen-
yeh]
skinny mršav [mershav]
ski-pants skijaške hlače
[skeeyashkeh Hlacheh]
ski pole skijaški štap
[skeeyashkee shtap]
ski run skijaška staza
[skeeyashka]
ski slope pista za skijanje
[peesta]
ski wax vosak za skije
[skeeyeh]
ski-pass pokazna karta za
skijanje
skirt suknja [sooknya]
sky nebo
sleep spavati [spavatee]
did you sleep well? jeste li
dobro spavali? [yesteh lee dobro
spavalee]
I need a good sleep
potrebno mi je da se dobro
ispavam [potrebno mee yeh da
seh dobro eespavam]
sleeper (rail) spavaća kola
[spavacha]
sleeping bag vreća za
spavanje [vrecha za spavan-yeh]
sleeping car spavaća kola
[spavacha]
sleeping pill pilula za spavanje
[peeloola]
sleepy: I'm feeling sleepy (said
by man/woman) pospan/pospana
sam

sleeve rukav [**roo**kav]

slide (photo) dijapozitiv
[deeyapo**zee**teev]

slip (under dress) kombine
[kom**bee**neh]

slippery klizav [**klee**zav]

Slovene (adj) slovenski
[slo**ven**skee]

(man) Slovenac [**slo**venats]

(woman) Slovenka

Slovenia Slovenija [slo**ven**eeya]

slow spor

slow down! (driving, speaking)
sporije [spo**ree**yeh]

slowly sporo

could you say it slowly? da li
biste to mogli reći sporije?
[lee **bee**steh to **mog**leh **rech**ee
spo**ree**yeh]

very slowly veoma sporo

small mali [**mal**ee]

smell: it smells smrdi
[**smerr**dee]

smile (verb) smiješiti se
[sm-**yes**heetee seh]

smoke (noun) dim [deem]

do you mind if I smoke?
smeta li vas ako pušim?
[**smet**a lee vas **ako** **poo**shem]

I don't smoke ne pušim [neh]

do you smoke? pušite li?
[**poo**sheetee lee]

snack: I'd just like a snack
nešto malo bih pojeo [**nesh**to
malo beeH po-yeo]

sneeze kihati [**kee**hatee]

snorkel (noun) cijev za disanje
[ts-yev za **dee**san-yeh]

snow snijeg [sn-yeg]

it's snowing pada snijeg

so: it's so expensive jako je
skupo [**yako** yeh **skoo**po]

it's so good jako je dobro

not so fast ne tako brzo
[**ber**zo]

so am I i ja sam [ee ya]

so do I i ja

so-so tako-tako

soaking solution (for contact
lensed) otopina za kontaktne
leće [**o**topeena za **kon**taktneh
lecheh]

soap sapun [**sa**poon]

soap powder deterdžent
[deter**J**ent]

sober trijezan [tr-**ye**zan]

sock čarapa [**charap**a]

socket (electrical) utičnica
[**oo**teech**neetsa**]

soda (water) soda

sofa sofa

soft (material etc) mekan

soft drink bezalkoholno piće
[**peech**eh]

soft lenses meke leće [**mek**eh
lecheh]

soft-boiled egg mekano
kuhano jaje [**koo**hano **yī**yeh]

sole (of shoe) đon [djon]

could you put new soles
on these? možete li ih
podoniti? [**mo**Jeteh lee eeH
pod**jon**eetee]

some: can I have some water/
rolls? mogu li dobiti vode/
pecivo? [**moo**goo lee **do**beetee
vodeh/**pet**seevo]

can I have some? mogu li

malo dobiti? [malo]
somebody, someone netko
something nešto [neshto]
  something to drink nešto za
  piće [peecheh]
sometimes katkad
somewhere negdje [negd-yeh]
son sin [seen]
song pjesma [p-yesma]
son-in-law zet
soon uskoro [ooskoro]
  I'll be back soon brzo ću se
  vratiti [berzo choo seh vrateetee]
  as soon as possible čim
  prije moguće [cheem preeyeh
  mogoocheh]
sore: it's sore boli me [bolee
  meh]
sore throat upaljeno grlo
  [oopal-yeno gerlo]
sorry: (I'm) sorry oprostite!
  [oprosteeteh]
  sorry? molim? [moleem]
sort: what sort of ...? koja
  vrsta ...? [ko-ya versta]
soup juha [yooha]
sour kiseo [keeseo]
south jug [yoog]
  in the south na jugu [yoogoo]
South Africa Južna Afrika
  [yooJna afreeka]
South African (adj)
  južnoafrižki [yooJnoafreechkee]
  (man) Južnoafrikanac
  [yooJnoafreekanats]
  (woman) Južnoafrikanka
  [yooJnoafreekanka]
southeast jugoistok [yoogo-
  eestok]

southwest jugozapad
  [yoogozapad]
souvenir suvenir [sooveneer]
spanner ključ [klyooch]
spare part rezervni dio (m)
  [rezervnee deeo]
spare tyre rezervna guma
  [rezervna gooma]
spark plug svjećica
  [sv-yecheetsa]
speak: do you speak English?
  govorite li engleski?
  [govoreeteh lee engleskee]
  I don't speak ... ne
  govorim ... [neh govoreem]

dialogue

can I speak to Roberto?
mogu li razgovarati s
Robertom? [mogoo lee
razgovaratee srobertom]
who's calling? tko zove?
[zoveh]
it's Patricia Patricia
I'm sorry, he's not in, can
I take a message? žao
mi je, nije ovdje; želite li
ostaviti poruku? [Jao mee
yeh, neeyeh ovd-yeh; Jeleeteh
lee ostaveeteh porookoo]
no thanks, I'll call back
later ne, hvala, nazvat ću
kasnije [neh Hvala nazvat choo
kasneeyeh]
please tell him I called
molim vas, kažite mu da
sam ga nazvala [moleem vas
kaJeeteh moo]

spectacles naočale [**na**ochaleh]

speed brzina [ber**zee**na]

speed limit ograničenje brzine [ogra**nee**chen-yeh ber**zee**neh]

speedometer brzinomjer [ber**zee**nom-yer]

spell: how do you spell it? kako se to piše? [**ka**ko seh to **pee**sheh]

see alphabet

spend (money) potrošiti [potro**shee**tee]

spider pauk [pa**ook**]

spin-dryer centrifuga [tsentree**foo**ga]

splinter (in finger) iver [**ee**ver]

spoke (in wheel) žbica [**Jbee**tsa]

spoon žlica [**Jlee**tsa]

sport sport

sprain: I've sprained my ... iščašio/iščašila sam ... [**ee**sh-chasheeo/**ee**sh-chasheela]

spring (of car, seat) opruga [**o**prooga]

(season) proljeće [prol-**yeche**h]

square (in town) trg [terg]

stairs stepenice [stepe**neet**seh]

stale (bread) star

stale (taste) bljutav [bly**oo**tav]

stall: the engine keeps stalling motor se stalno gasi [seh **stal**no **ga**see]

stamp marka

dialogue

a stamp for England, please marku za

Englesku, molim [**mar**koo za engle**skoo mo**leem]

what are you sending? što šaljete? [shto shal-**ye**teh]

this postcard ovu razglednicu [**o**voo ra**z**gledneetsoo]

---

standby stendbaj [stend**bī**]

star zvijezda [zv-**ye**zda]

start (noun) početak [po**che**tak]

when does it start? kad počinje? [po**cheen**-yeh]

the car won't start motor ne pali [neh **pa**lee]

starter (of car) anlaser [**an**las-er]

starving: I'm starving umirem od gladi [**oo**meerem od **gla**dee]

state (of country) država [der**Ja**va]

the States (USA) Sjedinjene Američke Države [s-ye**dee**n-yeneh ame**reech**keh der**Ja**veh]

station kolodvor

statue kip [keep]

stay: I'm staying at ... odsjeo sam u ... [**o**ds-yeo sam oo]

I'd like to stay another two nights (said by man/woman) želio/željela bih ostati još dvije noći [**Je**leeo/**Jel**-yela beeн **o**statee yosh dv-yeh **no**chee]

steak biftek [**bee**ftek]

steal ukrasti [**oo**krastee]

my bag has been stolen ukrali su mi torbu [**oo**kralee soo mee **to**rboo]

steep (hill) strm [sterm]

steering upravljanje
[**oo**pravlyan-yeh]

step: on the steps na
stepenicama [stepe**nee**tsama]

stereo stereo

sterling sterling [**ster**leeng]

steward (on plane) stjuard
[sty**oo**ard]

stewardess stjuardesa
[styoo**ar**desa]

sticking plaster flaster

still: I'm still here još sam tu
[yosh sam too]

I'm still waiting još čekam
[**che**kam]

is he still there? je li on još
tamo? [yeh lee]

keep still! budite mirni
[**boo**deeteh **meer**nee]

sting: I've been stung nešto
me ubolo [**nesh**to meh **oo**bolo]

stockings čarape [**char**apeh]

stomach želudac [**J**e**loo**dats]

stomach ache bol u želucu
[oo **J**e**loo**tsoo]

stone kamen

stop (verb) stati [**sta**tee]

please, stop here (to taxi driver
etc) molim vas, stanite ovdje
[**mo**leem vas, **sta**neeteh **o**vd-yeh]

do you stop near ...? stajete
li blizu ...? [**st**ī**yeteh lee
bl**ee**zoo?]

stop doing that! prestanite s
tim! [**pre**staneeteh s teem]

stopover prekid putovanja
[**pre**keed pootovanya]

storm oluja [o**loo**ya]

straight: straight ahead ravno

naprijed [**na**pr-yed]

a straight whisky nerazblažen
viski [nerazbla**J**en **vees**kee]

straightaway odmah [**o**dmaн]

strange (odd) čudan [**choo**dan]

stranger stranac [**stra**nats]
(woman) strankinja
[**stran**keenya]

I'm a stranger here ovdje
sam stranac [**o**vd-yeh]

strap remen

strawberry jagoda [**ya**goda]

stream potok

street ulica [**oo**leetsa]

on the street na ulici
[**oo**leetsee]

streetmap plan grada

string špaga [**shpa**ga]

strong jak [yak]

stuck zaglavljen [**za**glavl-yen]
the key's stuck zaglavio se
ključ [za**gla**veeo seh klyooch]

student student [**stoo**dent]
(female) studentica
[stoo**den**teetsa]

stupid glup [gloop]

suburb predgrađe [**pred**gradjeh]

subway (underground)
podzemna željeznica [**J**el-
yezneetsa]

suddenly naglo

suede antilop koža [an**tee**lop
koJa]

sugar šećer [**she**cher]

suit (noun) odijelo [o**d**-yelo]
it doesn't suit me (clothes etc)
ne stoji mi dobro [neh sto-yee
mee]

it suits you dobro vam stoji

suitcase kofer

summer ljeto [l-yeto]

in the summer ljeti [l-yetee]

sun sunce [soontseh]

in the sun na suncu [soontsoo]

out of the sun u hladu [oo Hladoo]

sunbathe sunčati se [soonchatee seh]

sunblock krema za sunčanje [soonchan-yeh]

sunburn opekotine [opekoteeneh]

sunburnt izgorio od sunca [eezgoreeo od soontsa]

Sunday nedjelja [ned-yelya]

sunglasses naočale za sunce [naochaleh za soontseh]

sun lounger ležaljka [leJalyka]

sunny sunčan [soonchan]

it's sunny sunčano je [yeh]

sun roof otvoren krov

sunset zalazak sunca [soontsa]

sunshade suncobran [soontsobran]

sunshine sunčev sjaj [soonchev syī]

sunstroke sunčanica [soonchaneetsa]

suntan preplanulost [preplanoolost]

suntan lotion losion za sunčanje [loseeon za soonchan-yeh]

suntanned preplanuo (od sunca) [preplanoo-o]

suntan oil ulje za sunčanje [ool-yeh]

super izvanredan [eezvanredan]

supermarket supermarket [soopermarket]

supper večera [vechera]

supplement (extra charge) doplata

sure siguran [seegooran]

are you sure? jeste li sigurni [yesteh lee seegoornee]

sure! naravno!

surname prezime [prezeemeh]

swearword psovka

sweater džemper [djemper]

sweatshirt majica [mīyeetsa]

Sweden Švedska [shvedska]

Swedish švedski [shvedskee]

sweet (dessert) desert
(adj: taste, wine) sladak

sweets slatkiši [slatkeeshee]

swelling otok

swim (verb) plivati [pleevateh]

I'm going for a swim idem na kupanje [eedem na koopan-yeh]

let's go for a swim idemo na kupanje [eedemo]

swimming costume kupaći kostim [koopachee kosteem]

swimming pool bazen

swimming trunks kupaće gaćice [koopachee gachetseh]

Swiss švicarski [shveetsarskee]

switch (noun) prekidač [prekeedach]

switch off isključiti [eesklyoocheetee]

switch on uključiti [oosklyoocheetee]

Switzerland Švicarska [shveetsarska]

swollen otekao

T

table stol
 a table for two stol za dvoje
 [dvo-yeh]
table cloth stolnjak [stolnyak]
table tennis stolni tenis
 [stolnee tenees]
table wine stolno vino [veeno]
tailback kolona vozila
 [vozeela]
tailor krojač [kroyach]
take uzeti [oozetee]
 can you take me to the
 airport? da li biste me
 odvezli na aerodrom? [lee
 beesteh meh odvezlee na a-
 erodrom]
 do you take credit cards?
 primate li kreditne kartice?
 [preemateh lee kredeetneh
 karteetseh]
 fine, I'll take it dobro, uzet ću
 [oozechoo]
 can I take this? mogu li to
 uzeti? [mogoo]
 how long does it take?
 koliko vremena treba za to?
 [koleeko]
 it takes three hours treba tri
 sata [tree]
 is this seat taken? je li ovo
 mjesto zauzeto? [yeh lee ovo
 m-yesto zaoozeto]
 pizza to take away pizza za
 van
 can you take a little off
 here? možete li ovdje malo

skratiti? [mojeteh lee ovd-yeh
 skrateetee]
talcum powder talk
talk (verb) govoriti [govoreetee]
tall (person) visok [veesok]
tampons tamponi [tamponee]
tan (noun) preplanulost
 [preplanoolost]
 to get a tan preplanuti
 [preplanootee]
tank (of car) spremnik
 [spremneek]
tap slavina [slaveena]
tape (cassette) traka
tape (sticky) ljepljiva [l-yepl-
 yeeva]
tape measure krojački
 centimetar [kroyachkee
 tsenteemetar]
tape recorder magnetofon
taste (noun) ukus [ookoos]
 can I taste it? mogu li
 probati? [mogoo lee probatee]
taxi taksi (m) [taksee]
 will you get me a taxi?
 molim vas, pozovite mi
 taksi [moleem vas pozoveeteh
 mee]
 where can I find a taxi? gdje
 mogu naći taksi [gd-yeh mogoo
 nachee]

dialogue

to the airport/to Hotel
Centrale please u zračnu
luku/hotel Central,
molim [oo zrachnoo lookoo/
hotel tsentral moleem]

how much will it be?
koliko će to biti? [koleeko
cheh to beetee]
100 kunas sto kuna [koona]
**that's fine, right here,
thanks** u redu je, ovdje,
hvala [oo redoo yeh ovd-yeh
Hvala]

taxi-driver taksist [takseest]
(woman) taksistkinja
[takseestkeenya]
taxi rank taksi stajalište [stī-
aleeshteh]
tea čaj [chī]
tea for one/two, please jedan
čaj/dva čaja, molim [yedan
– chīa, moleem]
teabags vrećice čaja
[vrecheetseh chīya]
teach: could you teach me?
možete li me naučiti?
[moJeteh lee meh naoocheetee]
teacher profesor
(woman) profesorica [-eetsa]
team momčad [momchad]
teaspoon mala žlica [Jleetsa]
tea towel kuhinjska krpa
[kooheenyska kerpa]
teenager tinejdžer [teenayjer]
telephone telefon
see **phone** and **speak**
television televizija
[televeezeeya]
tell: could you tell him ...?
da li biste mu rekli ...? [lee
beesteh moo reklee]
temperature (weather etc)
temperatura [temperatoora]

temple hram
tennis tenis [tenees]
tennis ball teniska loptica
[teneeska lopteetsa]
tennis court teniski teren
tennis racket teniski reket
tent šator [shator]
term (at school) tromjesječje
[trom-yes-yech-yeh]
terminus krajnja postaja
[krīnya ptosta-ya]
terrible grozan
terrific strašan [strashan]
text (message) tekstovna
poruka [porooka]
than* nego
smaller than manji nego
thanks, thank you hvala [Hvala]
thank you very much hvala
lijepo [l-yepo]
thanks for the lift hvala za
prijevoz [pr-yevoz]
no thanks ne, hvala [neh]

dialogue

thanks hvala [Hvala]
that's OK, don't mention it
molim [moleem]

that: that man taj čovjek [tī
chov-yek]
that woman ta žena [Jena]
that one onaj [onī]
I hope that ... nadam se
da ... [seh]
that's nice to je lijepo [yeh
l-yepo]
is that ...? je li to ...? [yeh lee]

that's it (that's right) tako je
[tako yeh]
the*
theatre kazalište [kazaleeshteh]
their njihov [n-yeehov]
their(s)* njihov
them*: for them za njih [zan-yeeH]
with them s njima [sn-yeema]
I gave it to them dao sam
njima [dao sam n-yeema]
who? – them tko? – oni
[onee]
then tada
there tamo
over there tamo
up there gore [goreh]
is there/are there …? ima
li …? [eema lee]
there is/there are … ima …
there you are izvolite
[eezvoleeteh]
thermometer termometar
thermos flask termos boca
[botsa]
these: these men ovi
muškarci [ovee mooshkartsee]
these women ove žene [oveh
Jeneh]
can I have these? molim vas
ove? [moleem]
they* oni [onee]
thick (cloth, traffic) debeo
thief lopov
thigh bedro
thin (cloth, hair) tanak
(person) mršav [mershav]
thing stvar
my things moje stvari [mo-yeh
stvaree]

think misliti [meesleetee]
I think so mislim da je tako
[meesleem da yeh]
I don't think so ne mislim da
je tako [neh]
I'll think about it razmislit
ću o tome [razmeesleechoo o
tomeh]
third treći [trechee]
third party insurance
osiguranje protiv treće
osobe [oseegooran-yeh proteev
trecheh osobeh]
thirsty: I'm thirsty žedan sam
[Jedan]
this ovaj [ovī]
this man ovaj muškarac
[mooshkarats]
this woman ova žena [Jena]
this one ovaj
this is my wife ovo je moja
žena [yeh mo-ya]
is this …? je li ovo …? [yeh
lee]
those oni [onee]
those men ovi muškarci
[ovee mooshkartsee]
those women ove žene [oveh
Jeneh]
those children ova djeca
[d-yetsa]
which ones? – those koje?
– ove [ko-yeh]
thread (noun) konac [konats]
throat grlo [gerlo]
throat pastilles pastile za grlo
[pasteeleh]
through kroz

does it go through ...?
prolazi li ...? [**pro**lazee lee]
throw (verb) baciti [**ba**tseetee]
throw away odbaciti
[**od**batseetee]
thumb palac [**pa**lats]
thunderstorm pljusak s
grmljavinom [**plyoo**sak s
germl-yaveenom]
Thursday četvrtak [chet**ver**tak]
ticket karta

dialogue

a return to Šibenik
povratnu za Šibenik
[**po**vratnoo za shee**be**neek]
coming back when? kada
se vraćate? [seh **vra**chateh]
today/next Tuesday
danas/sljedećeg utorka
[sleeye**de**cheg **oo**torka]
that will be 200 kunas to
je dvijesto kuna [**dvee**jesto
koona]

ticket office prodavaonica
karata [prodava**o**neetsa]
tie (necktie) kravata
tight tijesan [t-**ye**san]
it's too tight pretijesno je
[pret-**ye**sno yeh]
tights hula-hopke [**hoo**la-
hopkeh]
till (noun) blagajna [bla**gī**na]
time* vrijeme [vr-**ye**meh]
what's the time? koliko je
sati? [**ko**leeko yeh **sa**tee]
this time ovaj put [**o**vī poot]

last time prošli put [**pro**shlee]
next time sljedeći put
[sl-**ye**dechee]
four times četiri puta
[**che**teeree **poo**ta]
timetable red vožnje [**vo**Jn-yeh]
tin (can) konzerva
tin opener otvarač za
konzerve [**ot**varach za
konzerveh]
tinfoil aluminnijska folija
[aloom**ee**neeyska fo**lee**ya]
tiny malen
tip (to waiter etc) napojnica
[napoy**nee**tsa]
tired umoran [**oo**moran]
I'm tired umoran sam
tissues papirnate maramice
[papeer**na**teh mara**mee**tseh]
to: to Split/London za Split/
London
to Croatia/England u
Hrvatsku/Englesku [oo
hervatskoo/**en**gleskoo]
to the post office na poštu
[**po**shtoo]
toast (bread) tost
(drinking) zdravica [zdra**vee**tsa]
today danas
toe nožni prst [**no**Jnee perst]
together zajedno [**zī**yedno]
we're together mi smo
zajedno [mee]
can we pay together?
možemo li platiti zajedno?
[**mo**Jemo lee pla**tee**tee]
toilet zahod
where is the toilet? gdje je
zahod? [gd-yeh yeh]

I have to go to the toilet
moram ići na zahod [**ee**chee]

toilet paper toaletni papir
[toaletnee pa**peer**]

tomato rajčica [**rī**cheetsa]

tomato juice sok od rajčice
[**rī**cheetseh]

tomato ketchup kečap [**ke**chap]

tomorrow sutra [**soo**tra]

tomorrow morning sutra
ujutro [**oo**yootro]

the day after tomorrow
prekosutra [prekosootra]

toner toner

tongue jezik [**ye**zeek]

tonic (water) tonik [**to**neek]

tonight večeras [**ve**cheras]

tonsillitis angina [an**gee**na]

too (excessively) pre... [preh]
(also) također [ta**ko**jer]

too hot prevruć [prev**rooch**]

too much previše [pre**vee**sheh]

me too i ja, ja također [ee ya]

tooth zub [zoob]

toothache zubobolja
[zoobo**bo**lya]

toothbrush četkica za zube
[**chet**keetsa za **zoo**beh]

toothpaste pasta za zube

top floor najgornji kat [**nī**gorn-
yee]

top: on top of ... navrh
[**nav**erH]

at the top na vrhu [**ver**hoo]

topless toples

torch baterija [bate**ree**ya]

total (noun) ukupna svota
[**oo**koopna]

tour (noun) putovanje [pootovan-
yeh]
(shorter) izlet [**eez**let]

is there a tour of ...? imate li
izlet za ...? [**ee**mateh lee]

tour guide turistički vodič
[too**ree**steechkee **vo**deech]

tourist turist [**too**reest]
(woman) turistkinja
[too**ree**stkeenya]

tourist information office
turistički ured [too**ree**steechkee
oored]

tour operator turistička
agencija [too**ree**steechka
a**gent**seeya]

towards prema

towel ručnik [**rooch**neek]

tower kula [**koo**la]

town grad

in town u gradu [oo **gra**doo]

just out of town malo izvan
grada [**eez**van]

town centre središte grada
[sre**deesh**teh]

town hall gradska vijećnica
[v-**yech**neetsa]

toy igračka [**ee**grachka]

track kolosijek [kolos-**yek**]

tracksuit trenirka [tre**neer**ka]

traditional tradicionalan
[tradeetseeo**nal**an]

traffic promet

traffic jam prometni zastoj
[**pro**metnee **za**stoy]

traffic lights semafor

trailer prikolica [preeko**leet**sa]

train vlak

by train vlakom

111

dialogue

> is this train for ...? je li to
> vlak za...? [yeh lee]
> sure da
> no, you want that platform
> there ne, morate na onaj
> peron [neh morateh na onī]

trainers tenisice [teneeseetseh]
train station željeznički
kolodvor [Jel-yezneechkee]
tram tramvaj [tramvī]
translate prevesti [prevestee]
  could you translate that? da
  li biste mogli to prevesti?
  [lee beesteh moglee]
translation prijevod [pr-yevod]
translator prevoditelj
  [prevodeetel]
  (woman) prevoditeljica
  [prevodeetelyeetsa]
trashcan kanta za smeće
  [smecheh]
travel putovati [pootovatee]
  we're travelling around
  putujemo naokolo [pootooyemo]
travel agent's turistički agent
  [tooreesteechkee]
traveller's cheque putnički
  ček [pootneechkee chek]
tray plitica [pleetsa]
tree drvo [dervo]
tremendous izvanredan
  [eezvanredan]
trendy pomodan
trim: just a trim please molim
  vas, samo potšišati [moleem
  – potsheeshatee]

trip putovanje [pootovan-yeh]
  I'd like to go on a trip to ...
  volio bih otići na putovanje
  [voleeo beeH oteechee]
trouble (noun) problem
  I'm having trouble with ...
  imam problema s ... [eemam]
  sorry to trouble you oprostite
  što vam smetam [oprosteeteh
  shto]
trousers hlače [Hlacheh]
true: that's not true to nije
  istina [neeyeh eesteena]
trunk (US: of car) prtljažnik
  [pertl-yajneek]
  (big case) sanduk [sandook]
trunks (swimming) kupaće
  gaćice [koopacheh gacheetseh]
try probati [probatee]
  can I have a try? mogu li
  probati? [mogoo lee]
try on: can I try it on? mogu li
  probati?
T-shirt majica [mīyeetsa]
Tuesday utorak [ootorak]
tuna tuna [toona]
tunnel tunel [toonel]
turn: turn left/right skrenuti
  nalijevo/nadesno [skrenootee
  naleeyevo/nadesno]
turn off: where do I turn off?
  gdje trebam skrenuti [gd-yeh]
  can you turn the heating off?
  možete li isključiti grijanje?
  [moJeteh lee eeskl-yoocheetee
  greeyan-yeh]
turn on: can you turn the
  heating on? možete li
  uključiti grijanje? [ookl-

yoocheetee]

turning (in road) skretanje
[skretan-yeh]

TV televizija [televeezeeya]

tweezers pinceta [peentseta]

twice dvaput [dvapoot]

  twice as much dvaput toliko
  [toleeko]

twin beds dva kreveta

twin room dvokrevetna soba

twist: I've twisted my ankle
  uganuo sam nogu [ooganoo-o
  sam nogoo]

type (noun) vrsta [versta]

  a different type of ... drukčija
  vrsta ... [drook-cheeya]

typical tipičan [teepeechan]

tyre guma [gooma]

U

ugly ružan [rooJan]

ulcer čir [cheer]

umbrella kišobran [keeshobran]

uncle (mother's brother) ujak
  [ooyak]

  (father's brother) stric [streets]

unconscious nesvjestan [nesv-
  yestan]

under ispod [eespod]

underdone nepečen [nepechen]

underground (rail) podzemna
  željeznica [podzemna Jel-
  yezneetsa]

underpants gaće [gacheh]

understand razumjeti [razoom-
  yetee]

  I understand razumijem

[razoomeeyem]

  I don't understand ne
  razumijem [neh]

  do you understand?
  razumijete li? [razoomeeyeteh
  lee]

unemployed nezaposlen

United States Sjedinjene
  Države [s-yedeen-yeneh
  derJaveh]

university sveučilište
  [sveoocheeleeshteh]

unleaded petrol bezolovni
  benzin [bezolovnee benzeen]

unlimited mileage (on hire car)
  neograničena kilometraža
  [neograneechena keelometraJa]

unlock otključati
  [otklyoochatee]

unpack raspakirati [raspakeeratee]

until do

unusual neobičan
  [neobeechan]

up gore [goreh]

  up there tamo gore

  he's not up yet još nije ustao
  [yosh neeyeh oostao]

  what's up? što je? [shto yeh]

upmarket (restaurant, hotel, goods
  etc) luksuzan [looksoozan]

upset stomach pokvaren
  želudac [Jeloodats]

upside down naopako

upstairs gore [goreh]

urgent hitan [heetan]

us* nas

  with us s nama

  for us za nas

USA SAD [es a deh]

use (verb) upotrijebiti [oopotr-yebeetee]

  may I use ...? mogu li upotrijebiti ...? [mogoo lee]

useful koristan [koreestan]

usual običan [obeechan]

  as usual kao obično [kao obeechno]

  the usual kao obično

V

vacancy: do you have any vacancies? (hotel) imate li slobodnih soba? [eemateh lee slobodneeн soba]

vacation godišnji odmor [godeeshn-yee]

vaccination vakcinacija [vaktseenatseeya]

vacuum cleaner usisivač [ooseeseevach]

valid važeći [vaжechee]

  how long is it valid for? koliko važi? [koleeko vaжee]

valley dolina [doleena]

valuable dragocjen [dragots-yen]

  can I leave my valuables here? mogu li ostaviti ovdje svoje dragocjenosti? [mogoo lee ostaveetee ovd-yeh svo-yeh dragots-yenostee]

value vrijednost [vr-yednost]

van kombi [kombee]

vanilla vanilija [vaneelya]

  a vanilla ice cream sladoled od vanilije [vaneel-yeh]

vary: it varies zavisi [zaveesee]

vase vaza [vaza]

veal teletina [teleteena]

vegetables povrće [povercheh]

vegetarian (man) vegeterijanac [vegetereeyanats]

  (woman) vegeterijanka [vegetereeyanka]

vending machine automat [aootomat]

very vrlo [verlo]

  very little for me vrlo malo za mene [meneh]

  I like it very much jako mi se dopada [yako mee see]

vest (under shirt) potkošulja [potkoshoolya]

  (US: waistcoat) prsluk [perslook]

via preko

video video (m) [veedeo]

view pogled

villa vila [veela]

village selo

vinegar ocat [otsat]

vineyard vinograd [veenograd]

visa viza [veeza]

visit (verb) posjetiti [pos-yeteetee]

  I'd like to visit ... rado bih posjetio ... [rado beeн pos-yeteeo]

vital: it's vital that ... bitno je da ... [beetno yeh]

vodka votka

voice glas

voltage napon

vomit povraćati [povrachatee]

W

waist struk [strook]
waistcoat prsluk [perslook]
wait čekati [chekatee]
  wait for me čekajte me
  [chekite meh]
  don't wait for me nemojte me
  čekati [nemoyteh meh chekatee]
  can I wait until my wife/
  partner gets here? mogu li
  pričekati dok dođe moja
  žena/partner [mogoo lee
  preechekatee dok dojeh mo-ya
  Jena]
  can you do it while I wait?
  možete li to uraditi dok
  čekam? [moJeteh lee to
  ooradeetee]
  could you wait here for me?
  možete li me ovdje pričekati
  [meh ovd-yeh]
waiter konobar
  waiter! konobar!
waitress konobarica
  [konobareetsa]
wake: can you wake me up at
5.30? hoćete li me probuditi
u 5.30? [hocheteh lee meh
proboodeetee oo pet treedeset]
wake-up call telefonsko
buđenje [boojen-yeh]
Wales Vels
walk: is it a long walk? je li
daleko pješice? [yeh lee –
p-yesheetseh]
  it's only a short walk sasvim
je blizu pješice [sasveem yeh

bleezoo]
  I'll walk ići ću pješice [eechee
choo]
  I'm going for a walk idem
prošetati [eedem proshetatee]
Walkman® vokmen
wall zid [zeed]
wallet novčanik [novchaneek]
wander: I like just wandering
around volim lutati naokolo
[voleem lootatee]
want: I want a ... želim ...
[Jeleem]
  I don't want any ... ne
želim ... [neh]
  I want to go home želim ići
kući [eechee koochee]
  I don't want to ne želim
  he wants to ... želi...
[Jelee]
  what do you want? što
želite? [shto Jeleeteh]
ward (in hospital) odjel [od-yel]
warm topao
  I'm so warm tako mi je toplo
[mee yeh]
was*: he/she was on je bio/
ona je bila [yeh beeo/– beela]
  it was ono je bilo
  I was (said by man/woman) ja
sam bio/bila [ya]
wash (verb) oprati [opratee]
  can you wash these? možete
li ovo oprati? [moJeteh lee]
washer (for nut) podloška
[podloshka]
washhand basin umivaonik
[oomeevaoneek]
washing (clothes) prljavo rublje

[**per**l-yavo **roo**bl-yeh]
washing machine perilica
[pereel**eetsa**]
washing powder deterdžent
[**deter**jent]
washing-up liquid tekućina
za pranje suda [tek**oo**cheena za
pran-yeh **soo**ja]
wasp osa
watch (wristwatch) ručni sat
[**roo**chnee]
  **will you watch my things for
  me?** hoćete li mi pripaziti
  stvari? [**ho**cheteh lee mee
  pree**pa**zeetee st**var**ee]
  watch out! pazite!
  [**pa**zeeteh]
watch strap remen za sat
water voda
  may I have some water?
  molim vas malo vode
  [**mol**eem – **vo**deh]
waterproof nepromočiv
[nepro**mo**cheev]
waterskiing skijanje na vodi
[sk**ee**yan-yeh na **vo**dee]
wave (in sea) val
**way: could you tell me the
  way to ...?** da li biste mi
  mogli pokazati put za ...?
  [lee b**ee**steh mee **mo**glee po**ka**zatee
  poot]
  it's this way u ovom smjeru
  [oo **o**vom sm-**yer**soo]
  it's that way u onom
  smjeru
  is it a long way to ...? je li
  daleko do ...? [yeh lee]
  no way! ni govora! [nee]

dialogue

> **could you tell me the
> way to ...?** možete li mi
> reći kako ću doći do...?
> [**mo**jeteh lee mee **re**chee **ka**ko
> choo **do**chee]
> **go straight on until you
> reach the traffic lights**
> idite ravno do semafora
> [**ee**deeteh]
> **turn left** skrenite ulijevo
> [skre**nee**teh **oo**leeyevo]
> **take the first on the right**
> skrenite u prvu nadesno
> [oo **per**voo]
> **see where**

we* mi [mee]
weak (person) slab
weather vrijeme [vr-**yem**eh]

dialogue

> **what's the weather
> forecast?** kakva je
> vremenska prognoza?
> [yeh]
> **it's going to be fine** bit će
> lijepo [**bee**cheh leey**epo**]
> **it's going to rain** padat će
> kiša [**pada**cheh **kee**sha]
> **it'll brighten up later**
> razvedrit će se kasnije
> [razve**dree**cheh seh **kas**neeyeh]

website internetske
stranice [**ee**nternetskeh
str**a**neetseh]

wedding vjenčanje [v-yenchan-yeh]

wedding ring vjenčani prsten [v-yenchaneh persten]

Wednesday srijeda [sr-yeda]

week tjedan [t-yedan]

a week (from) today danas tjedan dana

a week (from) tomorrow sutra tjedan dana [sootra]

weekend vikend [veekend]

at the weekend preko vikenda

weight težina [teJeena]

weird čudan [choodan]

weirdo čudak [choodak]

welcome: welcome to … dobro došli u … [dobrodoshlee oo]

you're welcome nema na čemu [nema na chemoo]

well: I don't feel well ne osjećam se dobro [neh os-yecham seh dobro]

she's not well ne osjeća se dobro [os-yecha]

you speak English very well veoma dobro govorite engleski [govoreeteh engleskee]

well done! čestitam! [chesteetam]

this one as well i ovaj [ee ovī]

well well! vidi! vidi! [veedee]

dialogue

how are you? kako ste? [steh]

very well, thanks hvala, dobro [Hvala]

– and you? – a vi? [vee]

well-done (meat) dobro pečeno [dobro pecheno]

Welsh velški [velshkee]

I'm Welsh (said by man/woman) ja sam Velšanin/Velšanka [ya sam velshaneen/velshanka]

were*: we were bili smo [beelee]

you were bili ste [steh]

they were bili su [soo]

West Indian (adj) indijanski [eendeeyanskee]

west zapad

in the west na zapadu [zapadoo]

wet mokro

what? što? [shto]

what's that? što je to? [yeh]

what should I do? što da radim? [radeem]

what a view! kakav pogled!

what bus is it? koji je to autobus [ko-yee yeh to aootoboos]

wheel kotač [kotach]

wheelchair invalidska kolica [eenvaleedska koleetsa]

when? kada?

when we get back kad se vratimo [seh vrateemo]

when's the train/ferry? kada ide vlak/trajekt [eedeh]

where? gdje? [gd-yeh]

I don't know where it is ne znam gdje je to [neh – yeh]

dialogue

where is the cathedral?
gdje je katedrala? [gd-yeh
yeh]
it's over there tamo je
could you show me where
it is on the map? možete
li mi to pokazati na karti?
[moJeteh lee mee to pokazatee
na kartee]
it's just here točno ovdje
[tochno ovd-yeh]
see way

which: which bus? koji
autobus? [ko-yee aootoboos]
which one? koji?

dialogue

which one? koji? [ko-yee]
that one ovaj [ovī]
this one? ovaj? [ovaj]
no, that one ne, onaj [neh
onī]

while: while I'm here dok sam
ovdje [ovd-yeh]
whisky viski [veeskee]
white bijel [b-yel]
white wine bijelo vino [b-yelo
veeno]
who? tko?
who is it? tko je to? [yeh]
the man who ... čovjek
koji ... [chov-yek ko-yee]
whole: the whole week cijeli
tjedan [ts-yele t-yedan]

the whole lot sve [sveh]
whose: whose is this? čije je
ovo? [cheeyeh yeh]
why? zašto [zashto]
why not? zašto da ne? [neh]
wide širok [sheerok]
wife žena [Jena]
will*: will you do it for me?
možete li mi to učiniti?
[moJeteh lee mee to oocheeneetee]
wind (noun) vjetar [v-yetar]
window prozor
near the window blizu
prozora [bleezoo]
in the window (of shop) u
izlogu [oo eezlogoo]
window seat sjedalo pored
prozora [s-yedalo]
windscreen vjetrobran
[v-yetrobran]
windscreen wipers brisači
[breesachee]
windsurfing serfing [serfeeng]
windy: it's windy puše vjetar
[poosheh v-yetar]
wine vino [veeno]
can we have some more
wine? molim vas još malo
vina? [moleem vas yosh malo
veena]
wine list vinska karta [veenska
karta]
winter zima [zeema]
in the winter zimi
winter holiday zimski odmor
[zeemskee]
wire žica [Jeetsa]
wish: best wishes najbolje
želje [nībol-yeh Jel-yeh]
with s

I'm staying with ... odsjeo sam kod ... [ods-yeo sam kod ... [**ods**-yeo]

without bez

witness svjedok [sv-**ye**dok]
(woman) svjedokinja [sv-ye**do**keenya]

will you be a witness for me? hoćete li biti moj svjedok? [**ho**cheteh lee **bee**tee moy]

woman žena [**ye**na]

won't*: it won't start neće upaliti [**ne**cheh oo**pa**leetee]

wonderful divan [**dee**van]

wood (material) drvo [**der**vo]
(forest) šuma [**shoo**ma]

wool vuna [**voo**na]

word riječ [r-yech]

work raditi [**ra**deetee]
it's not working ne radi [neh]
I work in ... radim u ... [**ra**deem oo]

world svijet [sv-yet]

worry: I'm worried (said by man/woman) zabrinut/zabrinuta sam [**za**breenoot/**za**breenoota]

worse: it's worse gore je [**go**reh yeh]

worst najgori [**nī**goree]

worth: is it worth a visit? vrijedi li posjetiti? [vr-**ye**dee lee **pos**-yeteetee]

would: would you give this to ...? da li biste ovo dali ...? [lee **bee**steh **o**vo **da**lee]

wrap: could you wrap it up? da li biste mogli umotati? [lee **bee**steh **mo**glee oo**mo**tatee]

wrapping paper papir za umotavanje [**pa**peer za oomo**ta**van-yeh]

wrist ručni zglob [**rooch**nee]

write pisati [**pee**satee]
could you write it down? možete li to zapisati? [**mo**jeteh lee to za**pee**satee]
how do you write it? kako se to piše? [**pee**sheh]

writing paper papir za pisanje [**pa**peer za **pee**san-yeh]

wrong: it's the wrong key to je pogrešan ključ [yeh **po**greshan klyooch]
this is the wrong train ovo je krivi vlak [yeh **kree**vee]
the bill's wrong račun je pogrešan [**ra**choon]
sorry, wrong number žao mi je, pogrešan broj [**ja**o mee – broy]
sorry, wrong room oprostite, pogrešna soba [opro**stee**teh]
there's something wrong with ... nešto nije u redu s ... [**ne**shto **nee**yeh oo **re**doo]
what's wrong? što nije u redu? [shto]

X

X-ray rendgen

Y

yacht jahta [**yah**ta]

yard* (behind building) dvorište [**dvo**reeshteh]

year godina [**go**deena]
yellow žut [Joot]
yes da
yesterday jučer [**yoo**cher]
 yesterday morning jučer ujutro [**oo**yootro]
 the day before yesterday prekjučer [prekyoocheh]
yet: are we nearly there yet? jesmo li već blizu? [**ye**smo lee vech bl**ee**zoo]
 not yet ne još [neh yosh]

dialogue

is it here yet? jesmo li stigli? [**ye**smo lee st**ee**glee]
no, not yet nismo još [n**ee**smo yosh]
you'll have to wait a little longer yet morat ćete još malo pričekati [m**o**racheteh yosh malo pr**ee**chekatee]

yoghurt jogurt [**yo**goort]
you* (polite, singular, plural) vi [vee]
 (familiar, singular) ti [tee]
 this is for you ovo je za vas/tebe [tebeh]
 with you s vama/s tobom
young mlad
your(s)* (polite, singular, plural) vaš [vash]
 (familiar, singular) tvoj [tvoy]
youth hostel omladinski hotel [**o**mladeenskee]

Z

zero nula [n**oo**la]
zip patent-zatvarač [p**a**tent-z**a**tvarach]
 could you put a new zip on? da li biste mogli staviti novi patent-zatvarač? [lee b**ee**steh m**o**glee st**a**veetee n**o**vee]
zip code poštanski broj [p**o**shtanskee broy]
zoo zoološki vrt [zo-ol**o**shkee vert]

Croatian

→

English

Colloquialisms

The following are words you might well hear. You shouldn't be tempted to use any of the stronger ones unless you are sure of your audience.

boli me kurac! [bolee meh koorats] I don't give a damn!

dobit ćeš kurac [dobeechesh] you'll be lucky!, some hope!

dobiti po pički [dobeetee po peechkee] to get a thrashing

dovraga! blast!

drkati kurac [derkatee koorats] to bugger around, to do damn-all

evo ti kurac! [evo tee koorats] forget it!

fantastično! [fantasteechno] fantastic!

frajer/frajerica [frī-yer/frī-yereetsa] cool guy/cool chick

guba! [gooba] great!, wicked!, cool!

idi u kurac! [eedee oo koorats] get lost!

jebem ti mater! [yebem tee mater] fuck you!

jebi ga! [yebee] fuck!

kakva pička! [peechka] what a babe!

komad chick, bird; hunk

kurac [koorats] dick, prick

kurac! no way!

kurac na batini [bateenee] piece of junk

kurac od ovce [ovtseh] bum; loser

kurvo! [koorvo] bitch!

kvragu! [kvragoo] damn!

odjebi! [od-yebee] fuck off!

pičko! [peechko] cunt!

pizda ti materina! [peezda tee matereena] fuck you!

prokletstvo! damn!

pun mi je kurac! [poon mee yeh koorats] I'm fed up!

seronjo! [seronyo] arsehole!

sranje! [sran-yeh] shit!

tip [teep] guy, bloke

treba chick, bird

zajebati [zīyebatee] to fuck up

zezate me?, zezaš me? [zezateh meh, zezash] are you taking the mickey?, are you having me on?

This section is in Croatian alphabetical order:

a, b, c, č, ć, d, đ, e, f, g, h, i, j, k, l, lj, m, n, nj, o, p, r, s, š, t, u, v, z, ž

A

abeceda [abetseda] alphabet
aceton nail polish remover
adresa address
adresa za slanje pošte [slan-yeh poshteh] forwarding address
adresar address book
advokat lawyer
aerodrom airport
agencija agency
agent agent
agresivan aggressive
AIDS [eH-eeds] Aids
ako if
aktovka briefcase
akumulator [akoomoolator] battery
alat tool(s)
Albanac [albanats] Albanian
Albanija [albaneeya] Albania
Albanka [albanka] Albanian (woman)
albanski [albanskee] Albanian
alergičan [alergeechan] allergic
ali [alee] but
alkohol alcohol
alkoholno alcoholic
aluminijska folija [aloomeeneeyska foleeya] silver

foil
ambasada embassy
američki [amereechkee] American
Amerika [amereeka] America
amfiteatar [amfeeteatar] amphitheatre
amortizer [amorteezer] shock-absorber
ananas pineapple
angina [angeena] tonsillitis
angina pektoris angina
anlaser [anlas-er] starter (of car)
antibiotici [anteebeeoteetsee] antibiotics
antifriz [anteefreez] antifreeze
antihistaminik [anteeheestameeneek] antihistamine
antikvarnica [anteekvarneetsa] antique shop
antikvitet antique
antilop koža [anteelop koJa] suede
antiseptičan [anteesepteechan] antiseptic
aparat za brijanje [breeyan-yeh] shaver
aparat za gašenje požara [gashen-yeh] fire extinguisher
aperitiv [apereeteev] aperitif
apsolutno [apsolootno] absolutely
aspirin [aspeereen] aspirin
astma asthma
atletika [atleteeka] athletics
Australija [aoostraleeya] Australia
australski [aoostralskee]

Australian
Austrija [aoostreeya] Austria
Austrijanac [aoostreeyanats]
Austrian
Austrijanka [aoostreeyanka]
Austrian (woman)
austrijski [aoostreeskee]
Austrian
auto [aooto] car
autom by car
autobus [aootoboos] bus; coach
autobus za zračnu luku
[zrachnoo lookoo] airport bus
autobusna postaja [posta-ya]
bus stop
autobusna stanica [staneetsa]
bus stop
autobusni kolodvor
[aootoboosnee] bus station
autocesta [aootsesta]
motorway; highway
autokarta [aootokarta] road
map
automat [aootomat] vending
machine
automatski [aootomatskee]
automatic
autoservis [aootoservees]
garage (repairs)
autostopiranje hitchhiking
autostopirati hitchhike
avenija [aveneeya] avenue
avion aeroplane
avionom by air/airmail
avionska kompanija
[kompaneeya] airline
avionska koverta airmail
envelope

B

baciti [batseetee] throw; throw
away
badem almond
Badnjak [badnyak] Christmas
Eve
baka grandmother
balet ballet
balkon balcony
baloner raincoat; cagoule
banana banana
banka bank
bankomat automatic teller,
cash dispenser
bankovni račun [bankovnee
rachoon] bank account
bar bar; at least
barka boat
barka na vesla rowing boat
barmen barman
baš: baš ovdje [bash ovd-yeh]
just here
baterija [batereeya] battery;
torch
bazen swimming pool
beba baby
bedro thigh
Belgija [belgeeya] Belgium
benzin [benzeen] petrol, (US)
gas
benzinska crpka [tserpka]
petrol station, gas station
benzinska pumpa [poompa]
petrol station, gas station
benzinska stanica [staneetsa]
petrol station, gas station
Beograd Belgrade

bescarinski [bestsareenskee] duty-free

bescarinski dućan [doochan] duty-free shop

besplatan free of charge

bez without

bezalkoholan non-alcoholic

bezalkoholno piće [peecheh] soft drink

bezolovni benzin [bezolovnee benzeen] unleaded petrol

bež [beJ] beige

biber [beeber] pepper

bicikl [beetseekl] bicycle

biciklist [beetseekleest] cyclist

bijel [b-yel] white

bijela kava white coffee

bijeli kruh white bread

bijelo vino white wine

bijesan [b-yesan] furious

bik bull

bikini bikini

bili smo [beelee] we were

bili ste [steh] you were

bili su [soo] they were

bilo je zabavno [beelo] it was fun

bilježnica [beel-yeJneetsa] notebook

biljka [beelyka] plant

biljni čaj [beelynee chī] herbal tea

birati [beeratee] to choose; to dial

bistar clever; clear

bitan essential

bitno je da … it is essential that …

biti [beetee] be

biti prehlađen to have a cold

bjelilo [b-yeleelo] bleach

blag mild

blagajna [blagīna] cash desk; box office; ticket office; till

blagajnik [blagīneek] cashier

blagajnitsa [blagīneetsa] cashier (woman)

blagovaonica [blagova-oneetsa] dining room

blato mud

blenda shutter (camera)

blijed [bl-yed] pale

blizak close

blizanci [bleezantsee] twins

blizu [bleezoo] close, near

blokiran [blokeeran] blocked; jammed

bluza [blooza] blouse

bljutav [blyootav] stale

boca [botsa] bottle

bočica [bocheetsa] baby's bottle

Bog God

bog hello

bogat rich

boja [bo-ya] colour; paint

bojati se [bo-yatee seh] to be afraid

bojler [boyler] boiler

bokal jug

bol pain; ache

bol u leđima [bol oo leJeema] backache

bol u želucu [oo Jelootsoo] stomach ache

bolan painful

bolest illness, disease

bolestan ill, sick

bolnica [bolneetsa] hospital

bolničar [bolneechar] male nurse

bolničarka [bolneecharka] nurse

bolje mi je [bol-yeh mee yeh] I'm feeling better

boljeti [bol-yetee] to hurt

boli me [bolee meh] it's hurts

boli me uho I have earache

bolji [bol-yee] better

bomba bomb

bombon sweet, candy

boravak stay

Bosanac [bosanats] Bosnian

Bosanka Bosnian (woman)

bosanski Bosnian

Bosna Bosnia

Bosna i Hercegovina [ee hertsegoveena] Bosnia-Herzegovina

Božić [boJeech] Christmas

bračni krevet [brachnee] double bed

brada chin; beard

branik bumper, (US) fender

brašno [brashno] flour

brat brother

brava lock

brdo [berdo] hill

brendi brandy

breskva peach

briga worry

brijačnica [breejachneetsa] barber's

brijati se [breeyatee seh] to shave

brinuti se o to worry about; to look after

brisači [breesachee]

windscreen wipers

Britanija [breetaneeya] Britain

britanski [breetanskee] British

britva [breetva] razor

brkovi [berkovee] moustache

brod ship

brodom by ship

broj [broy] number; size

broj leta flight number

bronhitis [bronheetees] bronchitis

broš [brosh] brooch

brošura [broshoora] brochure

brz [berz] fast, quick

brzina [berzeena] speed; gear

brzina za vožnju unazad [voJn-yoo oonazad] reverse gear

brzinomjer [berzeenom-yer] speedometer

brzo [berzo] quickly

brzo ću se vratiti [berzo choo seh vrateetee] I'll be right back

bubrezi [boobrezee] kidneys

bučan [boochan] noisy

budan awake

budilica [boodeeleetsa] alarm clock

budite mirni [boodeeteh meernee] keep still!

budući da [boodoochee] since

budućnost [boodoochnost] future

Bugarska Bulgaria

bugarski Bulgarian

buha [booHa] flea

buka [booka] noise

C

carina [tsareena] Customs
celer [tseler] celery
Celzij [tselzee] Centigrade, Celsius
centar [tsentar] centre
centar grada city centre
centimetar [tsenteemetar] centimetre
centralno grijanje [tsentralno greeyan-yeh] central heating
centrifuga [tsentreefooga] spin-dryer
cesta [tsesta] road
cestarina toll
cigara [tseegara] cigar
cigareta [tseegareta] cigarette
cigla brick
cijeli [ts-yelee] whole, all; entire
cijena [ts-yena] price
cijena ulaznice [oolaznitseh] admission charge
cijepljenje [tseeyepl-yen-yeh] vaccination
cijev [ts-yev] pipe
cijev za disanje [deesan-yeh] snorkel
cikla beetroot
cipela [tseepela] shoe
crkva [tserkva] church
crn [tsern] black
Crna Gora [tserna] Montenegro
crni kruh [tsernee] brown bread
crno vino [tserno veeno] red

wine
Crnogorac [tsrnogorats] Montegran
Crnogorka Montegran (woman)
crnogorski Montegran
crtež [tserteJ] drawing
crven [tserven] red
crvena paprika [tservena] red pepper
crvenokos red-headed
cura [tsoora] girlfriend
curiti [tsooreetee] to leak
cvijet [tsveeyet] flower
cvjećarna [tsveeyecharna] florist
cvjetača [tsv-yetacha] cauliflower

Č

čaj [chī] tea
čaj s limunom [sleemoonom] lemon tea
čajna kuhinja [chīna] kitchenette
čajnik teapot
čak [chak] even
čak ako even if ...
čamac [chamats] boat
čamac na vesla rowing boat
čarape [charapeh] socks; stockings
čarter (izvanredni) let [charter] charter flight
časopis [chasopees] magazine
čaša [chasha] glass
čavao [chavao] nail
ček [chek] cheque, (US) check

čekaonica [cheka-**o**neetsa] waiting room

čekaonica za odlaske departure lounge

čekati [chekatee] to wait

čekajte me [chek**ī**te meh] wait for me

čekić [chekeech] hammer

čekirati [chekeeratee] to check in

čekovna kartica [chekovna karteetsa] cheque card

čekovna knjižica [chekovna k-n-y**ee**Jeetsa] cheque book

čelo [chelo] forehead

čep [chep] plug; cork

česma [chesma] (drinking) fountain

čestitam! [chesteetam] congratulations!, well done!

često [chesto] frequent; often

češalj [cheshal] comb

češnjak [cheshnyak] garlic

četiri [cheteeree] four

četka [chetka] brush

četka za kosu [ko**soo**] hairbrush

četkica za zube [chetkeetsa za **zoo**beh] toothbrush

četvrt [chetvert] quarter; area

četvrtak [chetvertak] Thursday

čeznuti za domom [cheznootee] to be homesick

čiji, čija, čije [cheeyee] whose

čije je ovo? [cheeyeh yeh] whose is this?

čim [cheem] as soon as

čim prije moguće [preeyeh mog**oo**cheh] as soon as possible

čips [cheeps] crisps, (US) potato chips

čir [cheer] ulcer

čist [cheest] clean

čistiti [cheesteetee] to clean

čitati [cheetatee] to read

čitav [cheetav] whole; all

čizma [cheezma] boot

čok [chok] choke

čokolada [chokolada] chocolate

čovjek [chov-yek] man

čudak [choodak] weirdo

čudan [choodan] odd, funny, strange

čuti [chootee] to hear

čuvati [choovatee] to take care (of)

čuvajte se! beware!

Ć

ćelav [chelav] bald

ćilim [cheeleem] rug

D

da yes

mislim da I think that

da li ...? question form

da li biste mu rekli ...? [lee beesteh moo reklee] could you tell him ...?

da li ste sami? [lee steh samee] are you on your own?

dagnje [dagn-yeh] mussels

dakle! [dakleh] well!

dalek far; far away

dalje [dal-yeh] further

daljina [dal-yeena] distance
 u daljini in the distance

dan day
 dan kasnije [kasneeyeh] the
 day after
 dan ranije [raneeyeh] the day
 before

danas today
 danas poslije podne
 [posleeyeh podneh] this
 afternoon

Danska Denmark

danski Danish

dar gift

daska board

daska za jedrenje [yedren-yeh]
 sailboard

dati [datee] give

datulje [datool-yeh] dates

datum date

debeo fat; thick

dečko [dechko] boy;
 boyfriend

definitivno [defeeneeteevno]
 definitely

deka blanket

depresivan depressed

desert dessert

deset ten

desno right
 s desne strane on the right
 (of)

deterdžent [deterJent] soap
 powder, washing powder

devet nine

dezinfekcijsko sredstvo
 [dezeenfekt-seeysko]
 disinfectant

dezodorans deodorant

dijabetičar [deeyabeteechar]
 diabetic

dijalekt [deeyaalekt] dialect

dijamant [deeyamant]
 diamond

dijapozitiv [deeyapozeeteev]
 slide

dijeliti [d-yeleetee] to share; to
 separate

dijeta [deeyeta] diet

dijete [deeyeteh] child

dijetetska hrana [deeyetetska
 Hrana] diabetic foods

dim smoke

dinja [deenya] melon

dio [deeo] part

direktan [deerektan] direct

direktor director; manager

direktorica [deerektoreetsa]
 manageress

disati [deesatee] to breathe

divan [deevan] lovely,
 wonderful

divljač [deevl-yach] game
 (hunting)

divlje [deevl-yeh] wild

dizalica [deezaleetsa] jack (for
 car)

dizalica [deezaleetsa] crane

dizalo [deezalo] lift, (US)
 elevator

dizel [deezel] diesel

dječak [d-yechak] boy

dječja hrana [d-yechya Hrana]
 baby food

Dj

djolja kolica [koleetsa]
pushchair; pram

dječja porcija [portseeya]
children's portion

dječja stolica [stoleetsa]
highchair

dječji bazen [d-yech-yee]
children's pool

dječji krevetić [kreveteech] cot

djed [d-yed] grandfather

Djed Mraz Father Christmas

djevojačko ime [d-yevoyachko
eemeh] maiden name

djevojčica [d-yevoycheetsa]
young girl

djevojka [d-yevoyka] girl;
girlfriend

dnevna soba living room

dnevnik diary; news

dnevno daily

dno bottom

do until; by

dob age

dobar good; kind

dobar tek! enjoy your meal!

dobiti [dobeetee] to get; to
receive; to win

dobra večer [vecher] good
evening

dobro good; fine; all right;
properly

dobro došli! [dobrodoshlee oo]
welcome!

dobro jutro [yootro] good
morning

dobro pečeno [pecheno] well-
done

doći [dochee] to come

dodirnuti to touch

dogoditi (se) [dogodeetee (seh)]
to happen

dogovor deal

dogovoreno! it's a deal, done

doista? [do-eesta] really?

dojiti [do-yeetee] to breastfeed

dojka [doyka] breast

dojmljiv [doym-lyeev]
impressive

dok while

dolasci arrivals

dolazak arrival

doletjeti [dolet-yetee] to fly in

dolina [doleena] valley

dolje [dol-yeh] down; below;
downstairs

dom home

domaći [domachee]
homemade; local

domaća radinost crafts

domaće vino house wine;
homemade wine

donijeti [doneeyetee] to bring

donje rublje [don-yeh roobl-yeh]
underwear

doplata supplement

dopustiti to let, to allow, to
permit

doručak [doroochak] breakfast

dosadan boring; annoying

dosadno mi je [mee yeh] I'm
bored

dosta enough, sufficiently;
rather

dostava delivery

dostaviti [dostaveetee] to
deliver

doviđenja! [doveejenya]
goodbye, cheerio

dovoljno [dovolyno] enough
dovraga! damn!
dozvola licence
dozvoliti to allow
drag dear
 drago mi je [mee yeh] nice to meet you; my pleasure
dragocjen [dragots-yen] valuable
drevan ancient
droga drug
drugdje [droogd-yeh] elsewhere
drugi [droogee] another; other; second
 nešto drugo [neshto] something else
drugi kat second floor
drugi razred [droogee] second class
drukčija vrsta ... [drook-cheeya versta] a different type of ...
društvo [drooshtvo] society, company
drvo [dervo] tree; wood
držati [derJatee] to hold; to keep
država [derJava] state (of country)
državljanstvo [derJavlyanstvo] nationality
državni praznik [derJavnee] public holiday
dubok [doobok] deep
duda [dooda] dummy, (US) pacifier
dug [doog] long
duga rainbow
dugme [doogmeh] button
dugo long

duhan tobacco
dunja [doon-ya] quince
duplo double
dužina [doosheena] length
dva two
dvaput [dvapoot] twice
dvokrevetna soba double room; twin room
dvorac [dvorats] castle
dvorište [dvoreeshteh] yard
dvosmjerna ulica two-way traffic
dvosmjerni promet two-way traffic
dvostruk [dvostrook] double
džem [jem] jam
džemper [jemper] jumper, sweater
džep [jep] pocket
džeparoš [jeparosh] pickpocket
džepna maramica [jepna marameetsa] handkerchief
džepni nož [jepnee noJ] penknife, pocket knife
džez [jez] jazz
džin [jeen] gin

Đ

đon [jon] sole (of shoe)

E

ej! [ay] hey!
ekonomska klasa economy class
elastika [elasteeka] elastic

elektični [elektreechnee] electric
električar [elektreechar]
  electrician
Engleska England
engleski [engleskee] English
Engleskinja [engleskeen-ya]
  English girl/woman
Englez Englishman
etiketa label
europski [eHooropskee]
  European
evo here is; here are

F

faks fax
faktor zaštite [zashteeteh]
  protection factor
fantastičan [fantasteechan]
  fantastic
far headlight
farma farm
farovi [farovee] headlights
feministkinja [femeeneestkeenya]
  feminist
fen frizura blow-dry
fen za kosu hair dryer
file [feeleh] fillet
fino fine; tasty
flaster sticking plaster,
  Bandaids®
fleš [flesh] flash
flomaster felt-tip (pen)
fontana fountain
forma: u formi fit
formular [formoolar] form;
  document
fotoaparat camera

fotografija [fotografeeya] photo
fotografirati to photograph
Francuska [frantsooska] France
francuski [frantsooskee] French
frape [frapeh] milkshake
frizer [freezer] hairdresser
frizura [freezoora] haircut
funta [foonta] pound

G

gaće [gacheh] underpants
gaćice [gacheetseh] panties;
  pants
gadan nasty
galeb seagull
garancija [garantseeya]
  guarantee
garaža [garaJa] garage (parking)
garderoba cloakroom; left
  luggage office
gazda boss; proprietor
gaziran [gazeeran] fizzy
gdje? [gd-yeh] where?
gel za kosu hair gel
gel za tuširanje [toosheeran-yeh]
  shower gel
gips [geeps] plaster cast
girica [geereetsa] pickerel
gitara [geetara] guitar
glačalo [glachalo] iron
glačati [glachatee] to iron
gladan hungry
glas voice
glasan loud
glava head
glavna cesta [tsesta] main
  road

glavna ulica [**oo**leetsa] main road

glavni [**glav**nee] main

glavni prekidač [preke**e**dach] mains switch

glavno jelo [**yelo**] main course

glavobolja [glavo**bolya**] headache

glazba music

glazbalo musical instrument

gledati to look (at); to watch

gležanj [gle**jan**] ankle

gljivična infekcija [gl-yee**veech**na eenfekt**seeya**] fungal infection; thrush

globa fine

gluh [glooH] deaf

glup [gloop] silly, stupid

glupost: to je glupost! [yeh gl**oo**post] that's rubbish!

gljive [gl-yee**veh**] mushrooms

gnjilo [g-nye**elo**] rotten

godina [**go**deena] year

godišnji odmor [**go**deeshn-yee] vacation

godišnjica [**go**deesh-nyeetsa] anniversary

gol naked; goal

gomila crowd

gorak bitter

gore [**go**reh] up; upstairs; worse

gorjeti [**go**r-yetee] to burn

gori [**go**ree] it's on fire

gospodarstvo farm

gospodin [gos**po**deen] gentleman; Mr

gospodine! sir; officer

gospođa [**go**spoja] lady; Mrs

gospođo! Madam

gospođica [**go**spojeetsa] Miss; Ms

gost guest

gostoprimstvo [gostopre**e**mstvo] hospitality

gotov ready; finished; done for

gotovo je [yeh] it's over

gotovina [goto**veena**] cash

gotovo almost; nearly

gotovo nikad [**nee**kad] hardly ever

govedina [**go**vedeena] beef

govoriti [govo**ree**tee] to speak, to talk

grad city; town; hail

gradska vijećnica [v-ye**chneetsa**] town hall

gradsko poglavarstvo town hall

grah [graH] beans

gramatika [grama**tee**ka] grammar

granica [gra**neetsa**] border; limit

grašak [gra**shak**] peas

grč [gerch] cramp

Grčka [**gerch**ka] Greece

grčki [**gerch**kee] Greek

grejpfrut [**grayp**froot] grapefruit

greška [**greshka**] fault; mistake

grickalica za nokte [gree>tskaleetsa za **nok**teh] nail clippers

grijač [**gree**yach] heater

grijanje [**gree**yan-yeh] heating

gripa [**gree**pa] flu

gristi to bite

Grk [gerk] Greek
Grkinja [gerkeenya] Greek
grlo [gerlo] throat
grmljavina [germl-yaveena] thunder
groblje [grobl-yeh] cemetery
grozan awful, terrible
groznica [grozneetsa] fever
grozničav [grozneechav] feverish
grožđe [grojjeh] grapes
grudi [groodee] chest; breasts
grudnjak [groodnyak] bra
grupa group
gubiti [goobeetee] to lose
  gubi se! go away!, get lost!
guma [gooma] rubber; gum; tyre
gumena pasica [goomena paseetsa] rubber band
gumeni čamac [goomenee chamats] dinghy
gumica [goomeetsa] elastic band
guraj push
gurati [gooratee] to push
guska [gooska] goose
gutati [gootatee] to swallow
gužva [gooJva] traffic jam

H

halo hello (on telephone)
haljina [hal-yeena] dress
hauba [haooba] bonnet, (US) hood
hidrantna krema moisturizer
hidrogliser [heedrogleeser] hydrofoil
higijenski uložak [heegeeyenskee ooloJak] sanitary napkins/towels
hitan [heetan] urgent
hitan slučaj [sloochī] emergency
hitno urgently; in a hurry; special delivery
hlače [Hlacheh] trousers, (US) pants
hlad [Hlad] shade
  u hladu in the shade
hladan [Hladan] cold
hladnjak [Hladnyak] fridge; radiator (in car)
hladovina [Hladoveena] shade
hobi [hobee] hobby
hobotnica [hobotneetsa] octopus
hoćete li …? [hocheteh lee] will you …?
hod unazad reverse gear
hodati to walk
hodnik [hodneek] corridor
holandski Dutch
hotelska soba hotel room
hrabar [Hrabar] brave
hrana [Hrana] food
hripavac [Hreepavats] whooping cough
hrkati [Herkatee] to snore
Hrvat [Hervat] Croatian
Hrvatica [Hervateetsa] Croatian (woman)
Hrvatska [Hervatska] Croatia
hrvatski [Hervatskee] Croatian
htjeti [Ht-yetee] to want

hula-hopke [hoola-hopkeh] tights, pantyhose

hvala [Hvala] thanks, thank you

hvala lijepo [l-yepo] thank you very much

I

i [ee] and

i ja [ya] me too

iako [yako] although

ići [eechee] to go

ideja [eedeh-ya] idea

idemo! [eedemo] let's go!

igla [eegla] needle

igra [eegra] game; dance

igračka [eegrachka] toy

igralište [eegraleeshteh] playground

igrati se [eegrate seh] to play

ikada ever

ili [eelee] or

ili ... ili ... either: either ... or ...

imati [eematee] to have

ima ... [eema] there is/there are ...

ima li ...? is there/are there ...?

imam problema s ... I'm having trouble with ...

imam 25 godina [godeena] I'm 25 years old

imate li ...? [eemateh lee] have you got ...?; is there ...?

ime [eemeh] name; first name

imitacija [eemeetatseeya] imitation

inače [eenacheh] otherwise

inč [eench] inch

indijanski [eendeeyanskee] West Indian

indijski [eendeeyskee] Indian

infarkt [eenfarkt] heart attack

infekcija [eenfektseeya] infection

informacija [eenformatseeya] information; directory enquiries

inozemstvo abroad

instant kava instant coffee

instruktor skijanja [eenstrooktor skeeyanya] ski instructor

inteligentan [eenteleegentan] intelligent

internetske stranice [eenternetskeh straneetseh] website

invalid [eenvaleed] disabled

invalidska kolica [eenvaleedska koleetsa] wheelchair

inzistirati [eenzeesteeratee] to insist

injekcija [een-yektseeya] injection

Irska [eerska] Ireland

irski [eerskee] Irish

iscrpljen [eestserpl-yen] exhausted

isključeno [eeskl-yoocheno] off

isključiti [eesklyoocheetee] to switch off

iskren sincere

iskusan [eeskoosan] experienced

ispit [**ee**speet] exam

ispod [**ee**spod] below, under

ispravan [**ee**spravan] correct, right; in working order

ispravljač [eesprav-lyach] adapter

ispred [**ee**spred] in front; in front of

ispričati se [eespr**ee**chatee seh] to apologize

isprika [ee**spree**ka] apology

isprva [**ee**sperva] at first

ispuniti [ee**spoo**neetee] to fill in

ispušna cijev [ee**spoo**shna ts**ee**yev] exhaust (pipe)

isti [**ee**stee] the same

istinit [ee**stee**neet] true

isto [**ee**sto] the same

isto toliko lijep koliko as beautiful as

istok [**ee**stok] east

istočno od [ee**sto**chno] east of

išta [**ee**shta] anything

Italija [eet**a**leeya] Italy

itko [**ee**tko] anybody

iver [**ee**ver] splinter

iza [**ee**za] behind; beyond; at the back

izaći [ee**za**chee] to get out; to go out

izbjeljivač [eezb-yel-y**ee**vach] bleach

izbočina [eez**bo**cheena] lump

izgledati to seem

izgorio od sunca [eez**go**reeo od **soo**ntsa] sunburnt

izgovoriti [eez**go**voreetee] to pronounce, to utter

izgubiti [eez**goo**beetee] to lose

izići [ee**zee**echee] to go out; to get out

izišao je [ee**zee**shao yeh] he's out

izlaz [**ee**zlaz] exit; gate

izlaz u nuždi [oo **noo**Jdee] emergency exit

izlaz u slučaju opasnosti [sl**oo**chī-yoo] emergency exit

izlet [**ee**zlet] trip

izlog [**ee**zlog] shop window

izložba [eez**lo**Jba] exhibition

između [**ee**zmejoo] between

iznad [**ee**znad] above

iznajmiti [eezn**ī**meetee] to rent; to hire out

iznajmljuje se [eesn**ī**ml-yooyeh seh] for hire

iznenađenje [eeznena-j**en**-yeh] surprise

iznos [**ee**znos] amount

izrađivati [eezra-je**e**vatee] to make

izvanredan [eez**va**nredan] tremendous; exceptional

izvolite [eez**vo**leeteh] here you are; there you are

J

ja [ya] I

jabuka [y**a**booka] apple

jabukovača [y**a**bookovacha] cider

Jadransko more [y**a**dransko **mo**reh] Adriatic

jagoda [y**a**goda] strawberry

jahanje konja [ya**Ha**n-yeh **ko**nya]

horse riding

jahta [yahta] yacht

jaje [yī-yeh] egg

jak [yak] strong

jakna [yakna] jacket

jako [yako] so

jako mi se dopada [mee seh] I like it so much

jako je dobro it's so good

jako puno very much

jamčevina [yamcheveena] guarantee

jamstvo [yamstvo] guarantee

janje [yan-yeh] lamb

janjetina [yan-yeteena] lamb

jarkocrven [yarkotserven] bright red

jasan [yasan] clear

jaslice [jasleetseh] crèche (for kids)

jastog [yastog] lobster

jastučnica [yastoochneetsa] pillow case

jastuk [yastook] pillow; cushion; couchette

javan [yavan] public

javni zahod [yavnee] public convenience

je [yeh] is

je li ...? is ...?

je li to ...? [lee] is it ...?, is that ...?

jedan [yedan] one

jedan smjer one-way street

jednobojan [yednoboyan] plain

jednodnevni izlet [yednodnevnee eezlet] day trip

jednokrevetna soba

[yednokrevetna] single room

jednom [yednom] once

jednosmjerna karta [yednosmyerna] one-way ticket

jednosmjerna ulica one-way street

jednostavan [yednostavan] simple

jedrenje [yedren-yeh] sailing

jedrenje na dasci [dastsee] sailboarding

jedrilica [yedreeleetsa] sailing boat

jedro [yedro] sail

jeftin [yefteen] cheap; downmarket

jeftiniji [yefteeneeyee] less expensive, cheaper

jelo [yelo] meal; dish; course

jelovnik [yelovneek] menu

jer [yer] because

jesen [yesen] autumn, (US) fall

jeste li ...? [yesteh lee] are you ...?; have you ...?

jesti [yestee] to eat

jetra [yetra] liver

jetrva [yeturva] sister-in-law

jezero [yezero] lake; pond

jezična škola [yezeechna shkola] language school

jezični tečaj [techī] language course

jezik [yezeek] language; tongue

jogurt [yogoort] yoghurt

još [yosh] more

još uvijek [ooveeyek] still

još jedno pivo another beer

Ju

još malo a little bit more
još nije [neeyeh] not yet
jučer [yoocher] yesterday
jug [yoog] south
jugoistok [yoogo-eestok]
southeast
jugozapad [yoogozapad]
southwest
juha [yooha] soup
juni June
jutro [yootro] morning
jutros this morning
Južna Afrika [yooJna afreeka]
South Africa
južni [yooJnee]
južno od south of

K

kabeli za punjenje
akumulatora [kabelee za poon-
yen-yeh akoomoolatora] jump
leads
kabina [kabeena] cabin
kablica [kableetsa] bucket
kaciga [katseega] helmet
kad when
kada? when?
kada bathtub
kafić [kafeech] bar; café
kakao cocoa
kakav what kind of
kakav pogled! what a view!
kako? how?
kako ide? how's it going?
kako se ovo zove? [seh
– zoveh] what's it called?
kako se zovete? [seh zoveteh]

what's your name?
kako si/ste? how are you?
kalendar calendar
kaloričan [kaloreechan] rich
kamen stone
kamera camcorder
kamion [kameeon] lorry
kamo? where?
kamp campsite; caravan site
kamp prikolica [preekoleetsa]
caravan
kamping campsite
kampiranje [kampeeran-yeh]
camping
kampirati [kampeeratee] to
camp
Kanada Canada
kanadski [kanadski] Canadian
kanal canal
kanta bin
kanta za benzin petrol can
kanta za smeće [smecheh]
dustbin, (US) trashcan
kanu [kanoo] canoe
kao like; as
velik kao as big as
kap drop; stroke (medical)
kapa cap
kapa za plivanje [pleevan-yeh]
bathing cap
kapak shutter
kapela chapel
kapetan captain
kapi za oči [kapee za ochee] eye
drops
kaput [kapoot] coat
karantena quarantine
karburator [karboorator]
carburettor

karta card; map; ticket
 karta u jednom smjeru single
 ticket
karton cardboard; card
kasa cash desk
kaseta cassette
kasetofon cassette player
kasni late
kasnije [kasneeyeh] afterwards;
 later
kasno late
kašalj [kashal] cough
kašljati [kashalatee] to cough
kašnjenje [kashn-yen-yeh] delay
kat floor, storey
katastrofa disaster
katedrala cathedral
katkad sometimes
katolički [katoleechkee]
 Catholic
katolik [katoleek] Catholic
kauč [kaooch] couch
kava coffee
kava bez kofeina [kofe-eena]
 decaffeinated coffee
kavana café
kazališna predstava
 [kazaleeshna] play; drama
kazališni komad play; drama
kazalište [kazaleeshteh] theatre
kazeta cassette
kazetofon cassette recorder
kći [kechee] daughter
kečap [kechap] ketchup
kej [kay] quay
keks biscuit, cookie
kemijska čistionica [kemeeyska
 cheesteoneetsa] dry-cleaner
kemijska olovka biro®,

ballpoint pen
keramika [kerameeka] pottery
kesten chestnut
kihati [keehatee] to sneeze
kikiriki [keekeereekee] peanuts
kilometar [keelometar]
 kilometre
kino [keeno] cinema, movie
 theater
kip [keep] statue
kiseo [keeseo] sour
kist paint brush
kiša [keesha] rain
kišiti [keesheetee] to rain
kišni mantil [keeshnee] raincoat
kišni ogrtač [ogertach] raincoat
kišobran [keeshobran] umbrella
klanac [klanats] pass
klasa class
klasična glazba/muzika
 [klaseechna] classical music
klavir [klaveer] piano
kliješta [kl-yeshta] pliers
klima climate
klimatizacija [kleemateezatseeya]
 air-conditioning
klimatizirano air-conditioned
klin [kleen] peg
klinika [kleeneeka] clinic
klizalište [kleezaleeshteh] ice
 rink
klizav [kleezav] slippery
ključ [klyooch] key; spanner
ključ za odvijanje [odveeyan-
 yeh] wrench
ključati [klyoochatee] to boil
knjiga [k-nyeega] book
knjižara [k-nyeejara] bookshop,
 bookstore

knjižnica [k-nyeeJneetsa] library

kobasica [kobaseetsa] sausage

kocka leda ice cube

kočiti [kocheetee] to brake

kočnica [kochneetsa] brake

kod code

kod: kod kuće [koocheh] at
home

kod vas at your place

kod Ane at Ann's

kofer suitcase

koji, koja, koje [ko-yee] which;
what; that (one)

bilo koji od njih [beelo ko-yee
od n-yeeh] either of them

koja vrsta ...? [ko-ya versta]
what sort of ...?

koje? – ove which ones?
– those

koka-kola Coke®

koktel cocktail

kolač [kolach] cake

koledž [kolej] college

kolica [koleetsa] buggy;
trolley; cart

kolica za bebu pram;
pushchair

kolica za prtljagu [pertl-yagoo]
luggage trolley, (US) baggage
cart

koliko? [koleeko] how many?;
how much?

koliko često? [chesto] how
often?

koliko dugo traje? [doogo tra-
yeh] how long does it take?

koliko imaš/imate godina?
[eemash/eemateh godeena] how
old are you?

koliko košta? [koshta] how
much does it cost?

kolodvor train station

kolona vozila [vozeela] tailback

kolonjska voda [kolonyska] eau
de toilette

kolosijek [kolos-yek] track

kolovoz August

koljeno [kol-yeno] knee;
generation

komad piece

komarac [komarats] mosquito

kombi [kombee] van

kombine [kombeeneh] slip (under
dress)

kompanija [kompaneeya]
company

kompas compass

kompjutor computer

komplet za prvu pomoć
[pervoo pomoch] first aid kit

kompliciran complicated

konac [konats] thread

konačno [konachno] eventually

koncert [kontsert] concert

kondom condom

konferencija [konferentseeya]
conference

konobar waiter

konobarica [konobareetsa]
waitress; barmaid

konop [konats] string

konop za sušenje rublja
[sooshen-yeh rooblya] clothes
line

kontaktirati [kontakeeratee] to
contact

kontaktne leće [kontaktneh
lecheh] contact lenses

kontracepcijsko sredstvo [kontratseptseeysko] contraceptive

konzerva tin, can

konzulat [konzoolat] consulate

konj [kon-yuh] horse

konjak [konyak] brandy

kopča za kosu [kopcha] hairgrip

koristan [koreestan] helpful; useful

kornet icecream cone

kosa hair

Kosovljanin, Kosovar [kosovl-yaneen] Kosovan

Kosovljanka, Kosovarka [kosovl-yanka] Kosovan (woman)

kosovski [kosovskee] Kosovan

kost bone

košara [koshara] basket

koštati [koshtatee] to cost

košulja [koshoolya] shirt

kotač [kotach] wheel

kotlet chop

kotlić [kotleech] kettle

kovanica [kovaneetsa] coin

kovčeg [kovcheg] case, suitcase; chest; box

koverta envelope

kovrčav [koverchav] curly

koza goat

kozji sir [koz-yee seer] goats' cheese

kozmetika [kozmeteeka] cosmetics

koža [koJa] leather; skin

krađa [kraja] theft

kraj [krī] end; district; by

kraj mora by the sea

krajnja postaja [krīnya ptosta-ya] terminus

krajnje [krīn-yeh] extremely

krajolik [kra-yoleek] scenery; landscape

kralj [kral] king

kraljica [kral-yeetsa] queen

krasan nice

krastavac [krastavats] cucumber

kratak short

kratke hlače [Hlacheh] shorts

kratkovidan shortsighted

krava cow

kravata tie, necktie

kreditna kartica [kredeetna karteetsa] credit card

kreker cracker

krema cream

krema poslije sunčanja [posleeyeh soonchanya] aftersun cream

krema za lice [leetseh] facial cream

krema za sunčanje [soonchan-yeh] sunblock

krema za usne [oozneh] lip salve

krevet bed

krevet za jednu osobu single bed

kreveti na kat bunk beds

krigla [kreegla] mug, beaker

krilo wing

kriška [kreeshka] slice, piece

kriv wrong

moja/njegova je krivnja it's my/his fault

krivotvorina [kreevotvoreena]
fake

križanje [kreeJan-yeh]
crossroads; junction

krojač [kroyach] tailor

krojački centimetar [kroyachkee
tsenteemetar] tape measure

krov roof

krovni prtljažnik [krovnee pertl-
yaJneek] roof rack

kroz through

krpa [kerpa] cloth

krpica za pranje lica [kerpeetsa
za pran-yeh leetsa] flannel

krstarenje [kerstaren-yeh] cruise

krug [kroog] circle

kruh [krooH] bread; loaf

kruh od cijelog zrna [tseeyelog
zerna] wholemeal bread

kruh s mekinjama wholemeal
bread

krumpir [kroompeer] potatoes

kruna [kroona] crown

kruška [krooshka] pear

kružni tok [krooJnee]
roundabout, (US) traffic
circle

krv [kerv] blood

krvarenje iz nosa [kervaren-yeh
eez] nosebleed

krvariti to bleed

krvna grupa [kervna] blood
group

krvni pritisak high blood
pressure

kuća [koocha] house

ići kući [eechee] to go home

kod kuće at home

kućna haljina [hal-yeena]

dressing gown

kućni broj [koochnee broy]
extension

kućni ogrtač [koochnee ogertach]
dressing gown

kuhano jaje [koohano yī-yeh]
boiled egg

kuhar cook

kuhati [koohatee] to cook

kuhinja [kooheenya] kitchen

kuhinjska krpa [kooheenyska
kerpa] dishcloth; teatowel

kuhinjska pomagala cooking
utensils

kuk [kook] hip

kukuruzne pahuljice
[kookooroozneh pahool-yeetseh]
cornflakes

kula [koola] tower

kunić [kooneech] rabbit

kupaće gaćice [koopachee
gachetseh] swimming trunks

kupaći kostim swimming
costume

kupanje [koopan-yeh] bath;
bathing; swimming

kupaonica [koopa-oneetsa]
bathroom

kupe [koopeh] carriage;
compartment

kupe za nepušače
[nepooshacheh] nonsmoking
compartment

kupiti [koopeetee] to buy

kupovina shopping

ići u kupovinu [eechee] to go
shopping

kupus [koopoos] cabbage

kurs [koors] exchange rate

kušet [**koo**shet] couchette

kušin couchette

kutija [**koo**teeya] box; carton

kutija s osiguračima [soseegoo**ra**cheema] fuse box

kvačilo [**kva**cheelo] clutch

kvaliteta [kva**lee**teta] quality

kvar breakdown

L

labav loose

ladica [**la**deetsa] drawer

lagan light; easy

lagati [**la**gatee] to lie

lak light

lak za kosu hair spray

lak za nokte [**nok**teh] nail varnish

lakat elbow

lako easy

lakom greedy

laksativ [**lak**sateev] laxative

laku noć [**la**koo noch] good night

lampa lamp

lanac [**la**nats] chain

lastik rubber band

laštilo [**lash**teelo] polish

laž [laJ] lie (untruth)

lažan [**la**Jan] false

leće [**le**cheh] lenses; lentils

leći [**le**chee] to go to bed; to lie down

led ice

ledena kava iced coffee

leđa [**le**ja] back

leptir butterfly

let flight

let na domaćoj liniji [**do**machoy **lee**neeyee] domestic flight

letak leaflet

letjeti [**let**-yetee] to fly

lezbijka [**lez**beeyka] lesbian

ležaj [**le**Ji] berth; bunk

ležaljka [**le**Jalyka] deckchair; sun lounger

ležati [**le**Jatee] to lie

lice [**leet**seh] face

lično [**leech**no] personally

liječnica [leeye**chneet**sa] doctor (woman)

liječnik [leeye**chneek**] doctor

lijek [**leey**ek] drug; medicine; cure

lijen [**leey**en] lazy

lijep [**leey**ep] beautiful; handsome

lijevak [**leey**evak] funnel

lijevo [**leey**evo] left

s lijeve strane on the left (of)

liker [**lee**ker] liqueur

limenka [**lee**menka] can, tin

limeta [**lee**meta] lime

limun [**lee**moon] lemon

limunada [leemoo**na**da] lemonade; fresh lemon juice

linija [**lee**neeya] line

lipanj [**lee**pan] June

list leaf; sheet; sole (fish)

lista list

listopad [**lee**stopad] October

listovni papir [**lee**stovnee **pa**peer] notepaper

litica [**lee**teetsa] cliff

litra [**lee**tra] litre

lizaljka [**lee**zalyka] lollipop

lokalni [lokalnee] local
lokot padlock
lom fracture
lonac [lonats] saucepan
lonci [lontsee] cooking
  utensils; pots
lopata spade, shovel
lopov thief
lopta ball
loptica [lopteetsa] (little) ball
losion [loseeon] lotion
losion poslije brijanja
  [posleeyeh breeyanya] aftershave
losion za sunčanje [soonchan-
  yeh] suntan lotion
losos salmon
loš [losh] bad; badly
loša probava [losha]
  indigestion
lubanja [looban-ya] skull
lud [lood] crazy, mad
luk [look] onion; arch
luka [looka] harbour, port
luksuz [looksooz] luxury
luksuzan [looksoozan]
  luxurious, upmarket
lula [loola] pipe
lunapark [loonapark] (fun)fair
lutka [lootka] doll

Lj

ljekarna [l-yekarna] pharmacy,
  chemist's
ljepilo [l-yepeelo] glue
ljepljiva [l-yepl-yeeva] (sticky)
  tape
ljepuškast [l-yepooshkast]

pretty
ljestve [l-yestveh] ladder
ljeto [l-yeto] summer
ljetovanje [–van-yeh] summer
  holidays
ljevak [l-yevak] left-handed
ljevoruk [l-yevorook] left-
  handed
ljubav [lyoobav] love
ljubazan [lyoobazan] kind
ljubičast [l-yoobeechast] purple
ljubomoran [lyoobomoran]
  jealous
ljudi [lyoodee] men
ljut [l-yoot] angry; hot, spicy

M

mačka [machka] cat; girl
mačo [macho] macho
maćeha [macheha] stepmother
mada although
madrac [madrats] mattress
Mađar [majar] Hungarian
Mađarica [majareetsa]
  Hungarian (woman)
Mađarska [majarska] Hungary
mađarski] Hungarian
magarac [magarats] donkey
magla fog; mist
magnetofon tape recorder
maj [mī] May
majica [mīyeetsa] sweatshirt;
  T-shirt
majka [mīka] mother
majoneza [mīyoneza]
  mayonnaise
maknuti to move

mala žlica [Jleetsa] teaspoon

male boginje [maleh bogeen-yeh] chickenpox

malen tiny, small

mali [malee] tiny, small

malo little; a little (bit)

mamurluk [mamoorlook] hangover

manje [man-yeh] less

manje pečen [man-yeh pechen] rare

marama head scarf

maramica [marameetsa] handkerchief

marka stamp; make

marmelada jam; marmalade

mart March

masan fatty

maslac [maslats] butter

mast fat; lard; ointment

mastan greasy

mašina [masheena] machine; engine

matica [mateetsa] nut (for bolt)

med honey

medeni mjesec [medenee m-yesets] honeymoon

medicinska sestra [medeetseenska] nurse

Mediteran [medeeteran] Mediterranean

meduza [medooza] jellyfish

među [mejoo] among

međugradski poziv [mejoogradskee pozeev] long-distance call

međunarodni [mejonarodnee] international

mehaničar [meHaneechara] mechanic

mekan soft

meni set menu

menstruacija [menstrooatseeya] period; menstruation

mentol bonboni [bonbonee] mints

mesnica [mesneetsa] butcher's

meso meat

metal metal

metar metre

metla broom

mi [mee] we

migrena [meegrena] migraine

mijenjati [m-yenyatee] to exchange; to change

miješati [m-yeshatee] to mix

mikrovalka [meekrovalka] microwave

milimetar [meeleemetar] millimetre

milja [meelya] mile

mineralna voda mineral water

minuta [meenoota] minute

miran [meeran] peaceful

miris smell; perfume

mirisati to smell

mirno still; quiet

misa mass

misliti [meesleetee] to think; to mean

mislim da I think that

miš [meesh] mouse

mišić [meesheech] muscle

mjehur [m-yehoor] bladder

mjenjač [m-yenyach] gearbox

mjenjačnica [m-yenyachneetsa] bureau de change

mjerilo [m-yereelo] measure, scale

mjesec [m-yesets] moon; moon

mjesto [m-yesto] place

mjesto sastanka meeting place

mlad young

mlak lukewarm

mliječna čokolada [mleeyechna [chokoladeh] milk chocolate

mlijeko [ml-yeko] milk

mlijeko za čišćenje lica [cheesh-chen-yeh leetsa] cleansing cream

mljeveno meso [ml-yeveno] minced meat

mnogo a lot, lots; much; many

mnoštvo [mnoshtvo] crowd

mobitel [mobeetel] mobile phone, cell phone

moći [mochee] to be able to

mogu li dobiti ... can I have ...?

može [moJeh] he/she can

možete li ...? [moJeteh lee] can you ...?

moda fashion

u modi fashionable

moderan modern

moderna galerija [galereeya] modern art gallery

modrica [modreetsa] bruise

moguć [mogooch] possible

moj, moja, moje [moy] my; mine

mokro wet

molim [moleem] please

molim? [moleem] pardon (me)?, sorry?

molo jetty

momčad [momchad] team

mora nightmare

morati to have to

moram ... I must ...

more [mooreh] sea

morska bolest sea-sickness

morska obala seafront

morska školjka [shkolyka] seashell

morska trava seaweed

morski jež [morskee yeJ] sea urchin

morski pas shark

morski specijaliteti [spetseeyaleeteetee] seafood

most bridge

motocikl motorbike

motor engine; motor

motorni čamac [motornee chamats] motorboat

možda [moJda] maybe, perhaps

mračan [mrachan] dark

mrav ant

mraz frost

mreža [mreJa] net

mrkva [merkva] carrot

mrlja [merlya] stain; spot

mršav [mershav] thin; skinny

mrtav [mertav] dead

mrziti [merzeetee] to hate

mučnina [moochneena] nausea

muha fly

munja [moonya] lightning

muslimanski [moosleemanskee] Muslim

muška odjeća [**moo**shka **o**d-yecha] menswear

muški [**moo**shkee] gents, men's room; masculine

mušule [**moo**shooleh] mussels

muzej [**moo**zay] museum

muzičar [**moo**zeechar] musician

muzika [**moo**zeeka] music

muž [mooJ] husband

N

na on; in; at; to;

naći [**na**chee] to find

  našao sam [**na**shao] I've found (it)

nada hope

nadajmo se [**na**dīmo seh] hopefully

nadati se [**na**datee seh] to hope

nadimak nickname

nadoplata excess fare

naglasak accent

naglo suddenly

naj- [nī] the most ...

najamnina [nīyamn**ee**na] rent

  za najam for rent

najbliži [nī**blee**Jee] the nearest

najbolji [nī**bol**-yee] (the) best

  najbolje želje [Jel-yeh] best wishes

najgori [nī**goree**] the worst

najgornji kat [nī**gorn**-yee] top floor

najkasnije [naika**sn**eeyee] the latest

najlon vrećica [**nī**lon vr**ee**cheetsa] plastic bag

najmanje [**nī**man-yeh] at least

najveći dio vremena [nī**vechee** deeo] most of the time

nakit [**na**keet] jewellery

naljepnica [**nal**-yepneetsa] label

namjerno [**nam**-yerno] deliberately

namještaj [**nam**-yeshtī] furniture

naočale [**na**ochaleh] glasses, spectacles

naočale za plivanje [pl**ee**van-yeh] goggles

naočale za sunce [**soon**tseh] sunglasses

naopako upside down

napad attack

napadački [napa**dach**kee] offensive

napisati to write

  napisao ... [na**pee**sao] written by ...

napojnica [na**poy**neetsa] tip

napon voltage

napuniti [napoo**nee**tee] to fill up

napustiti [nap**oo**steetee] to leave

naranča [na**ran**cha] orange (fruit)

narančast [naran**chast**] orange (colour)

naravno certainly, of course

  naravno da ne [neh] of course not

naročito [na**ro**cheeto] especially

narod people; nation

narodan national

narodna glazba folk music

narodna radinost [radeenost] craft shop

narodni ples folk dancing

naručiti [naroocheetee] to order

narukvica [narookveetsa] bracelet

nas us

nastavak leta connecting flight

nasuprot opposite, across from

naš [nash] our; ours

natečeno [natecheno] swollen

nategnuti to stretch

naušnice [naooshneetseh] earrings

navečer [navecher] in the evening

navijač [naveeyach] fan

navijačica [naveeyacheetsa] fan

navrh [naverH] on top of

navrtanj [naverHtan] nut (for bolt)

nazdravlje! [nazdravl-yeh] bless you!; cheers!

nazvati [nazvatee] to call back, to ring back

nažalost [naJalost] sorry

ne [neh] no; not

ne znam I don't know

nebo sky

nećak [nechak] nephew

nećakinja [nechakeenya] niece

nedaleko odavde near here, not far from here

nedavno recently

ne diraj! do not touch!

nedjelja [ned-yelya] Sunday; week

nedostajati [nedosta-yatee] to be missing; to lack

nedostaješ mi I miss you

negativ [negateev] negative

negdje [negd-yeh] somewhere

negdje drugdje [droogd-yeh] somewhere else

nego than

neispravan [neheespravan] faulty, out of order

neki dan [nekee] the other day

nekoliko [nekoleeko] a few; several

nemati not to have

nemam ... I don't have any ...

nema ... there isn't ...

nema na čemu you're welcome

nema problema! no problem!

nemoguć [nemogooch] impossible

ne naginji se kroz prozor do not lean out of the window

neobičan [neobeechan] extraordinary, unusual

neočekivano [neochekeevano] surprisingly

neograničena kilometraža [neograneechena keelometraJa] unlimited mileage

ne ometajte vozača do not disturb the driver

neoženjen [neoJen-yen] single

neparan odd

nepečen [nepechen] underdone

neprijatan [nepree-yatan] unpleasant

neprikladan [nepreekladan] inconvenient

nepromočiv [nepromocheev] waterproof

nepušač [nepooshach] non-
smoker

za nepušače non-smoking

ne radi out of order

neravni kolnik bad road
surface

nervozan nervous

nesanica [nesaneetsa] insomnia

neslužben [neslooJben]
informal

nesporazum [nesporazoom]
misunderstanding

nesreća [nesrecha] accident;
misfortune

nestati [nestatee] to disappear

nesvjestan [nesv-yestan]
unconscious

nešto [neshto] something;
some

netko somebody, someone

neudata [neoodata] single
(woman)

neuljudan [neool-yoodan] rude

neurotičan [neooroteechan]
neurotic

ne uznemiravajte do not
disturb

nevin [neveen] innocent

nevjerojatan [nev-yero-yatan]
incredible

nezaposlen unemployed

nezavisan independent

nezgodan embarrassing

neženja [neJen-ya] bachelor

ni ... ni ... neither ... nor ...

ni govora! [nee] no way!

nigdje [neegd-yeh] nowhere

nije [neeyeh] he/she/it isn't

nijedan [neeyedan] none;

neither

nije za prodaju not for sale

nikad [neekad] never

nimalo [neemalo] not in the
least

nisam I'm not; I haven't; I
didn't

ništa [neeshta] nothing

ništa za to never mind

ništa za carinjenje nothing to
declare

nitko [neetko] nobody

nizak [neezak] low

Nizozemska [neezozemska]
Netherlands

noć [noch] night

noću at night

noćenje s doručkom [nochen-
yeh s doroochkom] bed and
breakfast

noćni [nochnee] overnight, by
night

noćni lokal nightclub

noćni portir night porter

noga foot; leg

nogomet football

nogometna utakmica
[ootakmeetsa] football match

nokat fingernail; toenail

normalan normal

Norveška [norveshka] Norway

nos nose

nosiljka za bebu [noseelyka za
beboo] carry-cot

nositi [noseetee] to carry

nov new

Nova Godina [godeena] New
Year

novac [novats] money

novčanica [novchaneetsa] bank note, (US) bill

novčanik [novchaneek] purse; wallet

Novi Zeland [novee] New Zealand

novine [noveeneh] newspaper

novinski kiosk [noveenskee] newspaper kiosk

novo-novcato brand-new

nož [noJ] knife

nožni prst [noJnee perst] toe

nula [noola] zero

Nj

njega [n-yega] him

njegov, njegovo, njegova [n-yegov] his

Njemačka [n-yemachka] Germany

njemački German

njemu [n-yemoo] to him

njezin (njen), njezino (njeno), njezina (njena) [n-yezeen] her; hers

njih [n-yeeH] them

njihov, njihova, njihovo [n-yeehov] their; theirs

njoj [nyoy] to her

nju her

O

o against; about

oba, obje [ob-yeh] both

obala coast; shore

obavijestiti [obaveeyesteetee] to inform; to let know

obećati [obechatee] to promise

običaj [obeechī] custom; habit

običan [obeechan] usual; ordinary

obično usually

obilazak s vodičem [obeelazak s vodeechem] guided tour

obilaznica [obeelazneetsa] diversion

obitelj [obeetel] family

objasniti [obyasneetee] to explain

objed [ob-yed] meal

objektiv lens

oblačan [oblachan] cloudy

oblačiti [oblacheetee] to dress; to get cloudy

oblačiti se [seh] to get dressed

oblak cloud

obližnji [obleeJn-yee] nearby

oboriti [oboreetee] to knock over

obraz cheek

obrva [oberva] eyebrow

obući se [oboochee seh] to get dressed

ocat [otsat] vinegar

očekivati [ochekeevatee] to expect

očigledno [ocheegledno] obviously

očistiti [ocheesteetee] to clean

očuh [ochuH] stepfather

od by; of; from; since

   od Dubrovnika do Splita from Dubrovnik to Split

od jučer [yoocher] since yesterday

odbaciti [odbatseetee] to throw away

odbojnik [odboyneek] bumper

odgovor answer

odgovoran responsible

odgovoriti to answer

odijelo [od-yelo] suit

odjeća [od-yecha] clothes

odjel [od-yel] department; ward

odlasci departures

odlazak departure

odlazi! [odlazee] go away!

odletjeti [odlet-yetee] to fly out

odličan [odleechan] excellent

odlučiti [odloocheetee] to decide

odlučiti se [seh] to decide

odluka [odlooka] decision

odmah [odmaн] immediately; in a minute; just

odmor holiday; rest

odmoriti se to take a rest

odrasla osoba adult

odrastao adult

odredište [odredeeshteh] destination

odsjesti [ods-yestee] to stay

odvesti to take; to drive

odvijač [odveeyach] screwdriver

odvodna cijev [tseeyev] drain

odvojen [odvo-yen] separate

odvojeno separately

odvratan disgusting

ograda fence

ograničenje brzine [ograneechen-yeh berzeeneh] speed limit

ogrebotina [ogreboteena] scratch

ogrlica [ogerleetsa] necklace

ogroman enormous

ogrtač [ogertach] overcoat; coat

oko eye; about

okrenuti to turn

okrugao round

okuka bend

okus [okoos] flavour

olovka pencil

olovka za obrve [oberveh] eyebrow pencil

oluja [olooya] storm

omiljen [omeel-yen] favourite

omladina young people

omladinski hotel youth hostel

on he

ona she; that; that one

onaj, ona, ono [onī] that; that one; it

  onaj drugi the other one

onda then

onesvijestiti se [onesveeyesteetee seh] to faint

oni [onee] they; those

opasan dangerous

opasno po život! danger of death!

opasnost danger

opći [opchee] general

opekotina burn

operacija [operatseeya] operation

opet again

opis [opees] description

oprati [opratee] to wash

151

oprati rublje [roobl-yeh] to do the washing

oprati se [seh] to get washed

oprati suđe [soojeh] to wash the dishes

oprema equipment

oprez! caution!, beware!

oprezan careful

oprostite [oprosteeteh] excuse me; I'm sorry

opruga spring

optičar [opteechar] optician

opustiti se [opoosteetee seh] to relax

orah [oraH] walnut

oraščići [orash-cheecheeh] nuts

organizirati to organize

orkestar orchestra; band

ormar cupboard

osa wasp

osam eight

osamljen [osaml-yen] secluded

oseka low tide

osigurač [oseegoorach] fuse

osiguranje [oseegooran-yeh] insurance

osiguranje protiv treće osobe [proteev trecheh osobeh] third party insurance

osim [oseem] apart from, except

osip [oseep] rash

osjećaj [os-yechī] feeling

osjećati [os-yeh-chatee] to feel
  osjećati se [seh] to feel, to be feeling

osjetiti [os-yeteetee] to feel

osjetljiv [os-yetl-yeev] sensitive

oslobođen od carine [oslobojen od tsareeneh] duty-free

osoba person

osobna iskaznica [eezkazneetsa] ID card

osobni stereo [osobnee] personal stereo

osobno: ja/on osobno personally; myself; himself

osovina [osoveena] axle

ospice [ospeetseh] measles

ostatak rest

ostati [ostatee] to remain
  ostati u kvaru to break down

ostaviti [ostaveetee] to leave; to forget

oštar [oshtar] sharp

oštećen [oshtechen] damaged

oštetiti [oshteteetee] to damage

otac [otats] father

otekao swollen

otići [oteechee] to go away, to leave

otkad since

otkazati [otkazatee] to cancel

otključati [otklyoochateh] to unlock

otmjen [otm-yen] posh

otok island; swelling

otopina za kontaktne leće [otopeena za kontaktneh lecheh] soaking solution

otprilike [otpreeleekeh] roughly, approximately

otrov poison

otrovan poisonous

otvarač za boce [otvarach za botseh] bottle-opener

otvarač za konzerve [konzerveh] tin opener, can

opener
otvoren open
otvoren krov sun roof
otvorena karta open ticket
otvoriti [otvoreetee] to open
ovaj, ova, ovo [ovi] this; this
  one
ovako like this
ovca [ovtsa] sheep
ovdje [ovd-yeh] here
ovi, ove, ova these
ovisi [oveesee] it depends
ovo this; this one
ovratnik [ovratneek] collar
ozbiljan [ozbeelyan] serious
ozlijeđen [ozleeyejen] injured
oženjen [oJen-yen] married
ožujak [oJooyak] March

P

padati to fall; to drop
  pada kiša [keesha] it's raining
  pada snijeg [s-nyeg] it's
  snowing
pahuljice [pahool-yeetseh] cereal
paket package; parcel
paket aranžman [aranJman]
  package tour
paketić ... [paketeech] a pack
  of ...
pakirati [pakeeratee] to pack
  pakirati se [seh] to pack
pakistanski [pakeestanskee]
  Pakistani
palac [palats] thumb
palača [palacha] palace
paluba [palooba] deck

paljenje [pal-yen-yeh] ignition
pametan clever
pamuk [pamook] cotton;
  cotton wool
pansion [panseeon] guesthouse
papir [papeer] paper
papir za pisanje [peesan-yeh]
  writing paper
papir za umotavanje
  [oomotavan-yeh] wrapping
  paper
papirnata maramica
  [papeernata maramitsa] paper
  handkerchiefs
papirnica [papeerneetsa]
  stationer's
papuče [papoocheh] slippers
papučica za gas [papoocheetsa]
  accelerator, gas pedal
par couple; pair
parfem perfume
park park
parkiralište [parkeeraleeshteh]
  car park, (US) parking lot
parkirati [parkeeratee] to park
pas dog
pasta za cipele [tseepeleh]
  shoe polish
pasta za zube [zoobeh]
  toothpaste
pasti [pastee] to fall
pastile za grlo [pasteeleh za
  gerlo] throat pastilles
patent-zatvarač [zatvarach] zip,
  (US) zipper
patka duck
pauk [paook] spider
pazikuća [pazeekoocha]
  caretaker

pazi! look out!, caution!
paziti [pazeetee] to look after
pazite! [pazeeteh] look out!; be careful!
pazite malo! excuse me!, do you mind!
pažljiv [paJl-yeev] careful
pčela [pchela] bee
pecivo [petseevo] roll
peći [pechee] to bake
pećnica [pechneetsa] cave; oven
pedala gasa accelerator, gas pedal
pegla iron
peglati to iron
pejsaž [pay-saJ] scenery
pekara bakery
pekarnica [pekarneetsa] bakery
pekmez jam
pelena nappy, (US) diaper
peludna groznica [peloodna grozneetsa] hayfever
penzioner [penzeeoner] old-age pensioner
penjanje [penyan-yeh] climbing
pepeljara [pepelyara] ashtray
perad poultry
peraje [pera-yeh] flippers
perilica [pereeleetsa] washing machine
pero pen
peron platform
pet five
peta heel
petak Friday
pica [peetsa] pizza
piće [peecheh] drink
pidžama [peejama] pyjamas

pijan [peeyan] drunk
pijesak [p-yesak] sand
pikantno predjelo [peekantno pred-yelo] appetizer
piletina [peeleteena] chicken
pilula [peeloola] pill
pilula za spavanje [spavan-yeh] sleeping pill
pinceta [peentseta] tweezers
pipničar [peepneechar] barman
pisati [peesatee] to write
pismo [peesmo] letter; script
pismovna uložnica [ooloJneetsa] letterbox
pista za skijanje [skeeyan-yeh] ski slope
pištolj [pishtol] pistol
pita pie; tart
pitanje [peetan-yeh] question
pitati [peetatee] to ask
piti [peetee] to drink
pitka voda [peetka] drinking water
pivo [peevo] beer
pjena za brijanje [p-yena za breeyan-yeh] shaving foam
pjesma [p-yesma] song; poem
pješačka zona [p-yeshachka] pedestrian precinct
pješački prijelaz [p-yeshachkee pr-yelaz] pedestrian crossing; footpath
pješak [p-yeshak] pedestrian
pješčane dine [p-yesh-chaneh deeneh] sand dunes
pješice [p-yesheetseh] on foot
pješke [p-yeshkeh] on foot
pjevač [p-yevach] singer

pjevačica [p-yevacheetsa] singer (woman)

pjevati [p-yevatee] to sing

pladanj tray

plafon ceiling

plahta [plaнta] sheet

plakat poster

plakati [plakatee] to cry

plan map; plan

plan grada streetmap

planina [planeena] mountain

planinarenje [planeenaren-yeh] mountaineering; rock climbing

plastičan [plasteechan] plastic

plastična folija [plasteechna foleeya] cling film

plastična vrećica [plasteechna vrecheetsa] plastic bag

platiti [plateetee] to pay

platiti u gotovini to pay cash

plav blond; blue

plaža [plaja] beach

ples dance

plesati [plesatee] to dance

plesti to knit

plik [pleek] blister

plin [pleen] gas

plinska boca [pleenska botsa] camping gas; gas cylinder

plitak [pleetak] shallow

plitica [pleetsa] tray

plivanje [pleevan-yeh] swimming

plivati [pleevatee] to swim

ploča [plocha] disk; record; tablet

pločnik [plochneek] pavement, (US) sidewalk

plomba filling

plovak buoy

pluća [ploocha] lungs

pljusak [plyoosak] shower

pljusak s grmljavinom [germl-yaveenom] thunderstorm

pobijediti [pob-yedeetee] to win

poboljšati [pobol-shatee] to improve

početak [pochetak] start, beginning

početi [pochetee] to start, to begin

početnica [pochetneetsa] beginner (woman)

početnik [pochetneek] beginner

poći (po) [pochee] to fetch

pod floor

podizanje prtljage [podeezan-yeh pertl-yageh] baggage claim

podloga foundation cream; base

podloška [podloshka] washer (for nut)

podne [podneh] midday, noon

područje [podrooch-yeh] area; field

podrum [podroom] cellar; basement

poduka [podooka] lesson

podzemna željeznica [podzemna Jel-yezneetsa] underground, subway

pogled view

pogledati [pogledatee] to look at

pogodno convenient

pogreb funeral

pogreška [pogreshka] error, mistake

pohotan randy, horny

pojas [po-yas] belt

pojas za spašavanje [spashavan-yeh] lifebelt

pokazati to show

pokazna karta za skijanje [skeeyan-yeh] ski-pass

pokazna karta za žičaru [Jeecharoo] lift pass

poklon present

poklopac [poklopats] lid

pokraj [pokrī] next to

pokrasti to steal

pokrivač [pokreevach] blanket; cover

pokvaren želudac [Jeloodats] upset stomach

pokvariti se [pokvareetee seh] to break down

pola half

pola boce [botseh] half bottle

pola cijene [tseeyeneh] half price

poleđina [polejeena] back

polica [poleetsa] shelf

policajac [poleetsīyats] policeman

policajaka [poleetsīyaka] policewoman

policija [poleetseeya] police

policijska postaja [poeleetseeyska postīya] police station

policijska stanica [staneetsa] police station

politički [poleeteechkee] political

polovan second-hand

polupansion [poloopanseeon] half board

polusuho [poloosooHo] medium-dry

polje [pol-yeh] field

poljski krevet [pol-skee] campbed, (US) cot

poljubac [polyoobats] kiss

poljubiti [polyoobeetee] to kiss

pomaknuti [pomaknootee] to move

pomfrit [pomfreet] chips, French fries

pomoć [pomoch] help

pomoći [pomochee] to help

pomodan trendy

ponedjeljak [poned-yelyak] Monday

ponekad sometimes

poni [ponee] pony

ponijeti [poneeyetee] to carry away

ponoć [ponoch] midnight

ponosan proud

ponoviti [ponoveetee] to repeat

ponuditi to offer

popis list

pop glazba pop music

pop pjevač [p-yevach] pop singer

pop pjevačica [p-yevacheetsa] pop singer (woman)

poplava flood

poplun [poploon] duvet, quilt

popodne [popodneh] afternoon; p.m.

popraviti [**po**praveetee] to fix, to repair; to improve

poprsje [**po**pers-yeh] bust

popust [**po**poost] discount

poput like

porcija [**po**rtseeya] portion

porculan [ports**oo**lan] china

pored next to; in addition

porozne leće [**po**rozneh l**e**cheh] gas permeable lenses

portir [**po**rteer] porter

portret portrait

poruka [**po**rooka] message

posada crew

posao business; job

poseban special; separate

poseban popust special discount

posebna ponda special offer

posjeći se [pos-y**e**chee seh] to cut oneself

posjet [pos-yet] visit

posjetiti [pos-yet**ee**tee] to visit

posjetnica [pos-yetn**ee**tsa] business card

poslati to send; to forward

poslati poštom [p**o**shtom] to post

poslije [p**o**sleeyeh] after

poslije podne [p**o**dneh] afternoon

poslovni put business trip

posluga [pos**loo**ga] service

posluga u sobi room service

poslužiti [posl**oo**Jeetee] to serve

posljednji [p**o**sl-yedn-yee] last

pospan sleepy

posramljen [p**o**sraml-yen] ashamed

postati to become

posteljina [postel-y**ee**na] bed linen

posto per cent

postojati [p**o**sto-yatee] to be; to exist

postoji li popust [p**o**sto-yee lee] is there a discount?

postolar heelbar

postupno [p**o**stoopno] gradually

posuda [pos**oo**da] dish

posuditi [pos**oo**deetee] to borrow; to lend

posuđe [pos**oo**jeh] crockery, dishes

pošta [p**o**shta] mail, post; post office

poštanski broj [p**o**shtanskee broy] area code; postcode, (US) zip code

poštanski sandučić [p**o**shtanskee sand**oo**cheech] letterbox, mailbox; postbox

poštar [p**o**shtar] postman

pošten [p**o**shten] honest

pošto? [p**o**shto] how much?

potkošulja [potk**o**shoolya] vest, (US) undershirt

potok stream

potpis [p**o**tpees] signature

potpisati to sign

potpuno [p**o**tpoono] completely

potražite [p**o**traJeetee] to look for

potreban necessary

potreban mi je ... [mee yeh] I need a ...

potres concussion

potrošiti [potr**o**sheetee] to spend

potvrditi [potv**er**deetee] to confirm

povećanje [povechan-yeh] enlargement

povez bandage

povijest [pov-yest] history

povjetarac [pov-yetarats] breeze

povoj [povoy] dressing

povraćati [povrachatee] vomit
povraća mi se [seh] I feel sick

povratna karta return ticket, (US) round trip ticket

povrće [povercheh] vegetables

povrijeđen [povr-yedjen] injured; hurt

povući u slučaju opasnosti pull in case of emergency

povući zasun [povoochee] to bolt

poziciona svjetla [pozeetseeona sv-yetla] side lights

poziv [pozeev] invitation

pozivni broj [pozeevnee broy] dialling code

poznavati to know

pozvati to invite; to call

požar [poJar] fire

požarna uzbuna [**oo**zboona] fire alarm

požarni izlaz [**ee**zlaz] fire escape

požuriti [poJ**oo**reetee] to hurry
požurite! [poJ**oo**reeteh] hurry up!

praktičan [prakteechan] practical

pranje auta [pran-yeh **a**oota] carwash

pranje kose i frizura [koseh ee

freezoora] shampoo and set

praonica [pra**o**neetsa] laundry

praonica rublja [**roo**blya] launderette, laundromat

prase [praseh] pig

prašina [prasheena] dust

prašnjav [prashnyav] dusty

prati to wash
prati suđe [**soo**jeh] to wash the dishes

pratiti [pra**tee**tee] to accompany; to follow

pravac [pravats] direction

pravedan fair, just

pravi [pravee] genuine; real

praviti [pra**vee**tee] to make

pravnica [pravneetsa] lawyer (woman)

pravnik [pravneek] lawyer

prazan empty

praznik holiday, (US) vacation

pre... [preh] too ...
prebrz too fast

prečica [precheetsa] shortcut

preći [prechee] to cross

predaja prtljage [preda-ya pertl-yageh] baggage check

predak ancestor

predavati to teach

predgrađe [predgrajeh] suburb

prednost priority, right of way

prednji [predn-yee] front

predsjednica [preds-yedneetsa] president (woman)

predsjednik [preds-yedneek] president

predstaviti [predstaveetee] to

Croatian → English

introduce

predstavništvo
[predstavneeshtvo] agent;
representative

predujam [predooyam] deposit

predvorje [predvor-yeh] foyer,
lobby

prehlada [preHlada] cold

prehlađen sam [preHlajen] I
have a cold

prekid putovanja [prekeed
pootovanya] stopover

prekid struje [strooyeh] power
cut

prekidač [prekeedach] switch

prekjučer [prekyoocher] the day
before yesterday

preko via; across; over;
during

prekonoć [prekonoch]
overnight

prekosutra [prekosootra] the
day after tomorrow

prekrivač [prekeevats] quilt

prekuhan overdone

prema towards

premijer [premeeyer] prime
minister

premijerka [premeeyerka] prime
minister (woman)

preplanulost [preplanoolost]
suntan

preplanuo (od sunca)
[preplanoo-o (od soontsa)]
suntanned

preplanuti [preplanootee] to get
a tan

preporučeno [preporoocheno] by
registered mail

preporučiti [preporoocheetee] to
recommend

prepoznati [prepoznatee] to
recognize

prepun [prepoon] crowded

prerano too early

presjedati [pres-yedatee] to
change (trains/buses)

preskup too expensive

prestanak ograničenja brzine
end of speed limit

prestati [prestatee] to stop; to
finish

prestanite s tim! [prestaneeteh s
teem] stop doing that!

presvući se [presvoochee seh] to
get changed

preticati [preteetsatee] to
overtake

pretinac [preteenats] locker

pretjecati [pret-yetsatee] to
overtake

pretjerati [pret-yeratee] to
exaggerate

prevelik [preveleek] too big

prevesti [prevestee] to translate

previsoke cijene [preveesokeh
ts-yeneh] very high prices

previše [preveesheh] too much

prevoditelj [prevodeetel]
translator; interpreter

prevoditeljica [prevodeetel-
yeetsa] translator; interpreter
(woman)

prevoditi [prevodeetee] to
interpret

prevruć [prevrooch] too hot

prezervativ [prezervateev]
condom

prezime [prezeemeh] surname

pribadača [preebadacha] pin

pribor za jelo [preebor za yelo] cutlery

priča [preecha] story

prihvatiti [preeHvateetee] to accept

prijatan [preeyatan] nice; pleasant

prijatelj [preeyatel] friend

prijatelj za dopisivanje [dopeeseevan-yeh] penfriend

prijateljica [preeyatel-yeetsa] friend (female)

prijateljski [preeyatelyskee] friendly

prijava [preeyava] check-in

prijaviti se [preeyaveetee seh] to check in

prije [preeyeh] before

prije tri dana three days ago

prijelaz [preeyelaz] crossing

prijem [preeyem] reception

prijesan [pr-yesan] raw

prijevod [pr-yevod] translation

prikolica [preekoleetsa] trailer

prilično [preeleechno] fairly, quite, pretty

primati [preematee] to accept; to take

primjer [preem-yer] example

na primjer for example

pripadati to belong

pripremiti to prepare

pripremiti se [seh] to get ready

priroda countryside; nature

prirodan natural

pristajati [preesta-yatee] to fit

pristanište [preestaneeshteh] quayside

prišt [preesht] spot

pritužba [preetooJba] complaint

privatan [preevatan] private

privjesak za ključeve [preev-yesak za klyoocheveh] key ring

privlačan [preevlachan] attractive

prizemlje [preezem-lyeh] ground floor, (US) first floor

priznanica [preeznaneetsa] receipt

prljav [perlyav] dirty

prljavo rublje [roobl-yeh] laundry; washing

prljavština [perlyavshteena] dirt

probati to try (on); to taste

probuditi to wake

probuditi se [seh] to wake up

probušena guma [proboshena gooma] puncture

proći [prochee] to pass

proći kroz to go through

prodaja [prodiya] sale

za prodaju for sale

prodavač novina [prodavats] newsagent

prodavaonica [prodavaoneetsa] shop

prodavaonica karata ticket office

prodavaonica novina newsagent's

prodavati [prodavatee] to sell

produžni kabel [prodooJnee] extension lead

profesor teacher; professor

profesorica [profesoreetsa]
teacher; professor (woman)

prognoza vremena weather
forecast

prohladno [proHladno] cool

proizvedeno made in

prokletstvo! blast!

prolaz zabranjen no
thoroughfare; trespassers
will be prosecuted

proljeće [prol-yecheh] spring

proljev [prol-yev] diarrhoea

promet traffic

prometan busy

prometna gužva [gooJva] rush
hour

prometna nesreća [nesrecha]
road accident

prometni zastoj [zastoy] traffic
jam

prometni znak roadsign

promijeniti [prom-yeneetee] to
change

promjenljiv [proml-yenl-yeev]
changeable

propuh [propooH] draught

prosinac [proseenats]
December

prosječan [pros-yechan] average

prospekt leaflet

prostirka za plažu [prosteerka za
plaJoo] beach mat

prošlo [proshlo] past; last
prošle godine last year

protiv [proteev] against

provala burglary

provjeriti [prov-yereetee] to
check

prozor window

prsa [persa] breast

prsluk [perslook] waistcoat,
(US) vest

prsluk za spašavanje
[spashavan-yeh] life jacket

prst [perst] finger

prsten [persten] ring

prtljaga [pertl-yaga] baggage,
luggage

prtljažnik [pertl-yaJneek] boot,
(US) trunk

prva klasa [perva] first class

prva pomoć [pomoch] first aid

prvi [pervee] first

prvo firstly

pržen [perJen] fried

pržiti [perJeetee] to fry

psovka swearword

ptica [pteetsa] bird

publika audience; public

puce [pootseh] button

puder powder

puknuta cijev [pook-noota
tseeyev] burst pipe

pulover [poolover] pullover,
sweater

pumpa pump

pun [poon] full
puna sezona high season
puno umaka a lot of sauce
puno vam hvala na pomoći
thank you very much for
your help

punac [poonats] father-in-law

puni pansion [poonee panseeon]
full board

punica [pooneetsa] mother-
in-law

puniti [pooneetee] to fill

pustiti [**poo**steetee] to let

pušač [**poo**shach] smoker

za pušače smoking

pušenje dozvoljeno smoking
permitted

pušiti [**poo**sheetee] to smoke

puška [**poo**shka] gun; rifle

put path; road; journey;
occasion, time

četiri puta four times

putni kovčeg [**kov**cheg] suitcase

putnica [**poot**neetsa] traveller
(woman)

putnička agencija travel
agency

putnički ček [**poo**tneechkee chek]
traveller's cheque

putnik [**poot**neek] passenger;
traveller

putokaz [**poo**tokaz] signpost

putovanje [**poo**tovan-yeh]
journey; tour; trip

putovati [**poo**tovatee] to travel

putovnica [**poo**tovnitsa] passport

puž [pooJ] snail

R

račun [**ra**chun] bill; receipt

računalo [**ra**ch**oo**nalo]
computer

računar [**ra**ch**oo**nar] calculator

račvanje [**ra**chvan-yeh] fork,
turning

rad work

radijator radiator

radije [**ra**deeyeh] rather

radilica [**ra**deeleetsa] crankshaft

radio [**ra**deeo] radio

raditi [**ra**deetee] to do; to work

radno vrijeme [vr-**ye**meh]
opening times; business
hours

rado with pleasure

rado bih [beeн] I feel like

radostan glad

radovi na putu roadworks

rajčica [**rī**cheetsa] tomato

rak crab; cancer

rakija [**ra**keeya] brandy;
aquavit

rame [**ra**meh] shoulder

rampa level crossing, (US)
grade crossing

rana wound; sore; injury

rana u ustima [oo **oo**steema]
mouth ulcer

rano early

raskrižje [raskree**J**-yeh]
junction, intersection

raspakirati [raspak**ee**ratee] to
unpack

raspored schedule

rasprodaja sale

rastavljen [rasta**vl**-yen]
separated

rat war

ravan flat; straight

ravno naprijed [napr-**yed**]
straight ahead

razgledanje [razgledavan-yeh]
sightseeing tour

razglednica [razgledneetsa]
postcard

razgovor na račun primatelja
poziva [rachoon pr**ee**matelya
pozeeva] collect call

različit [razleecheet] different
razlika [razleeka] difference
razočaran [razocharan]
  disappointed
razočaravajući [razocharava-
  yoochee] disappointing
razred class
  prvi razred first class
razuman sensible
razumjeti [razoom-yetee] to
  understand
razveden divorced
razvijanje filma [razveeyan-yeh]
  film processing
razviti [razveetee] to develop
razvodnik paljenja [pal-yenya]
  distributor
rebrenice [rebreneetseh]
  shutters
rebro rib
recepcija [retseptseeya]
  reception
recepcioner [retseptseeoner]
  receptionist
recepcionerka receptionist
  (woman)
recept [retsept] prescription;
  recipe
reći [rechee] to say
red queue; order
  stajati u redu [stī-yatee] to
  queue
  u redu [oo redoo] OK
red vožnje [voJn-yeh] timetable
redovan let scheduled flight
regenerator [regenerator]
  conditioner
registarki broj [regeestarskee
  broy] number plate

registarske tablice [tableetseh]
  number plates
registracija putnika
  [regeestratseeya pootneeka]
  check-in
reket racket
religija [releegeeya] religion
remen belt, strap
remen ventilatora [venteelatora]
  fan belt
remen za sat watch strap
rendgen X-ray
rentakar car rental
rentgen X-ray
rep tail; queue
restauracija [restorats-ya]
  restaurant
restoran restaurant
retrovizor [retroveezor] rearview
  mirror
rezervacija [rezervatseeya]
  reservation
rezervirati [rezerveeratee] to
  reserve, to book
rezervna guma [gooma] spare
  tyre
rezervni dio [rezervnee deeo]
  spare part
rezervni djelovi [d-yelovee]
  spare parts
rezervoar tank
riba [reeba] fish
ribarnica [reebarneetsa]
  fishmonger's
ribarsko selo [reebarsko]
  fishing village
riblja kost [reebl-ya] fishbone
ribolov fishing
riječ [r-yech] word

Ri

163

rijedak [r-yedak] rare, uncommon

rijeka [r-yeka] river

rikverc [reekverts] reverse gear

riskantan [reeskantan] risky

riža [reeJa] rice

rječnik [r-yechneek] dictionary

rječnik fraza phrasebook

robna kuća [koocha] department store

rodbina relations, family

roditelji [rodeetel-yee] parents

roditi se [rodeetee seh] to be born

rođen sam 1963 I was born in 1963

rođak [rojak] cousin; relative

rođakinja [rojakeenya] cousin; relative (female)

rođendan [rojendan] birthday

rok upotrebe best before

rolete [roleteh] blinds

roman novel

roniti to dive

ronjenje [ron-yen-yeh] skin-diving

roštilj [roshteel] grill; barbecue

rub edge

rubeola [roobeola] German measles

rublje [roobl-yeh] laundry

ručak [roochak] lunch

ručica [roocheetsa] handle; lever; hand

ručica mjenjača [m-yenyacha] gear lever, gear shift

ručna kočnica [roochna kochneetsa] handbrake, parking brake

ručna prtljaga [pertlyaga] hand luggage

ručna torba handbag

ručni mjenjač [m-yen-yach] manual

ručni sat (wrist)watch

ručni zglob wrist

ručnik [roochneek] towel

ručnik za kupanje [koopan-yeh] bath towel

rujan [rooyan] September

ruka [rooka] arm; hand

rukav [rookav] sleeve

rukavice [rookaveetseh] gloves

rukovati se [rookovatee seh] to shake hands

ruksak rucksack

rumenilo za obraze [roomeneelo za obrazeh] blusher

Rumunjska [roomoon-yuh-ska] Romania

rumunjski Romanian

rupa [roopa] hole

Rusija [roseeya] Russia

ruski Russian

ruševine [roosheveeneh] ruins

ruta [roota] route

ruž za usne [rooJ za oosneh] lipstick

ruža [rooJa] rosé

ružan [rooJan] ugly

ružičast [rooJeechast] pink

S

s, sa with

SAD [es a deh] USA

sada now

sag carpet
sajam [sa-yam] (trade) fair
sako jacket
sakriti [sakreetee] to hide
salon lounge
salveta napkin, serviette
sam alone
  sam sam I'm on my own
samo just, only
  samo ravno straight ahead
samoposluga self-service;
  supermarket
samoposluživanje
  [samoposlooJeevan-yeh] self-
  service food store
samostan monastery
samo za članove members
  only
samo za pješake pedestrians
  only
san dream; sleep
sandale [sandaleh] sandals
sanduk [sandook] trunk, chest
sapun [sapoon] soap
sastanak appointment;
  meeting
sasvim [sasveem] altogether,
  quite
  sasvim je blizu pješice
  [bleezoo] it's only a short
  walk
sat clock; hour
  koliko je sati? [yeh] what
  time is it?
sav all
savjetovati [sav-yetovateh] to
  advise
savršen [savershen] perfect
saznati [saznateh] to find out

sedam seven
sedlo saddle
seks sex
seksi [seksee] sexy
sekunda second
selo village; countryside
selotejp [selotayp] Sellotape®,
  Scotch tape®
semafor traffic lights
sendvič [sendveech] sandwich
septičan [septeechan] septic
serfing [serfeeng]
  windsurfing
servis [servees] service charge
sestra sister
sezona season
sići [seechee] to get off; to get
  down
SIDA Aids
sidro anchor
siguran [seegooran] sure; safe
sigurnica [seegoorneetsa] safety
  pin
sigurnosni pojas [seegoornosnee
  po-yas] seat belt
siječanj [seeyechan] January
silovanje [seelovan-yeh] rape
simpatičan [seempateechan]
  nice
sin [seen] son
sinoć [seenoch] last night
sir [seer] cheese
siromašan [seeromashan] poor
sirov raw
sirup za kašalj [seeroop za
  kashal] cough medicine
sitniš [seetneesh] small change
siv [seev] grey
sjajan [sya-yan] brilliant

sjećati se [s-yechateh seh] to remember

sjeći [s-yechee] to cut

sjedalo [s-yedalo] seat

sjedalo pored prozora window seat

sjedalo uz prolaz aisle seat

sjedečnica [s-yedechneetsa] chair lift

Sjedinjene (Američke) Države [s-yedeen-yeneh (amereechkeh) derJaveh] United States (of America)

sjedište [s-yedeeshteh] seat; place

sjekira [s-yekeera] axe

sjenka [s-yenka] shadow

sjenilo za oči [s-yeneelo za ochee] eye shadow

sjesti [s-yestee] to sit down

sjetiti se [s-yeteetee seh] to remember

sjever [syever] north

sjeverno od north of

Sjeverna Irska [s-yeverna eerska] Northern Ireland

sjeverni [s-yevernee] northern

skandalozan shocking

skidač šminke [skeedach shmeenkeh] eye makeup remover

skija [skeeya] ski

skijanje [skeeyan-yeh] skiing

skijanje na vodi [vodee] waterskiing

skijaška staza [skeeyashka] ski run

skijaška žičara [Jeechara] ski-lift

skijaške cipele [tseepeleh] ski boots

skijaške hlače [Hlacheh] ski-pants

skijaški štap [shtap] ski pole

skijati se [skeeyatee seh] to ski

skije za vodu [skeeyeh] waterskis

skliznuti to skid; to slip

skočiti [skocheetee] to jump

skrenuti to turn

skrenite desno [skreneeteh] turn right

skretanje [skretan-yeh] turning

skup [skoop] expensive

skupina [skoopeena] group

skuter [skooter] scooter

slab weak

slabo mi je [slabo mee yeh] I'm going to be sick

sladak sweet

sladoled ice cream

sladoled na štapiću [shtapeechoo] ice lolly

slan savoury; salty

slap waterfall

slastičarnica [slasteecharneetsa] cake shop

slatkiši [slatkeeshee] sweets

slavan famous

slavina [slaveena] tap, (US) faucet

sličan [sleechan] similar

slijediti [sleeyedeetee] follow

slijedite me [meh] follow me

slijep [sleeyep] blind

slijepa ulica dead end

slika [sleeka] painting, picture

slikati [sleekatee] to paint; to

photograph
slobodan free
slobodno! come in!
slom živaca [Jeevatsa] nervous breakdown
slomiti [slomeetee] to break
slomljen [sloml-yen] broken
Slovenac [slovenats] Slovene
Slovenija [sloveneeya] Slovenia
Slovenka Slovene (woman)
slovenski Slovene
složeno [sloJeno] complicated
složiti se [sloJeetee seh] to agree
 slažem se I agree
slučajno [sloochino] by chance
slušalice [slooshaleetseh] headphones
slušati [slooshatee] to listen (to)
slušni aparat [slooshnee] hearing aid
slušno pomagalo [slooshno] hearing aid
služba pomoći na cesti [slooJba pomochee na tsestee] breakdown service
služben [slooJben] formal
službenica na recepciji [slooJbeneetsa na retseptseeyee] receptionist (woman)
službenik na recepciji [slooJbeneek] receptionist
sljedeći [sl-yedechee] next
 sljedeća ulica na lijevo the next street on the left
smeće [smecheh] rubbish; litter
smeđ [smej] brown

smetati [smetatee] to disturb; to annoy
smeta li vas ako pušim? [pooshem] do you mind if I smoke?
smijati se [smeeyatee seh] to laugh
smiješak [smeeyeshak] smile
smiješan [smeeyeshan] funny, amusing; ridiculous
smiješiti se [sm-yesheetee seh] to smile
smiriti se [smeereetee seh] to calm down
smjer [sm-yer] direction
smještaj [sm-yeshti] accommodation
smrdjeti [smerrd-yetee] to smell
smrdi [smerrdee] it smells
smrkava se [smerkava seh] it's getting dark
smrt [smert] death
smrznut [smerznoot] frozen
snaha [snaHa] daughter-in-law
snijeg [sn-yeg] snow
sniženje [sneeJen-yeh] sale; reductions
soba room
sobarica [sobareetsa] maid
soda soda (water)
sok juice
sok od ananasa pineapple juice
sok od greypfruta grapefruit juice
sok od naranče [narancheh] orange juice
sol salt

spakakirani ručak [spakeeranee roochak] packed lunch

spaliti [spaleetee] to burn

spasilac [spaseelats] lifeguard

spavaća kola [spavacha] sleeping car

spavaća soba bedroom

spavaćica [spavacheetsa] nightdress

spavati [spavatee] to sleep

specijalnost [spets-yalnost] speciality

spirala spiral; IUD

spomenik [spomeneek] monument

spomenuti [spomenootee] to mention

spor slow

sporije! [sporeeyeh] slow down!

sporedna ulica [ooleetsa] side street

sporo slowly

sportski objekti sports goods

sprava device

spremnik [spremneek] tank

spust [spoost] downhill skiing

spustiti se [spoosteetee seh] to land; lower oneself

spustite to tamo put it down over there

spuštena guma [spooshtena] flat tyre

sranje! [sran-yeh] shit!

Srbija [serbeeya] Serbia

Srbijanac [srbeeyanats] Serbian Serb

Srbijanka [srbeeyanka] Serbian Serb (woman)

Srbin [serbeen] Serb

srce [sertseh] heart

srčani napad [serchanee] heart attack

srebro silver

sreća [srecha] luck; happiness

srećom [srechom] fortunately

središnji [sredeeshn-yee] central

središte [sredeeshteh] centre

središte grada city centre

srednje [sredn-yeh] medium

srednje pečeno [pecheno] medium-rare

srednje veličine [veleecheeneh] medium-sized

srednji [sredn-yee] medium, middle

srednji vijek [veeyek] Middle Ages

sredstvo protiv bolova [proteev] painkillers

sredstvo protiv komaraca [komaratsa] mosquito repellent

sredstvo za čišćenje [cheeshchen-yeh] cleaning solution

sredstvo za kontracepciju [kontratseptseeyoo] contraceptive

sredstvo za pranje suđa [pran-yeh sooja] washing-up liquid, (US) dishwashing liquid

sredstvo za sunčanje [soonchan-yeh] sunblock

sredstvo za umirenje bolova [oomeeren-yeh] painkiller

sredstvo za zaštitu od insekata [zashteetoo] insect repellent

sresti [sʀestee] to meet
sretan happy
 sretan Božić! [boʒeech] happy
 Christmas!
 sretan put! have a good
 journey!
 sretan rođendan! [roʤendan]
 happy birthday!
 sretna Nova godina [godeena]
 Happy New year!
sretno! good luck!
srijeda [sʀ-yeda] Wednesday
srnetina [sʀneteena] venison
srpanj [sʀpan] July
Srpkinja [sʀpkeenya] Serb
 (woman)
srpski [sʀpskee] Serbian
srušiti [sʀoosheetee] to knock
 over
stajati [stʏyatee] to stand; to
 stop
 stajete li blizu ...? do you
 stop near ...?
staklenka jar
staklo glass
stambena zgrada block of
 apartments
stan apartment, flat
stanarina [stanaʀeena] rent
stančić [stancheech] flatlet,
 studio apartment
stanica [staneetsa] stop;
 station; cell
stanica za hitnu pomoć
 [heetnoo pomoch] casualty
 department
stanite! [staneeteh] stop!
stanovništvo [stanovneeshtvo]
 population

star old
Stara godina [godeena] New
 Year's Eve
stari grad [staʀee] old town
staromodan old-fashioned
starost age
stati [statee] to stop; to stand
staviti [staveetee] to put
staza lane; path; track
stendbaj [stendbɪ] standby
stepenice [stepeneetseh] stairs
stići [steechee] to arrive
stidljiv [steedl-yeev] shy
stijena [st-yena] rock; partition
stjuard [styooard] steward
stjuardesa [styooardesa]
 stewardess
stol table
stolac [stolats] chair
stolica [stoleetsa] chair
stolni tenis [stolnee tenees]
 table tennis
stolno vino [veeno] table
 wine
stolnjak [stolnyak] table cloth
stoljeće [stol-yecheh] century
stopalo foot
stopirati [stopeeʀatee] to
 hitchhike
straga at the back
strah [straH] fear
stran foreign
strana page; side
stranac [stʀanats] foreigner;
 stranger
strankinja [stʀankeenya]
 foreigner; stranger (woman)
strašan [stʀashan] horrible;
 terrific

stražna svjetla [straJna sv-yetla] rear lights

stražnjica [straJnyeetsa] bottom

stric [streets] uncle

strm [sterm] steep

stroj [stroy] machine

stroj za pranje rublja [pran-yeh roobl-ya] washing machine

strop ceiling

struja [strooya] electricity; current

struk [strook] waist

studeni [stoodenee] November

studentica [stoodenteetsa] student (female)

stupanj [stoopan] degree

stvar thing; cause

stvaran real

stvarati [stvaratee] to make

stvarno really

subota [soobota] Saturday

sudar [soodar] crash

sudoper [soodoper] (kitchen) sink

suh [sooH] dry

suknja [sooknya] skirt

sunce [soontseh] sun

suncobran [soontsobran] beach umbrella, sun shade

sunčan [soonchan] sunny

sunčanica [soonchaneetsa] sunstroke

sunčati se [soonchatee seh to sunbathe

sunčev sjaj [soonchev syī] sunshine

suprotan [sooprotan] opposite

suprug husband

supruga wife

susjed [soos-yed] neighbour

sušenje kose [sooshen-yeh koseh] blow-dry

sušilo za kosu [soosheelo] hairdryer

sušiti [soosheetee] to dry

sutra [sootra] tomorrow

sutra tjedan dana a week (from) tomorrow

sutra ujutro tomorrow morning

suženje puta road narrows

svak, svaka, svako each

svaki [svakee] every

svaki dan every day

svaki put every time

svatko everyone

sve [sveh] everything; all

sve cure [tsooreh] all the girls

sve to all of it

svećenik [svecheneek] priest

sve je uključeno [yeh ookl-yoocheno] all-inclusive

svekar father-in-law

svekrva mother-in-law

sveučilište [sveoocheeleeshteh] university

svi, sve, sva all

svi everyone; all

svi oni [onee] all of them

svibanj [sveeban] May

sviđati se [sveejatee seh] to like

sviđa li vam se ...? do you like ...?

sviđate mi se [sveejateh mee seh] I like you

svijeća [sveeyecha] candle

svijet [sv-yet] world

svijetao [sveeyetao] bright

svijetlo [sv-yetlo] light; pale

svila [sveela] silk

svjećica [sv-yecheetsa] spark plug

svjedok [sv-yedok] witness

svjedokinja [sv-yedokeenya] witness (woman)

svjestan [sv-yestan] conscious

svjetionik [sv-yeteeoneek] lighthouse

svjetlo [sv-yetlo] light

svjetlomjer [sv-yetlom-yer] light meter

svjetlucati [sv-yetlootsatee] flash

svjež [sv-yeJ] fresh; chilly

svinja [sveenya] pig

svo: svo mlijeko/pivo all the milk/beer

svoj one's own; my own; his/her own

svrbež [sverbez] itch

svuda [svooda] everywhere

Š

šah [shaH] chess

šal [shal] scarf

šala [shala] joke

šalica [shaleetsa] cup

šalter za informacije [shalter za eenformatseeyeh] information desk

šampon [shampon] shampoo

šator [shator] tent

šećer [shecher] sugar

šeri [sheree] sherry

šešir [shehsheer] hat

šest [shest] six

šetnja [shetnya] walk

šibice [sheebeetseh] matches

šiljilo [sheelyeelo] pencil sharpener

širok [sheerok] wide

šišanje [sheeshan-yeh] haircut

šiti [sheetee] to sew

škare [shkareh] scissors

škola [shkola] school

školjka [shkolykeh] shell; shellfish

Škotska [shkotska] Scotland

škotski [shkotskee] Scottish

šljiva [shlyeeva] plum

šljivovica [shl-yeevoveetsa] plum brandy

šminka [shmeenka] make-up

šogor [shogor] brother-in-law

šogorica [shogoreetsa] sister-in-law

šok [shok] shock

šovinistička muška svinja [shoveeneesteechka mooshka sveenya] male chauvinist pig

špaga [shpaga] string

Španjolska [shpanyolska] Spain

španjolski Spanish

špeceraj [shpetserī] grocer's

špilja [shpeelya] cave

štake [shtakeh] crutches

štakor [shtakor] rat

štednjak [shtednyak] cooker

šteta [shteta] damage

šteta! it's a pity

štipaljka [shteepalyka] clothes peg

štititi [sheeteetee] to protect

što? [shto] what?

što je? [yeh] what's up?

što je večeras? [vecheras]
what's on tonight?
štucanje [shtootsan-yeh] hiccups
šuma [shooma] forest; wood
šurjak [shooryak] brother-in-law
Švedska [shvedska] Sweden
švedski Swedish
Švicarska [shveetsarska]
Switzerland
švicarski Swiss

T

ta that
tabla čokolade [chokoladeh] bar
of chocolate
tacna [tatsna] tray
tada then
taj [tī] that
tajna [tīna] secret
tako so; like that
tako je [yeh] that's it, that's
right
također [takojer] also
tako-tako so-so
taksi [taksee] taxi
taksi stajalište [stīyaleeshteh]
taxi rank
taksist [takseest] taxi-driver
taksistkinja [takseestkeenya]
taxi-driver (woman)
talijanski [taleeyanskee]
Italian
talk talcum powder
taman dark
tamnomodra navy (blue)
tamo (over) there

tamo dolje [dol-yeh] down
there
tamo gore [goreh] up there
tamponi [tamponee] tampons
tanak thin
tanjur [tan-yoor] plate
tanjurić [tanyooreech] saucer
tapete [tapeteh] wallpaper
tast father-in-law
tata dad
tava frying pan
te [teh] you
tečajna lista [techīna] exchange
rate
tek only; not until
tek je šest sati [yeh shest satee]
it's only 6 o'clock
tek sam stigao I've only just
got here
tekstovna poruka [porooka]
text (message)
tekućina za čišćenje
[tekoocheena za cheesh-chen-yeh]
cleansing lotion
tekućina za pranje suđa [pran-
yeh sooja] washing-up liquid,
(US) dishwashing liquid
telefon [tele)phone
telefonirati [telefoneeratee] to
phone
telefonist [telefoneest] operator
telefonistkinja
[telefoneestkeenya] operator
(woman)
telefonska govornica
[govorneetsa] payphone;
cardphone
telefonska kartica [karteetsa]
phonecard

telefonske informacije
[telefonskeh eenformatseeyeh]
directory enquiries,
information

telefonski broj [broy] phone
number

telefonski imenik [eemeneek]
phone book

telefonsko buđenje [boojen-
yeh] wake-up call

televizija [televeezeeya]
television

temperatura [temperatoora]
temperature

tenis [tenees] tennis

tenisice [teneeseetseh] trainers,
(US) sneakers

teniska loptica [teneeska
lopteetsa] tennis ball

teniski reket tennis racket

teniski teren tennis court

tepih [tepeeH] carpet

tepison fitted carpet

teretana gym

termofor hot-water bottle

termometar thermometer

termos boca [botsa] thermos
flask

termosica [termoseetsa]
thermos flask

teško [teshko] badly; hardly

teškoća [teshkocha] difficulty

teta aunt

težak [teJak] difficult; heavy

težina [teJeena] weight

ti [tee] you

tih [teeH] quiet

tijekom [teeyekom] during

tijelo [teeyelo] body

tijesan [t-yesan] tight

tim with this; with that

tinejdžer [teenayjer] teenager

tipičan [teepeechan] typical

tiskanica [teeskaneetsa] printed
matter; printed form

tišina [teesheena] silence

tjedan [t-yedan] week

tjedno per week; weekly

tkanina [tkaneena] cloth,
material

tko? who?

tlo ground

to it; that

toaletni papir [toaletnee papeer]
toilet paper

točak [tochak] wheel

točan [tochan] accurate

točeno pivo [tocheno peevo]
draught beer

točno! [tochno] exactly!, that's
right!

toner toner

tonik [toneek] tonic (water)

tonuti [tonootee] to sink

topao warm

toples topless

torba bag; handbag

torba za spise [speeseh]
briefcase

tost toast

tradicija [tradeetseeya] tradition

tradicionalan [tradeetseeonalan]
traditional

trajan [tra-yan] lasting; durable

trajekt [tra-yekt] ferry

trajna [trina] perm

trak lane (on motorway)

traka tape

tramvaj [tramvī] tram

traperice [trapereetseh] jeans

trava grass

travanj [travan] April

trave [traveh] herbs

travnjak [travnyak] lawn

tražilo [traJeelo] viewfinder

tražiti [traJeetee] to search; to look for

trčanje [terchan-yeh] jogging

trčati [terchatee] to run

trebati [trebatee] to need

treba mi ... I need ...

treba tri sata it takes three hours

trebao je jučer stići he was due to arrive yesterday

treći [trechee] third

trenirka [treneerka] tracksuit, (US) sweats

trg [terg] square

trgovački centar [tergovachkee tsentar] shopping centre

trgovina darovima [tergoveena daroveema] gift shop

trgovina mješovitom robom [tergoveena m-yeshoveetom] grocer's

trgovina tehničkom robom [tergoveena teHneechkom] camera shop

trgovina zdravom hranom [trgoveena Hranom] health food shop

tri three

trijezan [tr-yezan] sober

trikotaža [treekotaJa] knitwear

trka [terka] race

tromjesječje [trom-yes-yech-yeh]

term

trošiti [trosheetee] to spend; to use

trovanje hranom [trovan-yeh Hranom] food poisoning

trovanje želuca [Jelootsa] food poisoning

truba [trooba] horn

trudna [troodna] pregnant

tržnica [terJneetsa] market

tucet [tootset] dozen

tuča [toocha] fight; hail

tući se [toochee seh] to fight

tunel [toonel] tunnel

tup [toop] dull

turist [tooreest] tourist

turistička agencija [tooreesteechka agentseeya] tour operator

turistički agent travel agent's

turistički aranžman [aranJman] package holiday

turistički ured [oored] tourist information office

turistički vodič [vodeech] tour guide

turistkinja [tooreestkeenya] tourist (woman)

turpija za nokte [toorpeeya za nokteh] nailfile

tuš [toosh] shower

tužan [tooJan] sad

tvoj, tvoja, tvoje [tvoy] your; yours

tvornica [tvorneetsa] factory

tvrd [tverd] hard; stubborn

tvrda stolica [stoleetsa] constipation

tvrde leće [lecheh] hard lenses

tvrđa [tverja] castle
tvrtka [tvertka] company, firm

U

u [oo] in; to; into; at
 u blizini down the road
 u subotu on Saturday
 u najam for hire
 u redu, hvala that's OK
 thanks
 u čemu je stvar? [oo chemo
 yeh] what's the matter?
ubiti [oobeetee] to kill
ubod sting
ubod insekta [oobod] insect
 bite
ubosti [oobostee] to bite; to
 sting
ubuduće [ooboodoocheh] in
 future
učiti [oocheetee] to learn
učtiv [oochteev] polite
ući [oochee] to enter; to get
 in; to get on
udaljenost [oodal-yenost]
 distance
udariti [oodareetee] to hit; to
 knock
udata married (woman)
udoban [oodoban] comfortable
udovac [oodovats] widower
udovica [oodoveetsa] widow
udvarati se [oodvaratee seh]
 to flirt
uđite [oojeeteh] to come in
uganuti [ooganootee] to sprain
ugao corner

ugasiti [oogaseetee] to switch
 off
ugašen [oogashen] off
uglavnom [ooglavnom] mostly
ugodan [oogodan] nice,
 enjoyable
 ugodan vam dan! have a nice
 day!
ugođaj [oogodī] mood;
 atmosphere
ugriz [oogreez] (insect) bite
uhapsiti [oohapseetee] to arrest
uho [ooHo] ear
uhvatiti [ooHvateetee] to catch
ujak [ooyak] uncle
ujesen [ooyesen] in the
 autumn
ujutro [ooyootro] in the
 morning
uključeno [ooklyoocheno]
 included
uključiti [ookloocheetee] to
 include
ukrasti [ookrastee] to steal
ukupna svota [ookoopna] total
ukus [ookoos] taste; flavour
ukusan [ookoosan] delicious;
 in good taste
u kvaru! out of order!
ulaz [oolaz] entrance
ulaz naprijed entrance at the
 front
ulaz otraga entrance at the
 rear
ulaz slobodan admission
 free
ulaz zabranjen keep out
ulica [ooleetsa] street
ulje [ool-yeh] oil

175

ulje za sunčanje [**soo**nchan-yeh] suntan oil

uljudan [**oo**l-yoodan] polite

umak [**oo**mak] gravy; sauce

umak za salatu [**sa**latoo] salad dressing

umirovljenica [oomeerovl-**ye**neetsa] pensioner, senior citizen (woman)

umirovljenik [oomeerovl-yen**ee**k] pensioner, senior citizen

umivaonik [oomeeva**o**neek] washhand basin

umjeren [**oo**m-yeren] reasonable

umjesto [**oo**m-yesto] instead

umjetan [**oo**m-yetan] artificial

umjetnica [**oo**m-yetneetsa] artist (woman)

umjetnička galerija [**oo**m-yetneechka ga**le**reeya] art gallery

umjetnik [**oo**m-yetneek] artist

umjetno zubalo [**oo**m-yetno **zoo**balo] dentures

umjetnost [**oo**m-yetnost] art

umoran [**oo**moran] tired

umotati [oom**o**tatee] to wrap

umrijeti [**oo**mreeyetee] to die

unajmiti [oon**ī**meetee] to hire, to rent

unajmljeni auto [oon**ī**ml-yenee **a**ooto] rented car

unaprijed [**oo**napreeyed] in advance

unuk [**oo**nook] grandson

unuka [**oo**nooka] granddaughter

unutarnja guma [**oo**nootarnya] inner tube

unutra [**oo**nootra] indoors;

inside

uostalom anyway

upala [**oo**pala] inflammation

upala pluća [pl**oo**cha] pneumonia

upala slijepog crijeva [sl**ee**yepog tsr**ee**yeva] appendicitis

upaliti [**oo**paleetee] to light; to switch on; to start

upaljač [**oo**palyach] cigarette lighter

upaljen [**oo**pal-yen] (switched) on; inflamed

upaljeno grlo [**oo**pal-yeno g**e**rlo] sore throat

upomoć! [**oo**pomoch] help!

upotrijebiti [oopotr-yeb**ee**tee] to use

upozorenje caution

upravljanje [**oo**pravlyan-yeh] steering; management

uraditi [oor**a**deetee] to do; to make

ured [**oo**red] office

ured za izgubljene stvari [**ee**zgoobl-yeneh st**va**ree] lost property (office), (US) lost and found

ured za prodaju karata [prod**ī**yoo] ticket office

usisivač [ooseese**e**vach] vacuum cleaner

uključiti [**oo**sklyoocheetee] to switch on

uskoro [**oo**skoro] soon

Uskrs [**oo**skers] Easter

usna lip

uspinjača [oospe**e**nyacha] ski-lift

U

uspjeh [**oo**sp-yeh] success

uspori slow down

usred [**oo**sred] in the middle of; among

usta [**oo**sta] mouth

ustati [**oo**statee] to get up

usuditi se [oos**oo**deetee seh] to dare

uštipak [**oo**shteepak] doughnut

utakmica [**oo**takmeetsa] match, game

utičnica [**oo**teechneetsa] power point, socket

utičnica za brijanje [beeyan-yeh] shaving point

utikač [**oo**teekach] plug; socket

utorak [**oo**torak] Tuesday

uvijek [**oo**veeyek] always; ever

uvredljiv [**oo**vredl-yeev] offensive

uvrijediti [**oo**vr-ye**d**eetee] to offend; to hurt

uz: uz more [ooz m**o**reh] by the sea

uzak [**oo**zak] narrow

uzbudljiv [oozb**oo**dl-yeev] exciting

uzbuna [**oo**zboona] emergency; alarm

uzeti [**oo**zetee] to take

uzletjeti [oozlet-y**e**tee] to take off

uznemiriti [**oo**znemeereetee] to disturb; to upset

uzorak [**oo**zorak] pattern

uzrok [**oo**rok] cause

užasan [**oo**Jasan] dreadful; appalling

uže [**oo**Jeh] rope

V

vadičep [vad**ee**chep] corkscrew

vagon carriage

vagon restoran restaurant car

vakcinacija [vaktseen**a**tseeya] vaccination

val wave

vani [v**a**nee] outdoors, outside

vanilija [van**ee**lya] vanilla

vaš, vaša, vaše [vash] your; yours

vata cotton wool

vatra fire

imate li vatre? [**ee**mateh lee v**a**treh] have you got a light?

vatrogasci [vatrog**a**stsee] fire brigade

vatrogasna služba [sl**oo**Jba] fire brigade

vatromet fireworks

vaza vase

važan [v**a**Jan] important

nije važno [n-yeh] it doesn't matter

važeći [v**a**Jechee] valid

večer [v**e**cher] evening

večera [v**e**chera] dinner, evening meal

večeras [v**e**cheras] this evening, tonight

večerati [v**e**cheratee] to have dinner

već [vech] already

jesmo li već blizu? are we nearly there yet?

većina [vech**ee**na] most (of); majority

vedro bucket; bright

vegeterijanac [vegetereeyanats] vegetarian

vegeterijanka [vegetereeyanka] vegetarian (woman)

veleposlanstvo embassy

veličina [veleecheena] size

velik [veleek] big; great

Velika Britanija [breetaneeya] Great Britain

Veliki petak [veleekee] Good Friday

Vels Wales

velški [velshkee] Welsh

veljača [velyacha] February

venerična bolest [venereechna] sexually transmitted disease

ventil valve

ventilator [venteelator] fan

veselim se [veseleem seh] to look forward to

vesta na kopčanje [kopchan-yeh] cardigan

veterinar vet

vez binding (for ski); embroidery

veza connection

vezice [vezeetseh] shoelaces

Vi, vi [vee] you

video [veedeo] video

vidi! vidi! [veedee] well well!

vidjeti [veed-yetee] to see

vidim I see

vidimo se kasnije [seh] see you later

vijak [veeyak] screw

vijest [v-yest] news

vijesti [v-yestee] news

vikati [veekatee] to shout

vikend [veekend] weekend

vila [veela] villa

vilica [veeleetsa] fork; jaw

vino [veeno] wine

vinograd [veenograd] vineyard

vinska karta wine list

visina [veeseena] height

viski [veeskee] whisky

visok [veesok] high; tall

visok krvni pritisak [kervnee preeteesak] high blood pressure

višak prtljage [veeshak pertl-yageh] excess baggage

više [veesheh] more

više od toga more than that

više voljeti to prefer

vitak slim

viza visa

vjenčani prsten [v-yenchaneh persten] wedding ring

vjenčanje [v-yenchan-yeh] wedding

vjerojatno [v-yero-yatno] probably

vjerovati [v-yerovatee] to believe

vješalica [v-yeshaleetsa] coathanger

vjetar [v-yetar] wind

vjetrobran [v-yetrobran] windscreen

vjetrovka [v-yetrovka] anorak

vlada government

vlak train

vlakom by train

vlasnica [vlasneetsa] owner (woman)

vlasnik [vlasneek] owner

vlažan [vlaJan] damp; humid

voćarna [vocharna] greengrocer's

voće [vocheh] fruit

voćni sok [vochnee] fruit juice

voda water

vodič [vodeech] courier; guide; guidebook

voditi [vodeetee] to lead

voditi ljubav [l-yoobav] make love

vodoinstalater [vodoeenstalater] plumber

vokmen Walkman®

volan steering wheel

voljeti [vol-yetee] love; like

volim ... [voleem] I love ...

volio bih ... [voleeo beeH] I'd like to ...

vosak za skije [skeeyeh] ski wax

votka vodka

vozač [vozach] driver

vozačica [vozacheetsa] driver (woman)

vozačka dozvola [vozachka] driving licence, driver's license

vozarina [vozareena] fare

vozilo [vozeelo] vehicle

vozilo hitne pomoći [Heetneh pomochee] ambulance

voziti [vozeetee] to drive

vožnja biciklom [voJnya beetseeklom] cycling

vožnja kanuom [kanoo-om] canoeing

vožnja u pripitom stanju [oo preepeetom stanyoo] drunken driving

vraćanje novca [vrachan-yeh novtsa] refund

vrat neck

vrata door; gate

vratar doorman

vratiti [vrateetee] to give back

vratiti se [seh] to come back; to go back; to get back

vrč [verch] jug

vreća za spavanje [vrecha za spavan-yeh] sleeping bag

vreće za smeće [vrecheh za smecheh] bin liners

vrećica [vrecheetsa] carrier bag

vrećice čaja [vrecheetseh chīya] teabags

vrh [verH] peak; top

na vrhu at the top

vrhnje [verHn-yeh] cream

vrijednost [vr-yednost] value

vrijeme [vr-yemeh] time; weather

na vrijeme on time

za vrijeme during

vrijeme je odmaklo it's getting late

vrijeme dolaska arrival time

vrijeme polaska departure time

vrisnuti [vreesnootee] to scream

vrlo [verlo] very

vrsta [versta] type

vrt [vert] garden

vrtjeti [vert-yetee] to spin; to revolve

vrti mi se [vertee mee seh] I feel dizzy

vruć [vrooch] hot

vruća čokolada [vroocha chokoladeh] hot chocolate
vrućina [vroocheena] heat
vuci pull
vući [voochee] to pull
vuna [voona] wool

Z

za for
  za dva dana in two days from now
  za Split / London to Split/ London
  za noć per night
zabava party
zabavljati se [zabavlyatee seh] to enjoy oneself, to have fun
zaboraviti [zaboraveetee] to forget
zabraniti [zabraneetee] to forbid, to prohibit
zabranjen [zabranjen] forbidden, prohibited
zabranjen pristup no access
zabranjena prodaja duhanskih proizvoda osobama mlađim od 18 godina sale of tobacco to persons under 18 is not allowed
zabranjeno parkiranje no parking
zabranjeno pušenje no smoking
zabranjeno zaustavljanje no stopping
zabrinut [zabreenoot] worried
začin [zacheen] spice

začin za salatu [za salatoo] salad dressing
zadnji [zadn-yee] last; rear
zadovoljan [zadovolyan] glad, pleased
zadržati [zaderJatee] to keep
zagađen [zagajen] polluted
zaglavljen [zaglavl-yen] stuck
zahod toilet, rest room
zahtjev [zaHt-yev] demand
zahvalan [zaHvalan] grateful
zahvaliti se [zaHvaleetee seh] to thank
zajedno [zīyedno] together
zakasniti [zakasneetee] to be late
  zakasniti na to miss
zaključati [zaklyoochatee] to lock
zakon law
zalazak sunca [soontsa] sunset
zaljev [zal-yev] bay
zamak castle
zamijeniti [zameeyeneetee] to change
zamisao [zameesao] idea
zamrzivač [zamerzeevach] freezer
zamrznuto [zamerznooto] frozen
  zamrznuta hrana [Hrana] frozen food
zanima me ... [zaneema meh] I'm interested in ...
zanimljiv [zaneeml-yeev] interesting
zauzet [zaoozet] occupied
zaova sister-in-law
zapad west
  zapadno od west of

Vr

zapanjujući [zapan-yooyoochee] astonishing

za prodaju for sale

zaptivač glave motora [zapteevach glaveh] cylinder head gasket

zaraditi [zaradeetee] to earn

zaraza infection

zarazan infectious

zarez comma; (decimal) point

zaručen [zaroochen] engaged

zaručnica [zaroochneetsa] fiancée

zaručnik [zaroochneek] fiancé

zasitan [zaseetan] rich; filling

zastava [zastava] flag

zastoj [zastoy] delay

zastoj u prometu traffic jam

zasun [zasoon] bolt

zašto [zashto] why?

zašto da ne? [neh] why not?

zato što [shto] because

zatvarati [zatvaratee] to shut

zatvor prison

zatvoren closed; constipated

zatvoreni bazen [zatvorenee] indoor pool

zatvoreno closed

zatvoriti [zatvoreetee] to close

zauške [zaooshkeh] mumps

zauzet [zaoozet] busy; engaged; occupied

zauzeto [zaoozeto] occupied

za van to take away, to go

zaveži! [zavejee] shut up!

zavisi [zaveesee] it varies; it depends

zavjese [zav-yeseh] curtains

zavoj [zavoy] bend; bandage

završiti [zaversheetee] to finish

zbirka collection; anthology

zbog because of

zbogom goodbye

zbrka mess; confusion

zdjela [zd-yela] bowl

zdrav healthy

zdravica [zdraveetsa] toast

zdravo hello

zec [zets] rabbit

zelen green

zelena karta green card

zelena salata lettuce

zelena paprika green pepper

zeleni karton green card

zemlja [zemlya] country; earth; soil

zemljano posuđe [posoojeh] crockery

zet son-in-law

zgodan pretty

zgrada building

zid [zeed] wall

ziherica [zeehereetsa] safety pin

zima [zeema] winter; cold

zimi in the winter

zimski odmor [zeemskee] winter holiday

zlatar jeweller's; goldsmith

zlatarna jeweller's

zlato gold

zmajarstvo [zma-yarstvo] hang-gliding

zmija [zmeeya] snake

znamenitosti ... [znameneetostee] the sights of ...

znanost science

znati [znatee] to know

znojiti se [znoyeetee seh] to sweat

zoološki vrt [zo-oloshkee vert] zoo

zora dawn

zračna luka [zrachna looka] airport

zračnica [zrachneetsa] inner tube

zrak air

zrakoplov airplane

zrakoplovom by air

zrakoplovna kompanija [kompaneeya] airline

zrcalo [zertsalo] mirror

zreo ripe

zub [zoob] tooth

zubar [zoobar] dentist

zubarica [zoobareetsa] dentist (woman)

zubobolja [zoobobolya] toothache

zvati [zvatee] to call

zvati se [seh] to be called

zovem se Ivan my name is Ivan

zvijezda [zv-yezda] star

zvono bell

Ž

žaliti se [Jaleetee seh] to complain

žalost [Jalost] sorrow, sadness

na žalost unfortunately

žaluzine [Jaloozeeneh] shutters

žao mi je [Jao mee yeh] sorry

žarulja [Jaroolya] light bulb

žbica [Jbeetsa] spoke

žbuka [Jbooka] plaster

žeđ [Jej] thirst

žedan sam I'm thirsty

želudac [Jeloodats] stomach

željeti [Jeletee] to want

želi... he wants ...

želim ... I want ...

želio bih ... [beeн] I would like ...

želite li...? would you like ...?

željezarija [Jel-yezareeya] hardware shop

željeznica [Jel-yezneetsa] railway

željeznicom [Jel-yezneetsom] by rail

željeznički kolodvor [Jel-yezneechkee] train station

željezo [Jel-yezo] iron

žemlja [Jemlya] roll

žena [Jena] woman; wife

ženska odjeća [Jenska od-yecha] ladies' wear

ženski [Jenskee] ladies' (toilets)

žica [Jeetsa] wire

žica za osigurač [oseegoorach] fuse wire

žičara [Jeechara] cable car

židovski [Jeedovskee] Jewish

žilet [Jeelet] razor blade

živ [Jeev] alive

živahan [Jeevahan] lively

živjeli! [Jeev-yelee] cheers!

živjeti [Jeev-yetee] to live

život [Jeevot] life

životinja [Jeevoteenya] animal

žlica [Jleetsa] spoon
žmigavac [Jmeegavats]
 indicator
žohar [Johar] cockroach
žučkasta [Joochkasta] cream
žuriti [Jooreetee] to hurry
žut [Joot] yellow
žvakaća guma [Jvakacha gooma]
 chewing gum

ŽV

Menu Reader:
Food

Essential terms

appetizer pikantno predjelo [peekantno pred-yelo]
bread kruh [krooH]
butter maslac [maslats]
dessert desert
fish riba [reeba]
fork vilica [veeleetsa]
glass čaša [chasha]
knife nož [noJ]

main course glavno jelo [yelo]
margarine margarin [margareen]
meat meso
menu jelovnik [yelovneek]
pepper biber [beeber]
plate tanjur [tan-yoor]
salad salata
salt sol (f)
set menu meni
soup juha [yooha]
spoon žlica [Jleetsa]
starter predjelo [pred-yelo]
table stol
vegetables povrće [povercheh]

can I have ...? mogu li dobiti ...? [mogoo lee dobeetee]
waiter! konobar!
another ..., please još jedno ..., molim [yosh yedno – moleem]
could I have the bill, please? račun, molim! [moleem]

This section is in Croatian alphabetical order:

a, b, c, č, ć, d, đ, e, f, g, h, i, j, k, l, lj, m, n, nj, o, p, r, s, š, t, u, v, z, ž

ajvar [īvar] relish made of
aubergine/eggplant and
peppers

ananas pineapple

bademi [bademee] almonds

bakalar cod

baklava rich cake in syrup
made of thin layers of
pastry filled with walnuts

barbun [barboon] red mullet

brza hrana [berza Hrana] fast
food

batak (pileći) [peelechee] leg
(of poultry)

bečki odrezak [bechkee]
Wiener Schnitzel

biftek beefsteak

biftek tartarski steak tartare

bešamel umak [beshamel
oomak] sauce béchamel

bijeli [beeyelee] white

bijela riba [reeba] white fish

bijeli kruh [krooH] white bread

bijeli luk [look] garlic

bijelo meso breast (of
poultry)

blitva Swiss chard

blitva s krumpirom [s
kroompeerom] Swiss chard
with potato

blitva kuhana boiled Swiss
chard tops

bjelance [b-yelantseh] egg-
white

borovnice [borovneetseh]
blackcurrants

bosanski lonac [bosanskee
lonats] Bosnian hot-pot

brašno [brashno] flour

bravetina [braveteena] mutton

breskve [breskveh] peaches

brizl [breezl] sweetbreads

brodet fish stew

brodet na dalmatinski način
[nacheen] bouillabaisse
Dalmatian-style, fish stew

bubrezi [boobrezee] kidneys

bučino ulje [boocheeno ool-yeh]
pumpkin oil

bundeva [boondeva]
pumpkin

burek s mesom minced meat
in puff pastry

burek sa sirom cheese in puff
pastry

burek s jabukama [yabookama]
apples in puff pastry

but [boot] leg

celer listaš [tseler leestash]
celery

cikla [tseekla] beetroot, red
beet

cikorija [tseekoreeya] chicory

cimet [tseemet] cinnamon

cipal [tseepal] grey mullet

Colbert juha [tsolbert yooha]
clear soup with an egg yolk

cjenik [tsyeneek] price list

crni kruh [tsernee krooH] brown
bread, wholewheat bread

crno ulje [tserno ool-yeh]
pumpkin oil

crvena paprika [tservena
papreeka] paprika (spice)

crveni luk [tservenee look]
onion

čajno pecivo [chīno petseevo]
cookies, biscuits

čokoladna torta [chokoladna]
chocolate gâteau

čokoladno čajno pecivo
[chokoladno chīno petseevo]
chocolate biscuits

češnjak [cheshn-yak] garlic

ćevapčići [chevap-cheechee]
small grilled rolls of minced
meat

ćevapčići s lukom grilled tiny
rolls of minced meat, served
with chopped raw onions

dagnje [dagn-yeh] mussels

desert dessert

dimljen [deeml-yen] smoked

dimljeni bakalar smoked cod

dimljeni sir [seer] smoked
cheese

dinja [deen-ya] melon

divljač [deevl-yach] game

dobar tek! enjoy your meal!

dobro pečen [pechen] well-
done

domaće kobasice na žaru
[domacheh kobaseetseh na Jaroo]
grilled home-made sausages

domaći [domachee] home-made

domaći rezanci [rezantsee]
home-made noodles

doručak [doroochak] breakfast

doručkovati [doroochkovatee] to
have breakfast

drevna hrvatska jela [Hervatska
yela] old Croatian dishes

dunja [doonya] quince

đuveč [joovech] dish made
of meat, rice and various
vegetables

fazan pheasant

feferoni hot chillies

francuska salata [frantsooska]
French salad - mixed
vegetables and ham in
mayonnaise

gibanica sa sirom [geebaneetsa
sa seerom] layered cheese pie

gibanica s jabukama
[yabookama] layered apple pie

girica [geereetsa] whitebait

glavno jelo [yelo] main course

gljive [gl-yeeveh] mushrooms

gljive na roštilju [roshteelyoo]
grilled mushrooms

gorak bitter

gorak okus [okoos] bitter taste

gostionica [gosteeoneetsa] inn,
a type of restaurant where
the food will be homemade
and normally cheaper

gotova jela [yela] set dishes
(items on menu immediately
available)

goveđa juha [goveja yooha]
beef soup

goveđa juha s rezancima
[yooha s rezantseema] beef soup
with noodles

goveđe pečenje [govejeh
pechen-yeh] roast beef

goveđi gulaš [govejee goolash]
beef goulash

goveđi jezik [yezeek] ox

tongue

govedina [govedeena] beef

govedina s hrenom [Hrenom] cold beef with horseradish

goveđi odrezak s lukom [lookom] beef steak with onion

govedska juha s domaćim rezancima [govedska yooha s domacheem rezantseema] beef soup with home-made noodles

govedski beef …

gradele: na gradele [gradeleh] grilled

grah [graH] beans

grah s kuhanim kobasicama [koohaneem kobaseetsama] bean stew with boiled

grah s pečenim kobasicama [pecheneem kobaseetsama] bean stew with fried sausages

grah sa suhim rebrecima [sooheem rebretseema] bean stew with smoked ribs

grah varivo [vareevo] bean stew

grašak [grashak] peas

grašak varivo [vareevo] pea stew

grejpfrut [grayfroot] grapefruit

grgeč [gergech] perch

grožđe [grojeh] grapes

grožđice [grojeetseh] raisins

gulaš [goolash] stew, goulash (Hungarian style)

gusji [goos-yee] goose …

guska [gooska] goose

guščetina [goosh-cheteena] goose meat

guščja jetra [goosh-chya yetra] goose liver

guščji [goosh-chee] goose …

heljdina (hajdinska) kaša [hel-ydeena (hīdeenska) kasha] buckwheat

hladan [Hladan] cold

hladna zakuska [zakooska] mixed hors d'œuvre

hladno predjelo [pred-yelo] cold starter

hrana [Hrana] food

hrana u konzervi [oo konzervee] canned food

hren [Hren] horseradish

hrenovke [Hrenovkeh] frankfurters; hot-dogs

istarski brodet [eestarskee] Istrian spicy fish stew

jabuke [yabookeh] apples

jagode [yagodeh] strawberries

jagode sa šlagom [shlagom] strawberries with cream

jaja sa slaninom [slaneenom] bacon and eggs

jaja sa šunkom [ya-ya sa shoonkom] ham and eggs

jaje [yī-yeh] egg

jaje na oko fried egg, sunny side up

janjeća jetra na žaru [yan-yecha yetra na Jaroo] grilled lamb's liver

janjeća juha [yooha] lamb soup

janjeća kapama braised lamb with spinach

janjeća koljenica [kol-yeneetsa] lamb shank

janjeći ... [yan-yechee] lamb ...

janjeći but [boot] leg of lamb

janjetina [yan-yeteena] lamb

jarebica [yarebeetsa] partridge

jastog [yastog] lobster

jegulja [yegoolya] eel

jela od riba i ljuskara [yela od reeba ee l-yooskara] fish and shellfish

jela po narudžbi [naroojbee] à la carte dishes

jela s roštilja [roshteelya] grilled dishes

jelo [yelo] dish; food

jelovnik [yelovneek] menu

jetra [yetra] liver

jetra na žaru [Jaroo] grilled liver

jetrena pašteta [yetrena pashteta] liver pâté

jezik [yezeek] tongue

jogurt [yogoort] yoghurt

juha [yooha] soup

juha od gljiva [gl-yeeva] mushroom soup

juha od graška [grashka] pea soup

juha od rajčica [rīcheetsa] tomato soup

juha od šparoga [shparoga] asparagus soup

juha od vrganja [vrgan-ya] bolete mushroom soup, porcini mushroom soup

juneći odrezak u povrću s prilogom [yoonechee odrezak oo povrchoo s preelogom] beef with vegetables and garnish

junetina [yooneteena] young beef

kajgana [kīgana] scrambled eggs

kajmak [kīmak] rich creamy cheese

kalorije [kaloreeyeh] calories

kamenice [kameneetseh] oysters

kamenice s limunom [leemoonom] oysters with lemon

karfiol [karfeeol] cauliflower

kaštradina [kashtradeena] smoked mutton cooked with cabbage, potatoes and beans

kečiga [kecheega] sterlet (fish)

keks biscuit, cookie

kelj [kel-yuh] savoy cabbage, kale

kelj varivo [vareevo] stew made with savoy cabbage

kelj s hrenovkama [Hrenovkama] stew made with savoy cabbage served with frankfurters

kesten chestnut

kesten pire [peereh] chestnut purée

kiflice [keefleetseh] sweet filled croissants

kiflice s makom sweet filled croissants with poppy seeds

kiflice s orasima [oraseema] sweet filled croissants with walnuts

kikiriki peanuts

kisele paprike [keeseleh papreekeh] pickled peppers

kiseli krastavci [keeselee krastavtsee] pickled gherkins

kiseli kupus [koopoos] sauerkraut

kiseli kupus s grahom [grahom] sauerkraut with beans

kiselo mlijeko [mleeyeko] sour milk

kiselo vrhnje [verHnyeh] sour cream

knedla [k-nedla] dumpling

knedle od sira [knedleh od seera] cheese dumplings

knedle od šljiva [shlyeeva] plum dumplings

kobasica [kobaseetsa] sausage

kokice [kokeetseh] popcorn

kokice slane [slaneh] salty popcorn

kokice slatke [slatkeh] sweet popcorn

kokošja juha [kokosh-ya yooha] chicken soup

kolači [kolachee] cakes

komadić kruha [komadeech krooha] slice of bread

komadić mesa piece of meat

kompot stewed fruit, compote

kompot od stewed ...

kompot od bresaka [bresaka] stewed peaches

kompot od jabuka [yabooka] stewed apples

kompot od marelica [mareleetsa] stewed apricots

kompot od šljiva [shl-yeeva] stewed plums

konzervirana hrana [konzerveerana Hrana] canned food

kost bone

kosani odrezak [kosanee] minced meat steaks

kotlet chop, cutlet

kotleti na žaru [kotletee na Jaroo] grilled pork chops

kotleti sa šampinjonima [shampeenyoneema] grilled pork chops with mushrooms

kotlovina [kotloveena] pork and potatoes stew

kozji sir [koz-yee seer] goat cheese

krafni [krafnee] doughnuts

krastavac [krastavats] cucumber

krastavci s vrhnjem [krastavtsee s verHhn-yem] cucumber salad with sour cream

krem juha od gljiva [yooha od gl-yeeva] cream of mushroom soup

krem juha od povrća [povrcha] cream of vegetable soup

krem-karamel crème caramel

kremšnita [kremshneeta] squares of custard cream between two layers of puff pastry krepka juha s jajem [yooha s yīyem] consommé with egg

krilce, krilo [kreeltseh, kreelo] wing

krpice s kupusom [kerpeetseh s koopoosom] small square-shaped pasta pieces with cabbage

krpice sa sirom small square-shaped pasta pieces with cheese

kruh [krooH] bread

krumpir [kroompeer] potato

krumpir paprikaš [papreekash] potato stew

krumpir pire [peereh] mashed potatoes

krupica (griz) [kroopeetsa (greez)] semolina

kruške [krooshkeh] pears

krvav [kervav] rare

krvavica [kervaveetsa] black pudding

kuglice sladoleda [koogleetseh sladoleda] scoops of ice cream

kuhan [koohan] boiled, cooked

kuhana govedina s povrćem [koohana govedeena s povrchem] boiled beef with vegetables

kuhane kobasice [koohaneh kobaseetseh] boiled sausages

kuhani krumpir [koohanee kroompeer] boiled potato

kuhano jaje [yīyeh] boiled egg

kuhano povrće [koohano povrcheh] boiled vegetables

kukuruz [kookoorooz] sweet corn

kukuruz kuhani [koohanee] boiled corn on the cob

kukuruz pečeni [pechenee] roast corn on the cob

kukuruzni kruh [krooH] corn bread

kukuruzno brašno [brashno] corn meal

kupine [koopeeneh] blackberries

kupus [koopoos] cabbage

kvasac [kvasats] yeast

lagana hrana [Hrana] low-calorie food

leća [lecha] lentils

lepinja [lepeenya] type of pitta bread

lički kupus sa suhim mesom [leechkee koopoos sa sooheem] cabbage from Lika with smoked meat (layers of sauerkraut and smoked pork or ribs of mutton)

lignja [leegnya] squid

lignje na buzaru [leegn-yeh na boozaroo] squid in savoury sauce

lignje na pariški [pareeshkee] Parisian style squid (in batter)

lignje pržene [leegn-yeh perJeneh] fried squid

lignje punjene [poon-yeneh] stuffed squid usually with parma ham, cheese and olives

lignje s roštilja [roshteelya] grilled squid

limun [**lee**moon] lemon

list [leest] sole

lješnjaci [l-**yesh**n-yatsee]
hazelnuts

losos salmon

lovački gulaš [**lo**vachkee **goo**lash]
hunter's stew

lubenica [**loo**ben**ee**tsa]
watermelon

luk [look] onion

mahune [mah**oo**neh] French
beans

majoneza [**mï**yoneza]
mayonnaise

mak poppy seed

makovnjača [ma**ko**vn-yacha]
poppy seed cake

maline [ma**lee**neh] raspberries

marelice [mare**lee**tseh] apricots

margarin [marga**reen**]
margarine

mariniran [mareen**ee**ran]
marinated

marinirana skuša [sk**oo**sha]
marinated mackerel

marinada od skuša marinated
mackerel

marmelada marmalade

maslac [**mas**lats] butter

masline [**mas**leeneh] olives

maslinovo ulje [**mas**leenovo **ool**-
yeh] olive oil

masna hrana [**Hra**na] high-
calorie food, fatty food

mast pork fat, lard

med honey

medenjaci [**med**en-yatsee]
honey biscuits/cookies

meko kuhano jaje [**koo**hano
yïyeh] soft-boiled egg

mesna jela [**ye**la] meat courses

meso meat

meso divljači [**deevl**-yàchee]
venison

miješana salata [mee**ye**shana]
mixed salad

miješano meso na žaru [**Ja**roo]
grilled meat selection

miješano povrće [**pov**rcheh]
mixed vegetables

mladi grašak [**mla**dee **gra**shak]
early peas, new peas

mladi krumpir [**kro**ompeer] new
potatoes

mladi krumpir s janjećim
mesom [**yany**-echeem] new
potatoes with roast lamb

mladi (kravlji) sir [(**kra**vl-yee)
seer] cottage cheese

mliječni proizvodi [ml**ee**yechnee
pro-eezvodee] dairy products

mlinci [**ml**eentsee] flat savoury
pastry made from flour,
eggs and water

mljevena govedina [ml-**ye**vena
govedeena] minced beef

mljeveno meso minced meat

morska riba [**reeba**] sea fish

morski račići [**ra**cheechee]
shrimps

mrkva [**mer**kva] carrot

musaka od krumpira
[**kro**ompeera] potato
moussaka

musaka od patlidžana
[**patleejana**] aubergine/
eggplant moussaka

musaka od tikvica [**teek**veetsa] courgette/zucchini moussaka

na gradele [gra**del**eh] grilled

na maslacu [**mas**latsoo] in butter

na ražnju [ra**J**nyoo] on the spit

na roštilju [**r**oshteelyoo] barbecued; grilled

na ulju [**oo**lyoo] in oil

na žaru [**J**aroo] grilled

namaz spread

naranča [na**ran**cha] orange

naravni odrezak [na**ra**vnee **o**drzak] plain veal escalope

naresci [**na**restsee] cold cuts

narezak a cut, a slice of something (ham, sausages etc)

nezaslađeno [nezasla**je**no] unsweetened

njoki [n-**yo**kee] dumplings, gnocchi

njoki sa škampima [shk**am**peema] dumplings with scampi

njoki s tartufima [tart**oo**feema] dumplings with truffles

njoki a la formaggio [form**a**djeeo] dumplings with four different kinds of cheese

objed [**ob**-yed] lunch

ocat [**ot**sat] vinegar

odojak [**o**do-yak] sucking pig

odrezak [**o**drezak] steak

odrezak u umaku od vrhnja i gljiva [**oo**makoo od **ver**Hn-ya ee gl-**yee**va] steak in mushroom

and sour cream sauce

okruglice od mesa u umaku od rajčica [ok**roo**gleetseh od **me**sa oo **oo**makoo od **r**ĭcheetsa] meatballs in tomato sauce

omlet s gljivama [gl-**yee**vama] mushroom omelette

omlet s krumpirom [kr**oo**mpeerom] potato omelette

omlet sa sirom [**see**rom] cheese omelette

omlet sa šunkom [sh**oo**nkom] ham omelette

orahnjača [**o**rahn-yacha] walnut cake

orasi [**o**rasee] walnuts

oslić [**o**sleech] hake

ovčetina [**o**vcheteena] mutton

ovčji sir [**o**vchyee seer] ewe's milk cheese

palačinke [pala**chee**nkeh] pancakes

palačinke punjene sirom i šunkom [**poo**n-yeneh **see**rom ee sh**oo**nkom] pancakes filled with cheese and ham

palačinke s čokoladom [choko**l**adom] pancakes with chocolate

palačinke s orasima [**o**raseema] pancakes with ground walnuts

palačinke s pekmezom [**pek**mezom] pancakes with jam

palačinke sa sirom [**see**rom] pancakes with cheese

palenta polenta (side dish or porridge-like dumpling eaten with milk)

papar pepper

papreno peppery, hot

paprika pepper

paprika slatka sweet pepper

paprika ljuta [l-yoota] hot pepper

paprikaš [papreekash] bean or lentil stew with smoked meat

paprike [papreekeh] red or green peppers

paprike punjene sirom [poonyeneh seerom] peppers stuffed with cheese

paradajz [paradīz] tomato

pariški odrezak [pareeshkee odrezak] Parisian style escalope, escalope in batter

paški sir [pashkee seer] cheese from the island of Pag

pašteta [pashteta] pâté

pašticada [pashteetsada] Dalmatian braised beef with chard and potatoes

pastrva trout

pastrnak parsnip

patka duck

pečen ... [pechen] roast ...

pečena patka s mlincima [mleentseema] roast duck with 'mlinci'

pečena piletina [pechena peeleteena] roast chicken

pečena purica s mlincima [pooreetsa] roast turkey with 'mlinci'

pečene brizle [pecheneh breezleh] baked sweetbreads

pečene kobasice [kobaseetseh] fried/grilled sausages

pečene paprike [papreekeh] fried peppers

pečeni kesteni [pechenee kestenee] roasted chestnuts

pečeni krumpir [kroompeer] roast potatoes

pečeni odojak [pechenee odoyak] roast sucking pig

pečenjarnica [pechen-yarneetsa] type of café serving 'ćevapčići' made on the premises

pečeno jaje [pecheno yīyeh] fried egg

pecivo [petseevo] roll, bun

pekara bakery

pekmez [pekmez] jam

pekmez od jagode [yagodeh] strawberry jam

pekmez od marelice [mareleetseh] apricot jam

pekmez od šipka [sheepka] rosehip jam

peršun [pershoon] parsley

piknik picnic

pile [peeleh] chicken

pileća jetrica [peelecha yetretsa] chicken liver

pileća juha [yooha] chicken soup

pileća prsa [persa] chicken breast

pileća prsa u vinu [oo veenoo] chicken breast in wine sauce

pileći [peelechee] chicken

pileći temeljac [temel-yats] chicken stock

piletina [peeleteena] chicken

piletina na roštilju [roshteelyoo] barbecued chicken

piletina u umaku od rajčica [oo oomakoo od rīcheetsa] chicken in tomato sauce

pire [peereh] purée

pire od ... mashed, puréed

pire od krumpira [kroompeera] mashed potatoes

pire od spanaća sa prženicama [spanacha sa perJeneetsama] creamed spinach with French toast

pire od špinata [shpeenata] creamed spinach

pirjan [peer-yan] braised

pita pie made with layers of thin puff pastry with sweet or savoury fillings

pita od jabuka [yabooka] apple pie

pita od oraha [oraha] walnut pie

plava riba [reeba] oily fish

plavi patlidžan [plavee patleejan] aubergine

pljeskavica [pl-yeskaveetsa] large hamburger

pljeskavica s lukom [lookom] spicy beefburger with onion

podvarak roast meat on sauerkraut

pogača [pogacha] type of flat, round bread

pogačice sa čvarcima [pogacheetseh sa chvartseema] flat, flaky buns with crackling

pohan [pohan] dipped in flour, egg and breadcrumbs and fried

pohane jabuke [pohaneh yabookeh] sliced apples coated in sweet batter and fried

pohani kruh [krooH] bread fried in batter

pohani patlidžani [patleejanee] aubergines/eggplants fried in batter

pohani pilići [peeleechee] spring chicken fried in batter

pohani sir [seer] cheese fried in batter

pohani svinjski odrezak [sveenyskee odrezak] pork escalope fried in batter

pohani teleći odrezak [telechee] veal escalope fried in batter

polubijeli kruh [poloobeeyelee krooH] semi-white bread, plain bread

pomfrit [pomfreet] French fries

porcija ... [portseeya] portion of ...

poriluk [poreelook] leeks

poriluk sa svinjskim mesom [sveenyskeem] leeks with pork

poriluk varivo [vareevo] stewed leeks

poširana jaja [posheerana yīya] poached eggs

poslije jela [**po**sleeyeh **ye**la] after
meals

povrće [**po**vrcheh] vegetables

predjela [**pr**ed-yela] starters

predjela hladna [Hladna] cold
starters

predjela topla hot starters

prepelica [prepe**le**etsa] quail

prije jela [**pr**eeyeh **ye**la] before
meals

prilog [**pr**eelog] side dish

prokulice [pro**ko**oleetseh]
Brussel sprouts

pršut [**per**shoot] smoked ham

prstaci [**per**statsee] date-shells
(like mussels)

pržen [**per**Jen] fried

pržen kruh [krooH] croûtons

pržene lignje [**per**Jeneh **le**egn-
yeh] fried squid

prženi krumpirići
[kr**oo**mpeereechee] fried new
potatoes

prženo jaje [**yī**yeh] fried egg

pšenični kruh [**p**she**nee**chnee
krooH] wheat bread

pšenično brašno [**br**ashno]
wheat flour

puding [**po**odeeng]
blancmange-type pudding

punjen [**po**on-yen] stuffed

punjena jaja [**po**on-yena **yī**ya]
stuffed eggs

punjena paprika [**pa**preeka]
peppers stuffed with minced
meat in tomato sauce

puran [**po**oran] turkey

pureća prsa [**po**orecha **pe**rsa]
turkey breast

puretina u umaku od kopra
[**po**oreteena oo **oo**makoo] turkey
steak in dill sauce

purica [**po**oreetsa] turkey

puslice [**po**osleetseh] small
meringues

rahatlokum [rahatlo**ko**om]
Turkish delight

rajčica [**rī**cheetsa] tomato

rajčica s mozzarelom i
avokadom tomato with
mozzarella and avocado,
served as starter

rak/rakovica [rako**ve**etsa] crab

ramstek [**ra**mstek] rump
steak

raženi kruh [ra**Je**nee krooH] rye
bread

ražnjići [**ra**Jn-yeechee] kebab

ražnjići s lukom [**lo**okom] kebab
served with chopped raw
onion

ražnj: na ražnju [**ra**Jnyoo] on
the spit

rebra ribs

restoran restaurant

rezanci sa sirom [**re**zantsee
sa **se**erom] tagliatelle with
cottage cheese

rezanci s makom tagliatelle
with poppy seeds

rezanci s orasima [o**ra**seema]
tagliatelle with walnuts

rezanci za juhu [**yo**ohoo] thin
egg noodles used in soup

riba [**re**eba] fish

ribe, rakovi i školjke [**re**ebe,
rako**ve**e ee shko**ly**keh] seafood

riba na gradele [gradeleh] barbecued fish

ribane tikvice [reebaneh teekveetseh] grated courgettes/zucchinis

ribizle [reebeezleh] blackcurrants

riblja juha [reeblya yooha] fish soup

riblja kost [reeblya kost] fish bone

riblji ... [reebl-yee] fish ...

riblji paprikaš [papreekash] fish stew (made with red paprika, Hungarian style)

riblji restoran fish restaurant

ričet [reechet] thick barley broth with beans

riječna riba [reeyechna reeba] freshwater fish

rizi-bizi [reezo] rice with peas

rizoto [reezoto] risotto

riža [reeja] rice

riža s povrćem [povrchem] rice with vegetables

rižot [reeJot] risotto

rižot crni [tsernee] risotto with cuttlefish

rižot s gljivama [gl-yeevama] risotto with mushrooms

rižot s plodovima mora [plodoveema] risotto with 'fruits of the sea'

rižot s tartufima [tartoofeema] risotto with truffles

roštilj [roshteel] grilled, barbecued

rotkvica [rotkveetsa] radish

rožata [roJata] caramel pudding

ručak [roochak] lunch

ručati [roochatee] to have lunch

ruska salata [rooska] Russian salad

salata [salata] salad; lettuce

salata od cikle [tseekleh] beetroot salad

salata od graha [graha] bean salad

salata od hobotnice [hobotneetseh] octopus salad

salata od kiselih krastavaca [keeseleeh krastavatsa] pickled gherkin salad

salata od kiselog kupusa [keeselog koopoosa] sauerkraut salad

salata od krastavaca [krastavatsa] cucumber salad

salata od krumpira [kroompeera] potato salad

salata od rajčice [rīcheetseh] tomato salad

salata od slatkog kupusa [koopoosa] cabbage salad

sardele [sardeleh] anchovies

sarma stuffed cabbage leaves

sataraš [satarash] egg dish with onions, tomatoes, peppers, served as a starter or side dish

savijača [saveeyacha] strudel

savijača od jabuka [yabooka] apple strudel

savijača od sira [seera] cottage
cheese strudel

savijača od trešanja [treshanya]
cherry strudel

senf mustard

servirati hladno [serveeratee
Hladno] serve cold

servirati toplo serve hot

sipa [seepa] cuttlefish

sir [seer] cheese

sirna plata cheese board

sirni namaz [seernee] cheese
spread

sir s vrhnjem [verHn-yem]
cottage cheese with sour
cream

skuša [skoosha] mackerel

slačica [slacheetsa] mustard

sladak sweet ...

sladoled od ... [sladoled] ... ice
cream

sladoled od čokolade
[chokoladeh] chocolate ice
cream

sladoled od jagode [yagodeh]
strawberry ice cream

sladoled od vanilije
[vaneeleeyeh] vanilla ice
cream

sladoled s tučenim vrhnjem
[toocheneem verHn-yem] ice
cream with whipped cream

slani štapići [slanee shtapeechee]
savoury sticks

slanina [slaneena] bacon

slastice [slasteetseh] dessert

slastičarnica [slasteecharneetsa]
cake shop

slatki [slatkee] sweet ...

smokve [smokveh] figs

smrznuta hrana [Hrana] frozen
food

smrznuti grašak [smerznootee
grashak] frozen peas

smrznuto povrće [povrcheh]
frozen vegetables

smuđ [smooj] pike-perch

soja [so-ya] soya beans

sojino ulje [so-yeeno ool-yeh]
soya oil

sol salt

som catfish

suhe kobasice [sooheh
kobaseetseh] smoked
sausages

suncokretovo ulje
[soontsokretovo ool-yeh]
sunflower oil

svinjetina [sveen-yeteena] pork

svinjski ... [sveenyskee]
pork ...

svinjski kotlet pork chop

svinjski kotleti na samoborski
[samoborskee] pork chops in
garlic sauce

svinjski ražnjići [raJn-yeechee]
pork kebab

svinjsko pečenje [sveenysko
pechen-yeh] roast pork

svjež [svyeJ] fresh

svježe povrće [sv-yeJeh
povrcheh] fresh vegetables

svježe voće [vocheh] fresh
fruit

svježi grašak [sv-yeJee grashak]
fresh peas, garden peas

šampinjoni [shampeenyonee]
mushrooms

šampita [shampeeta] soft meringue between two layers of pastry, whipped-cream pie

šaran [sharan] carp

šaran na roštilju [roshteelyoo] grilled carp

šećer [shecher] sugar

škampi [shkampee] scampi

škampi na buzaru [boozaroo] 'buzara' style scampi (fried in olive oil with onion, garlic and parsley and cooked in wine)

škampi na žaru [Jaroo] grilled scampi

šlag [shlag] whipped cream

šljive [shl-yeeveh] plums

šnita kruha [shneeta krooha] slice of bread

šopska salata [shopska] mixed salad with feta cheese

špageti [shpagetee] spaghetti

špar(o)ga [shpar(o)ga] asparagus

špinat [shpeenat] spinach

štrudli od ... [shtroodlee od] ... strudel

štrudli od jabuka [yabooka] apple strudel

štruklji [shtrookl-yee] sweet or savoury pastry, boiled with curd cheese filling and served with sour cream

štuka [shtooka] pike

štuka sa slaninom [slaneenom] pike with bacon

šumske jagode [shoomskeh yagodeh] wild strawberries

šunka [shoonka] ham

šunka s hrenom [Hrenom] ham with horseradish

šunka s jajima [yīyeema] ham and eggs

tartar-sos tartar sauce

tartufi [tartoofee] truffles

teleća juha [telecha yooha] veal soup

teleća ragu juha [ragoo] veal ragout soup

teleće grudi [telecheh groodee] breast of veal

teleće pečenje [pechen-yeh] roast veal

teleći ... [telechee] veal ...

teleći medaljon u umaku od šampinjona [telechee medalyon oo oomakoo od shampeenyona] veal fillet with mushroom sauce

teleći odrezak [odrezak] veal escalope

teleći paprikaš [papreekash] veal stew

teleći ragu [ragoo] veal ragoût

teletina [teleteena] veal

temeljac od povrća [temel-yats od povrcha] vegetable stock

tikva [teekva] marrow; pumpkin

tikvice [teekveetseh] courgettes, zucchinis

tjestenina [t-yesteneena] pasta

tjestenina s plodovima mora [plodoveema] pasta with 'fruits of the sea'

tjestenina s vrganjima i špekom [**ver**ganyeema ee shpekom] pasta with porcini mushrooms and bacon

torta gâteau

trapist sir [trapeest seer] cheese similar to Port Salut

trešnje [treshn-yeh] cherries

tučeno vrhnje [toocheno verHn-yeh] whipped cream

tuna/tunj/tunjevina [toona/toony/toonyeveena] tuna

tuna na gradele [gradeleh] barbecued tuna

tvrdo bareno jaje [tverdo bareno yīyeh] hard-boiled egg

tvrdo kuhano jaje [koohano] hard-boiled egg

ukusan [ookoosan] tasty

ulje [ool-yeh] oil

umak [oomak] sauce

u umaku [oo oomakoo] with sauce

valjušci od krumpira [valyooshtsee od kroompeera] potato dumplings

valjušci od mesa [valyooshtsee od mesa] meat dumplings

varivo [vareevo] stew

varivo od poriluka [poreelooka] stewed leeks

varivo s mesom meat stew

večera [vechera] dinner

večerati [vecheratee] to have dinner

vegeta® Vegeta cooking condiment

vegetarijanska jela [vegetareeyanska yela] vegetarian dishes

višnje [veeshn-yeh] morello cherries

voće [vocheh] fruit

voćna salata [vochna] fruit salad

voćni kolač [vochnee kolach] fruit cake

voćni kup fruit coupe

vrhnje [verHn-yeh] cream

zabatak upper leg (of poultry)

zagrebački odrezak [zagrebachkee odrezak] cordon bleu veal, cheese inside veal slices, breaded and fried

zapečene punjene rajčice [zapecheneh poon-yeneh rīcheetseh] baked stuffed tomatoes

zapečeni grah [zapechenee graH] baked beans

zapečeni grah s kobasicama [kobaseetsama] baked beans with sausages

zapečeno povrće [zapecheno povrcheh] baked vegetables

zajutrak [zīyootrak] breakfast

zakuska [zakooska] mixed starter (cold meat, cheese)

zec/zečevina [zets/zecheveena] hare; rabbit

zelena salata lettuce

zobeni kolač [kolach] oatmeal cake

zobeni kruh [zobenee krooн] oatmeal bread

zubatac [zoobatats] dentex (fish)

žar: na žaru [Jaroo] grilled

žganci [Jgantsec] polenta, corn hard-boiled into a yellowish porridge-like mush

žumanjak [Joomanyak] yolk

Menu Reader:
Drink

Essential terms

beer pivo [**peevo**]
bottle boca [**bo**tsa]
brandy konjak [**ko**nyak]
  (local variety) rakija [**ra**keeya]
coffee kava
cold hladan [**H**ladan]
cup šalica [**sha**leetsa]
drink piće [**pee**cheh]
gin džin [jeen]
glass čaša [**cha**sha]
half bottle pola boce [**bo**tseh]
ice led
milk mlijeko [ml-**ye**ko]
mineral water mineralna voda [mee**ne**ralna]
red wine crno vino [tserno **vee**no]
rosé ruža [**roo**Ja]
rum rum [room]
Scotch škotski viski [**shko**tskee **vee**skee]
soda (water) soda
soft drink bezalkoholno piće [**pee**cheh]
sugar šećer [**she**cher]
tea čaj [chī]
tonic (water) tonik [**to**neek]
water voda
whisky viski [**vee**skee]
white wine bijelo vino [b-**ye**lo **vee**no]
wine vino [**vee**no]
wine list vinska karta [**vee**nska]

a cup of ..., please šalicu ... molim [**mo**leem]
a glass of ... čaša ...
a gin and tonic, please džin i tonik, molim [**mo**leem]
with ice s ledom
no ice bez leda [**mo**leem]
another beer, please još jedno pivo, molim [yosh yedno **pee**vo, **mo**leem]

alkoholna pića [peecha] wines and spirits

bijela kava [beeyela] white coffee
bijelo vino [beeyelo veeno] white wine
boca [botsa] bottle
brendi [brendee] brandy

crna kava [tserna] black coffee
crno vino [veeno] red wine
čaj [chī] tea
čaj s limunom [leemoonom] tea with lemon
čaj od bazge [bazgeh] elderflower tea
čaj od jagode [yagodeh] strawberry tea
čaj od kamilice [kameeleetseh] camomile tea
čaj od lipe [leepeh] lime-flower tea
čaj od marelice [mareleetseh] apricot tea
čaj od metvice [metveetseh] mint tea
čaj s rumom [roomom] tea with rum
čaj od šipka [sheepka] rose-hip tea
čaj s medom tea with honey
čaša [chasha] glass

desertno vino sweet wine, dessert wine
džin [jeen] gin

engleski čaj [eengleskee chī] English tea

gazirana pića [gazeerana peecha] fizzy drinks
gemišt [gemeesht] wine mixed with mineral water

jabukovača [yabookovacha] cider
jogurt [yogoort] drinking yoghurt

kafić [kafeech] café
kava coffee
kava s mlijekom [mleeyekom] coffee with milk/macchiato
kava s vrhnjem [verHn-yem] coffee with cream
kava sa šlagom [shlagom] coffee with whipped cream
kapuciner [kapootseener] cappuccino
kavana café
kakao [kakao] cocoa

kisela voda [keesela voda] mineral water
klekovača [kleekovacha] juniper brandy
komovača [komovacha] grappa
komovica [komoveetsa] grape brandy
konjak [konyak] cognac
konjak s jajem [yīyem] eggnog liqueur
kruškovača [krooshkovacha] pear brandy

kuhana rakija [**koo**hana ra**kee**ya] mulled brandy

kuhano vino [**vee**no] mulled wine

liker [**lee**ker] liqueur

limunada [leemoo**na**da] lemon squash

lipov čaj [**lee**pov chī] lime-flower tea

loza/lozovača [**lo**za/lo**zo**vacha] grape brandy

mineralna voda [**vo**da] mineral water

mlijeko [**mlee**yeko] milk

mlijeko hladno [**Hl**adno] cold milk

mlijeko toplo hot milk

narančin sok [na**ran**cheen] orange juice

obična voda [o**bee**chna **vo**da] tap water

oranžada [oran**J**ada] orange drink

osvježavajuća pića [osv-ye**J**ava-**yoo**cha **pee**cha] soft drinks

piće [**pee**cheh] drink

pivo [**pee**vo] beer

pivo bezalkoholno non-alcoholic drink

pjenušavo vino/pjenušavac [p-ye**noo**shavo **vee**no/ p-ye**noo**shavats] sparkling wine

prirodna limunada [pree**rod**na leemoo**na**da] freshly squeezed lemon juice

prirodni sok od naranče [na**ran**cheh] freshly squeezed orange juice

promiješati [pro**mee**yeshatee] stir

punjeno u ... [**poon**-yeno oo ...] bottled in ...

rakija [ra**kee**ya] brandy

rakija od jabuka [**ya**booka] apple brandy

rakija od krušaka [**kroo**shaka] pear brandy

rakija od marelica [mare**leetsa**] apricot brandy

rose vino [**ro**seh **vee**no] rosé wine

slamka/slamčica [**slamka/slam**cheetsa] drinking straw

sok od ananasa [a**nanasa**] pineapple juice

sok od borovnice [bo**rov**neetseh] blackcurrant juice

sok od breskve [**bresk**veh] peach juice

sok od jabuke [**ya**bookeh] apple juice

sok od jagode [**ya**godeh] strawberry juice

sok od maline [ma**leeneh**] raspberry juice

sok od marelice [mare**leetseh**] apricot juice

sok od naranče [na**ran**cheh] orange juice

sok od rajčice [rīcheetseh] tomato juice

sok od višnje [veeshn-yeh] sour cherry juice

stono vino [veeno] table wine

suho vino dry wine

šalica [shaleetsa] cup, mug

šalica čaja [chīya] cup of tea

šalica kave [kaveh] cup of coffee

šampanjac [shampanyats] champagne

šipkov čaj [sheepkov chī] rose-hip tea

šljivovica [shl-yeevoveetsa] plum brandy

špricer [shpreetser] spritzer (wine and soda)

travarica [travareetsa] herb-flavoured brandy

turska kava [toorska] Turkish coffee

vinjak [veenyak] wine brandy

vino [veeno] wine

vinska karta [veenska] wine list

viski [veeskee] whisky

voćni sok [vochnee] fruit juice

voda water

voda za piće [peecheh] drinking water

votka vodka

votka s narančinim sokom [narancheeneem] vodka with orange juice, screwdriver

votka sa sokom od rajčice [rīcheetseh] vodka with

tomato juice, bloody Mary

vrč [verch] jug

vrč vina [veena] jug of wine

vrč vode [vodeh] jug of water

žestoka pića [Jestoka peecha] spirits

žličica [Jleecheetsa] tea spoon

207

How the Language Works

Pronunciation

In this phrasebook, the Croatian has been written in a system of imitated pronunciation so that it can be read as though it were English, bearing in mind the notes on pronunciation given below:

ay	as in m**ay**
ch	as in **ch**ildren
e, eh	as in g**e**t
g	always hard as in **g**oat
H	a guttural 'ch' as in the Scottish way of pronouncing lo**ch**
ī	as the 'i' sound in m**i**ght
j	as in **j**ot
J	as the 's' sound in mea**s**ure
o	as in n**o**t
oo	as in b**oo**k
oy	as in b**oy**
uh	'u' as in b**u**t
y	as in **y**es

Letters given in bold type indicate the part of the word to be stressed.

Croatian pronunciation

aj	'i' as in m**i**ght
c	'ts' as in ha**ts**
č	'ch' as in **ch**ocolate
ć	'ch' as in **ch**ocolate
đ	'j' as in **j**am
dž	'j' as in **j**am
ej	'ay' as in m**ay**
j	'y' as in **y**es
lj	like the 'll' in mi**ll**ion
nj	like the 'nu' in **nu**isance

oj	'oy' as in b**oy**
š	'sh' as in **sh**op
ž	's' as in mea**s**ure

When **e** occurs at the end of a Croatian word, it is always pronounced, for example **piće** (drink) is pronounced 'p**ee**ch**eh**'.

Abbreviations

A	accusative	m	masculine
adj	adjective	N	nominative
D	dative	n	neuter
f	feminine	nom	nominative
G	genitive	pl	plural
I	instrumental	sing	singular
L	locative	V	vocative

The Croatian Alphabet

The Croatian-English section and Menu Reader are in Croatian alphabetical order which is as follows:

a, b, c, č, ć, d, đ, e, f, g, h, i, j, k, l, lj, m, n, nj, o, p, r, s, š, t, u, v, z, ž

Note

An asterisk (*) next to a word in the English-Croatian or Croatian-English means that you should refer to the **How the Language Works** section or conversion tables for further information.

Articles

There are no articles in Croatian, no words for 'a' or 'the'. So, for example,

> **stan**

Can mean either 'a flat' or 'the flat' depending on the context. For example:

> **želim iznajmiti stan**
> I want to rent a flat

> **stan se nalazi u centru grada**
> the flat is situated in the centre of town

Nouns

Gender

Nouns can be masculine, feminine or neuter.

Most masculine nouns end in a consonant:

grad	**hotel**	**muž**
town	hotel	husband

but some masculine nouns end in **-o**:

auto	**radio**
car	radio

and some words of foreign origin ending in **-i**, **-e** or **-u** are masculine:

taksi	**intervju**	**pire**
taxi	interview	mashed potatos

Feminine nouns usually end in **-a**:

sestra	**plaža**
sister	beach

But some feminine nouns (mostly abstract) end in a consonant:

ljubav
love

noć
night

Neuter nouns end in -o or -e:

selo
village

dijete
child

more
sea

In the English-Croatian part of this book we have marked all feminine nouns ending in a consonant with (f) and all masculine nouns ending in -i, -o, -e or -u with (m).

Plurals

To form the plurals of nouns, follow the rules given below:

Masculine nouns

Masculine nouns ending in a consonant: add -i

hotel/hoteli
hotel/hotels

Masculine nouns of one syllable ending in a "hard" consonant: add -ovi

grad/gradovi
town/towns

Masculine nouns of one syllable ending
in a "soft" consonant (j, lj, nj, c, ć, č, š, dž, đ, ž): add -evi

muž/muževi
husband/husbands

Masculine nouns ending in -k change the final consonant into -c before adding the plural ending -i:

potok/potoci
stream/streams

otok/otoci
island/islands

Feminine nouns

Feminine nouns ending in -a: change -a to -e

žena/žene	**plaža/plaže**
woman/women	beach/beaches

Feminine nouns ending in a consonant: add -i

noć/noći
night/nights

Neuter nouns

Neuter nouns: change -o or -e into -a

vino/vina	**jaje/jaja**
wine/wines	egg/eggs

A small number of neuter nouns insert **-en-** between the stem and the plural ending:

ime/imena	**rame/ramena**
name/names	shoulder/shoulders

Some neuter nouns insert **-et-** between the stem and the other case endings in the singular:

dijete (child)	**uže** (rope)	**dugme** (button)
djeteta	**užeta**	**dugmeta**

Some nouns exist only in a plural form (and take a plural verb and plural adjective endings) although they are singular in meaning, for example:

leđa	**novine**	**vrata**
back	newspaper	door

Some nouns have an irregular plural:

brat/braća	**čovjek/ljudi**	**dijete/djeca**
brother/brothers	man/men	child/children

oko/oči	**uho/uši**
eye/eyes	ear/ears

The Declension of Nouns

Croatian is an inflected language. This means that nouns, pronouns and adjectives change their endings according to their function in the sentence. There are seven cases:

nominative, genitive, dative, accusative, vocative, locative, instrumental

The NOMINATIVE is used for the subject of a sentence, for example:

> *moj muž* nije ovdje
> *my husband* isn't here

The GENITIVE is one of the most frequently used cases in Croatian. Phrases in the genitive may denote origin and possession (of), for example:

> **kuća mojih roditelja** **on je iz Hrvatske** (nom: Hrvatska)
> my parents' house   he is from Croatia

> **ovo je djelo Ivana Meštrovića**
> this is a work of Ivan Meštrović

It is also used after some prepositions (**od** from; **iza** behind; **bez** without; **blizu** near; **do** until etc), for example:

> **iza hotela** **od Londona do Zagreba**
> behind the hotel   from London to Zagreb

> **kava bez šećera** **blizu kuće**
> coffee without sugar   near the house

The genitive is also used after **evo** (here is), **eno** (there is), and **koliko** (how many), after adverbs of quantity (**nekoliko** some; **mnogo** much; **malo** a little) and nouns of measurement (**kilogram** kilogram; **komad** piece), for example:

> **eno Petra**
> there's Peter

komad kruha	**kilogram šećera**	**litra mlijeka**
(nom: **kruh**)	(nom: **šećer**)	(nom: **mlijeko**)
a piece of bread	a kilo of sugar	a litre of milk

The DATIVE is used to denote direction towards someone or something. It is used for the indirect object with verbs of giving, sending etc, often preceded in English by the preposition "to", for example:

dao sam ključ *direktoru*
I gave the key *to the manager*

The ACCUSATIVE is used for the direct object of a sentence, for example:

ne znam *njegovo ime*
I don't know *his name*

It is also used after some prepositions when they convey the idea of motion or direction (**kroz** through; **pod** under; **pred** in front of; **u** in; **niz** down, **na** on), for example:

idem kroz grad	**idem na krov**
I am going through town	I'm going up onto the roof

The VOCATIVE is used for addressing animate creatures (people and animals), for example:

bok Ivane!	**bok Ivana!**
hello Ivan!	hello Ivana!

In these two examples, the people's names are Ivan and Ivana.

The LOCATIVE is used after prepositions denoting location, for example:

u Splitu	**na plaži**
in Split	on the beach

The INSTRUMENTAL is used to denote the means by which an action is carried out, for example:

on je pokazao *prstom*
he pointed *with his finger*

It is also used for the idea of being together with, or in the company of, other persons or objects, for example:

bio sam *s Nadom* u kinu
I went to the cinema *with Nada*

It is also in several expressions of time, for example:

nedjeljom	**mjesecima**	**godinama**
on Sundays	for months	for years

Here are declension tables for Croatian nouns:

Masculine nouns

	hotel hotel			**prijatelj** friend	
	sing	pl		sing	pl
N	hotel	hoteli		prijatelj	prijatelji
G	hotela	hotela		prijatelja	prijatelja
D	hotelu	hotelima		prijatelju	prijateljima
A	hotel	hotele		prijatelja	prijatelje
V	hotele	hoteli		prijatelju	prijatelji
L	hotelu	hotelima		prijatelju	prijateljima
I	hotelom	hotelima		prijateljem	prijateljima

	grad town, city			**muž** husband	
	sing	pl		sing	pl
N	grad	gradovi		muž	muževi
G	grada	gradova		muža	muževa
D	gradu	gradovima		mužu	muževima
A	grad	gradove		muža	muževe
V	grade	gradovi		mužu	muževi
L	gradu	gradovima		mužu	muževima
I	gradom	gradovima		mužem	muževima

The accusative singular ending of masculine nouns differs depending on whether they are animate (indicating persons and animals) or inanimate. If the noun is inanimate the accusative is the same as the nominative (**hotel, grad**); if the noun is animate it is the same as the genitive (**prijatelja, muža**).

Masculine nouns which end in **-k** change the **-k** into **-c** before adding **-i** or **-ima**. For example:

singular:	putnik		
pl:	**N** putnici	**V** putnici	
	G putnika	**L** putnicima	
	D putnicima	**I** putnicima	
	A putnike		

Masculine nouns which end in **-k** and **-g** change the final consonant into **-č** and **-ž** respectively in front of **-e** in the vocative singular case, for example:

putnik	putniče	traveller
drug	druže	friend, comrade

Feminine nouns

	žena woman, wife		**noć** night	
	sing	pl	sing	pl
N	žena	žene	noć	noći
G	žene	žena	noći	noći
D	ženi	ženama	noći	noćima
A	ženu	žene	noć	noći
V	ženo	žene	noći	noči
L	ženi	ženama	noći	noćima
I	ženom	ženama	noći	noćima

Feminine nouns ending in **-ka**, **-ga** and **-ha** change these into **-ci**, **-zi** and **-si** respectively in the dative and locative, for example:

majka	majci	mother
knjiga	knjizi	book
snaha	snasi	daughter-in-law

Neuter Nouns

selo village, countryside　　more sea

	sing	pl	sing	pl
N	selo	sela	more	mora
G	sela	sela	mora	mora
D	selu	selima	moru	morima
A	selo	sela	more	mora
L	selu	selima	moru	morima
I	selom	selima	morem	morima

ime name

	sing	pl
N	ime	imena
G	imena	imena
D	imenu	imenima
A	ime	imena
L	imenu	imenima
I	imenom	imenima

The noun **dijete** (child) has the irregular plural form **djeca**.
Djeca is declined as a feminine singular noun, but it takes a
plural verb.

Adjectives

Adjectives agree with the nouns they refer to in gender,
number, and case. In Croatian there are two forms of most
adjectives – indefinite and definite. In the English-Croatian section of this book we have given the masculine indefinite form
of the adjective. In general practice the indefinite form is used
when the adjectives are used after the noun, for example:

> **moj novi kaput je *crven***
>
> my new coat is *red*

The definite form is used when the adjective comes before the
noun, for example:

> **moj *crveni* kaput je nov**
>
> my *red* coat is new

To form the feminine and neuter forms of an adjective add **-a** to the masculine indefinite form for the feminine and **-o** for the neuter. The indefinite declension is:

	m	f	n
red	crven	crvena	crveno
new	nov	nova	novo
old	star	stara	staro

The plurals of the adjectives are formed by the addition of the endings **-i** for masculine, **-e** for feminine and **-a** for neuter to the masculine indefinite form.

m	f	n
crveni	crvene	crvena
novi	nove	nova
stari	stare	stara

The declension of definite adjectives

mladi young

singular

	m	f	n
N	mladi	mlada	mlado
G	mladog(a)	mlade	mladog
D	mladom	mladoj	mladom
A	mladi, mladog	mladu	mlado
V	mladi	mlada	mlado
L	mladom(e,u)	mladoj	mladom
I	mladim	mladom	mladim

plural

	m	f	n
N	mladi	mlade	mlada
G	mladih	mladih	mladih
D	mladim(a)	mladim(a)	mladim(a)
A	mlade	mlade	mlada
V	mladi	mlade	mlada
L	mladim(a)	mladim(a)	mladim(a)
I	mladim(a)	mladim(a)	mladim(a)

Examples:

> **došao sam sa svojom mladom sestrom**
> I came with my younger sister

> **to je za moju mladu sestru**
> that's for my young sister

Comparatives (bigger, better etc)

Most comparatives are formed by the addition of the endings
-iji (m), -ija (f) and -ije (n) to the indefinite adjective. In the
plural the feminine ending is changed to -ije, the neuter ending to -ija, and the masculine remains the same:

	singular		
	m	f	n
red	crven - crveniji	crvenija	crvenije
new	nov - noviji	novija	novije
old	star - stariji	starija	starije

	plural		
	m	f	n
red	crveniji	crvenije	crvenija
new	noviji	novije	novija
old	stariji	starije	starija

These words take the normal adjective case endings (see page
232).

ona je starija	**ona je sa starijom sestrom**
she's older	she's with her older sister

To express 'than' use **od** + genitive:

> **ona je starija od mene**
> she's older than me

Other adjectives have the ending -ji, although it is not always
'visible' because of regular consonant changes:

d + j	gives	đ	tvrd	tvrđi	(hard-harder)
g + j	gives	ž	drag	draži	(dear-dearer)
h + j	gives	š	tih	tiši	(quiet-quieter)
k + j	gives	č	jak	jači	(strong-stronger)
t + j	gives	ć	ljut	ljući	(hot, angry-hotter, angrier)

Most adjectives ending in **-ak, -ek, -ok** drop this ending in the comparative:

blizak (fem. bliska)	bliži	(close-closer)
dalek	dalji	(far-further)
dubok	dublji	(deep-deeper)
kratak	kraći	(short-shorter)
plitak	plići	(shallow-shallower)
sladak	slađi	(sweet-sweeter)
širok	širi	(broad-broader)
težak	teži	(hard, heavy-harder, heavier)
uzak	uži	(narrow-narrower)

Some common adjectives have irregular comparative forms:

dobar	bolji, bolja, bolje	(good-better)
loš	gori, gora, gore	(bad-worse)
velik	veći, veća, veće	(big-bigger)
malen	manji, manja, manje	(small-smaller)

Superlatives (biggest, best etc)

The superlatives are formed by adding the prefix **naj-** to the comparative:

bliži	najbliži	(close-closest)
slađi	najslađi	(sweet-sweetest)
bolji	najbolji	(better-best)
veći	najveći	(bigger-biggest)

najskuplji hotel u gradu
the most expensive hotel in town

Possessive Adjectives (my, your etc)

They are:

moj	my
tvoj	your (singular familiar)
njegov	his, its
njezin, njen	hers, its
naš	our
vaš	your (singular polite, plural familiar and polite)
njihov	their

vaš can also be written **Vaš** in the singular polite form.

In the following tables the forms given in brackets are optional alternatives and are especially common in the written language.

The declension of "moj"

singular

	m	f	n
N	moj	moja	moje
G	mojeg(a) mog(a)	moje	mojeg(a mog(a)
D	mojem(u) mom(u/e)	mojoj	mojem(u) mom(u/e)
A	moj, mojeg(a) mog(a)	moju	moje
L	mojem(u) mom(u/e)	mojoj	mojem(u) mom(u/e)
I	mojim	mojom	mojim

plural

	m	f	n
N	moji	moje	moja
G	mojih	mojih	mojih
D	mojim(a)	mojim(a)	mojim(a)
A	moje	moje	moja
L	mojim(a)	mojim(a)	mojim(a)
I	mojim(a)	mojim(a)	mojim(a)

Tvoj and **svoj** are declined in the same way.

The declension of "njegov"

singular

	m	f	n
N	njegov	njegova	njegovo
G	njegovog(a)	njegove	njegovog(a)
D	njegovom(u/e)	njegovoj	njegovom(u/e)
A	njegov, njegovog(a)	njegovu	njegovo
L	njegovom(e/u)	njegovoj	njegovom(e/u)
I	njegovim	njegovom	njegovim

plural

	m	f	n
N	njegovi	njegove	njegova
G	njegovih	njegovih	njegovih
D	njegovim(a)	njegovim(a)	njegovim(a)
A	njegove	njegove	njegova
L	njegovim(a)	njegovim(a)	njegovim(a)
I	njegovim(a)	njegovim(a)	njegovim(a)

Njen and njihov are declined in the same way.

The declension of "naš"

singular

	m	f	n
N	naš	naša	naše
G	našeg(a)	naše	našeg(a)
D	našem(u)	našoj	našem(u)
A	naš, našeg(a)	našu	naše
L	našem(u)	našoj	našem(u)
I	našim	našom	našim

plural

	m	f	n
N	naši	naše	naša
G	naših	naših	naših
D	našim(a)	našim(a)	našim(a)
A	naše	naše	naša
L	našim(a)	našim(a)	našim(a)
I	našim(a)	našim(a)	našim(a)

Vaš is declined in the same way.

moj bicikl	**moja prijateljica**
my bicycle	my friend (female)

u našem automobilu	**u našim automobilima**
in our car	in our cars

There are two forms for the accusative masculine singular in all these declensions. The one identical with the genitive is used if the noun is animate:

vidim naš hotel	**vidim našeg prijatelja tamo**
I can see our hotel	I can see our friend over there

There is in Croatian a reflexive possessive adjective **svoj** (one's own). It is used when the possessed object or person belongs to the subject of the sentence:

uzet ću svoj auto	**uzet će svoj auto**
I'll take my (own) car	he'll take his (own) car

Demonstrative Adjectives (this, that etc)

See section on Demonstrative Pronouns (page 230) as the forms are the same.

Pronouns

Personal Pronouns

sing:	ja	I
	ti	you (singular familiar)
	on	he
	ona	she
	ono	it

pl:	mi	we
	vi	you (singular polite, plural polite and familiar)
	oni	they (m)
	one	they (f)
	ona	they (n)

vi and it related forms can also be written Vi etc in the singular polite form.

The declension of personal pronouns

singular

N	ja	ti	on	ona	ono
G	mene, me	tebe, te	njega, ga	nje, je	njega, ga
D	meni, mi	tebi, ti	njemu, mu	njoj, joj	njemu, mu
A	mene, me	tebe, te	njega, ga	nju, je, ju	njega, ga
L	meni	tebi	njemu	njoj	njemu
I	mnom, mnome	tobom	njime , njim	njom, njome	njime , njim

plural

N	mi	vi	oni, one, ona
G	nas	vas	njih, ih
D	nama, nam	vama, vam	njima, im
A	nas	vas	njih, ih
L	nama	vama	njima
I	nama	vama	njima

As you can see, in some cases personal pronouns have two forms. The long, stressed forms are used for emphasis and after prepositions; the short forms are not stressed, and cannot start a sentence. The accusative of **ona** has two short forms: **je** and **ju**. **Je** is the form which is generally used; **ju** is used only when the preceding word ends in -**je**, or the following word begins with **je**-.

to je za mene	**daj to meni**	**dao sam ih njoj**
that's for me	give it to me	I gave them to her

Croatian often omits the personal pronoun when it is the subject of a sentence, for example:

gdje je?
where is he/she/it?

ne mogu
I can't

n želim
I don't want to

But the pronoun is used for emphasis:

on ne radi, a ja radim
he's not working but I am

You

There are two ways of saying 'you' in Croatian. They are:

ti (sing)   used for addressing a child, a relative, a friend; it is also used between young people.

vi (pl)   used more formally to address a person the speaker does not know well.
It is also the plural form of **ti**. The verbs used are always in the plural.

ti si moj prijatelj
you are my friend

jeste li Vi direktor?
are you the manager?

svo vi ste moji prijatelji
all of you are my friends

Reflexive Pronouns (myself, yourself etc)

There is only one reflexive pronoun in Croatian: **se** (or **sebe**) and it corresponds to all English reflexive pronouns. It is used instead of a personal pronoun when the verb refers to the subject of the sentence:

on se stalno gleda
he's always looking at himself

ja sam se zatvorio u kući
I locked myself in the house

Croatian uses many more verbs reflexively than English. Some are truly reflexive, i.e. **se** refers to the subject:

perem se svaki dan
I wash (myself) every day

Others are reflexive in form only:

bojim se vode
I am afraid of the water

sjećam se mora
I remember the sea

šetali smo se po gradu
we walked around the city

The declension of the reflexive pronoun

There is no nominative or vocative case. The same forms are used for both the singular and the plural:

G	sebe, se
D	sebi, si
A	sebe, se
L	sebi
I	sobom

govorio sam sam sa sobom
I was just talking to myself

Possessive Pronouns (mine, yours etc)

Possessive pronouns have the same form as possessive adjectives (see page 224).

Like the possessive adjectives, possessive pronouns agree in gender, number and case with the noun they replace:

ovi koferi su vaši?
are these suitcases yours?

ovo nije tvoja torba
moja je!

that's not your handbag
it's mine!

Demonstrative Pronouns

These are: **ovaj, ova, ovo** (this); **onaj, ona, ono** (that over there); **taj, ta, to** (that). They are all declined in the same way.

	singular		
	m	f	n
N	ovaj	ova	ovo
G	ovog(a)	ove	ovog(a)
D	ovom(u/e)	ovoj	ovom(u/e)
A	ovaj, ovog(a)	ovu	ovo
L	ovom(e/u)	ovoj	ovom(e/u)
I	ovim	ovom	ovim

	plural		
	m	f	n
N	ovi	ove	ova
G	ovih	ovih	ovih
D	ovim(a)	ovim(a)	ovim(a)
A	ove	ove	ova
L	ovim(a)	ovim(a)	ovim(a)
I	ovim(a)	ovim(a)	ovim(a)

neću ovaj auto, hoću onaj
> I don't want this car,
> I want that one

pošto su ove?
> how much are these?

Interrogative Pronouns

The interrogative pronouns are **tko** (who), **što** (what), **koji** (which) and **čiji** (whose).

The declension of "tko" and "što"

N	tko	što
G	koga, kog	čega, čeg
D	kome, komu, kom	čemu
A	koga, kog	što
L	kom(e), kom	čemu
I	kim(e)	čim(e)

kome si dao?

who did you give it to?

Netko (somebody) and nitko (nobody) are declined like tko.
Ništa (nothing) is declined like što; nešto (something) is also
declined like što, except that in the accusative it has the same
form as the nominative, nešto.

The declension of "koji"

singular

	m	f	n
N	koji	koja	koje
G	kojeg(a), kog(a)	koje	kojeg(a), kog(a)
D	kojem(u), kom(u/e)	kojoj	kojem(u), kom(u/e)
A	koji/kojeg(a), kog(a)	koju	koje
L	kojem(u), kom(u/e)	kojoj	kojem(u), kom(u/e)
I	kojim	kojom	kojim

plural

	m	f	n
N	koji	koje	koja
G	kojih	kojih	kojih
D	kojim(a)	kojim(a)	kojim(a)
A	koje	koje	koja
L	kojim(a)	kojim(a)	kojim(a)
I	kojim(a)	kojim(a)	kojim(a)

u kojoj sobi?

in which room?

Čiji is declined in the same way.

Verbs

Present Tense

There is only one form of the present tense in Croatian and it has three main sets of endings. It is important to know the 1st person singular, present tense of every verb in order to determine the endings (see the list on page 237).

	imati	govoriti	putovati
	(to have)	(to speak)	(to travel)
(ja)	imam	govorim	putujem
(ti)	imaš	govoriš	putuješ
(on, ona, ono)	ima	govori	putuje
(mi)	imamo	govorimo	putujemo
(vi)	imate	govorite	putujete
(oni, one, ona)	imaju	govore	putuju

Personal pronouns are rarely used in Croatian as subjects, except for emphasis (see also page 226):

govorim engleski
I speak English

The verbs are made NEGATIVE by placing **ne** immediately before the verb:

ne govorim, ne govoriš, ne govori etc; **ne pišem, ne pišeš, ne piše** etc:

ne govorim hrvatski
I don't speak Croatian

But the verb **imati** (to have) has its own negative form: **nemam, nemaš, nema, nemamo, nemate, nemaju:**

nemam novaca
I don't have any money

The verb 'to be' (biti)

	(long form)	(short form)	(negative)
(ja)	jesam	sam	nisam
(ti)	jesi	si	nisi
(on, ona, ono)	jest	je	nije
(mi)	jesmo	smo	nismo
(vi)	jeste	ste	niste
(oni, one, ona)	jesu	su	nisu

The long forms are used for emphasis, at the beginning of a sentence or when answering a question with a simple 'yes, I am' etc:

jesi li Englez?	are you English?
jesam	yes, I am
jesu li Englezi?	are they English?
jesu	yes, they are

Some other important verbs are irregular:

htjeti* (to want, wish)

	(long form)	(short)	(negative)
(ja)	hoću	ću	neću
(ti)	hoćeš	ćeš	nećeš
(on, ona, ono)	hoće	će	neće
(mi)	hoćemo	ćemo	nećemo
(vi)	hoćete	ćete	nećete
(oni, one, ona)	hoće	će	neće

*This verb is also used as an auxiliary for the future tense (see page 235).

	moći (to be able to)	**ići** (to go)
(ja)	mogu	idem
(ti)	možeš	ideš
(on, ona, ono)	može	ide
(mi)	možemo	idemo
(vi)	možete	idete
(oni, one, ona)	mogu	idu

The Past Tense

There is only one past tense in common use in Croatian. It is composed of the short form of the present tense of the verb **biti** (sam, si, je, smo, ste, su) and the past participle of the verb concerned. In all verbs ending in -ti (**imati, govoriti, putovati**), the participle is formed by replacing **-ti** with the following endings:

	sing	pl
masc.	ima-o	ima-li
fem.	ima-la	ima-le
neut.	ima-lo	ima-la

	sing	pl
masc.	govori-o	govori-li
fem.	govori-la	govori-le
neut.	govori-lo	govori-la

	sing	pl
masc.	putova-o	putova-li
fem.	putova-la	putova-le
neut.	putova-lo	putova-la

The past participle used agrees in number and gender with the subject of the sentence:

ja sam putovao   I travelled (said by a man)
ja sam putovala   I travelled (said by a woman)

If the infinitive of a verb does not end in -ti but, for example, in -sti or -ći it is best to learn the part participle as you come across it (see the list on page 238).

The verb 'to be'

ja sam bio/bila (I was)   **mi smo bili/bile** (we were)
ti si bio/bila (you were)   **vi ste bili/bile** (you were)
on je bio (he was)   **oni su bili** (they were)
ona je bila (she was)   **one su bile** (they were)
ono je bilo (it was)   **ona su bila** (they were)

Word order

Normally the personal pronoun is omitted and the word order reversed when the past tense expression comes at the beginning of a sentence:

bio sam žedan (said by a man)
I was thirsty

bila sam žedna (said by a woman)
I was thirsty

imao je puno novaca
he had a lot of money

stigle su rano
they arrived early (feminine form)

The negative form of the past tense

The negative form of the past tense is composed of the negative form of the verb to be (**nisam, nisi, nije, nismo, niste, nisu**) and the past participle of the verb concerned:

nisam otputovao	I didn't leave
nije došao	he didn't arrive
nisu jele	they didn't eat (feminine form, plural)

The Future Tense

The future tense is formed from the short form of the present tense of the verb **htjeti** (see page 233) and the infinitive of the verb concerned. For the negative form use the negative form of the verb **htjeti** and the infinitive. For example:

biti (to be)

ja ću biti	I will be
ti ćeš biti	you will be
on/ona/ono će biti	he/she/it will be
mi ćemo biti	we will be
vi ćete biti	you will be
oni/one/ona će biti	they will be

ja neću biti	I will not be
ti nećeš biti	you will not be
on/ona/ono neće biti	he/she/it will not be
mi nećemo biti	we will not be
vi nećete biti	you will not be
oni/one/ona neće biti	they will not be

When the personal pronoun is omitted, the word order changes, the final -i of the infinitive is omitted and the auxiliary verb is added:

bit ću, bit ćeš, bit će, bit ćemo, bit ćete, bit će (I will be etc)
radit ću, radit ćeš, radit će, radit ćemo, radit ćete, radit će (I will work etc)

But verbs ending in -ći do not drop their ending:

doći ću, doći ćeš, doći će, doći ćemo, doći ćete, doći će (I will come etc)
moći ću, moći ćeš, moći će, moći ćemo, moći ćete, moći će (I will be able etc)

The Imperative (Commands, Suggestions)

There are three forms, the second person singular and the first and second persons plural. They are formed by adding the endings -i, -imo, -ite or -j, -jmo, -jte to the verb stem (see page 238).

First set:

govoriti	to speak	govori, govorimo, govorite
kupiti	to buy	kupi, kupimo, kupite
pisati	to write	piši, pišimo, pišite
jesti	to eat	jedi, jedimo, jedite

The second set of ending is used with verbs which have the vowel **a** in the ending of the present tense, and with verbs in which the present tense stem in the third person of plural ends in -j:

pitati	to ask	**pitaj, pitajmo, pitajte**
slušati	to listen	**slušaj, slušajmo, slušajte**
piti	to drink	**pij, pijmo, pijte**
čitati	to read	**čitaj, čitajmo, čitajte**

kupi kruha
buy some bread

idemo jesti
let's go and eat

govorite engleski
speak English

The negative imperative is formed by placing **ne** in front of the imperative:

ne govorite tako brzo
don't speak so fast

Questions

To form a question put the interrogative particle **li** after the verb:

imate li ... ?	do you have ...?
pliva li on?	does he swim?
jeste li iz Hrvatske?	are you from Croatia?

Alternatively you can use use the following pattern:

da li + the appropriate tense of the verb.

| **da li imate ... ?** | do you have ...? |
| **da li pliva?** | does he/she swim? |

Here is a list of common verbs, giving the parts that you will need to know in order to form the tenses given on the preceding pages.

Infinitive		1st person sing present	past participle
biti	to be	jesam	bio
činiti	to do	činim	činio
čitati	to read	čitam	čitao
dati	to give	dam	dao
dobiti	to get (obtain)	dobijem	dobio
doći	to come	dođem	došao
donijeti	to bring	donesem	donio
držati	to hold	držim	držao
gledati	to look at, watch	gledam	gledao
govoriti	to speak	govorim	govorio
gurati	to push	guram	gurao
hodati	to walk	hodam	hodao
htjeti	to want	hoću	htio
imati	to have	imam	imao
ići	to go	idem	išao
izgubiti	to lose	izgubim	izgubio
jesti	to eat	jedem	jeo
kupiti	to buy	kupim	kupio
misliti	to think	mislim	mislio
moći	to be able	mogu	mogao
ostati	to stay	ostanem	ostao
otvoriti	to open	otvorim	otvorio
pitati	to ask	pitam	pitao
piti	to drink	pijem	pio
početi	to begin	počnem	počeo
pomaknuti	to move (something)	pomaknem	pomaknuo
pomoći	to help	pomognem	pomogao
poslati	to send	pošaljem	poslao
praviti	to make	pravim	pravio
putovati	to travel	putujem	putovao
raditi	to work	radim	radio

Infinitive		1st person sing present	past participle
razumjeti	to understand	razumijem	razumio
reći	to say	rečem/reknem	rekao
smijati se	to laugh	smijem se	smijao se
spavati	to sleep	spavam	spavao
staviti	to put	stavim	stavio
trčati	to run (person)	trčim	trčao
uzeti	to take	uzmem	uzeo
vidjeti	to see	vidim	vidio
voljeti	to like, love	volim	volio
voziti	to drive	vozim	vozio
vući	to pull	vučem	vukao
zatvoriti	to close	zatvorim	zatvorio
znati	to know	znam	znao
željeti	to want	želim	želio

jeste li imali …?
did you have …?

je li se kupao/kupala?
did he/she go swimming?

hoćete li se vratiti dogodine?
will you be coming back next year?

Dates

Use the numbers on page 242 to express the date:

prvi rujna [pervee rooyna] the first of September
drugi prosinca [droogee proseentsa] the second of December
trideseti svibnja [treedesetee sveebnya] the thirtieth of May
tridesetprvi svibnja [treedesetpervee sveebnya] the thirty-first of
  May

Days

Sunday nedjelja [ned-yelya]
Monday ponedjeljak [poned-yelyak]
Tuesday utorak [ootorak]
Wednesday srijeda [sreeyeda]
Thursday četvrtak [chetvertak]
Friday petak
Saturday subota [soobota]

Months

January siječanj [seeyechan]
February veljača [velyacha]
March ožujak [oJooyak]
April travanj [travan]
May svibanj [sveeban]
June lipanj [leepan]
July srpanj [serpan]
August kolovoz
September rujan [rooyan]
October listopad [leestopad]
November studeni [stoodenee]
December prosinac [proseenats]

Time

what time is it? koliko je sati? [koleeko yeh satee]
one o'clock jedan sat [yedan]
two o'clock dva sata
it's one o'clock jedan je sat
it's two o'clock dva su sata
it's ten o'clock deset je sati
five past one jedan i pet [ee]
ten past two dva i deset
quarter past one jedan i četvrt [chetvert]
quarter past two dva i četvrt
*half past ten pola jedanaest [yedanaest]
twenty to ten dvadeset do deset
quarter to ten četvrt do deset
at eight o'clock u osam sati
at half past four u pola pet
2 a.m. dva ujutro, dva sata [ooyootro]
2 p.m. dva poslije podne, četrnaest sati [posleeyeh podneh, cheterna-est satee)
6 a.m. šest ujutro
6 p.m. šest poslije podne
noon podne
midnight ponoć [ponoch]
an hour sat
a minute minuta [meenoota]
two minutes dvije minute [dveeyeh meenooteh]
a second sekunda [sekoonda]
a quarter of an hour četvrt sata [chetvert]
half an hour pola sata
three quarters of an hour tri četvrt sata [tree]

* Note the difference here. Croatian for 'half past two/three/four' etc is, literally, 'half three/four/five' etc.

Numbers

0 nula [noola]
1 jedan [yedan]
2 dva
3 tri [tree]
4 četiri [cheteeree]
5 pet
6 šest [shest]
7 sedam
8 osam
9 devet
10 deset
11 jedanaest [yedana-est]
12 dvanaest [dvana-est]
13 trinaest [treena-est]
14 četrnaest [cheterna-est]
15 petnaest [petna-est]
16 šesnaest [shesna-est]
17 sedamnaest [sedamna-est]
18 osamnaest [osamna-est]
19 devetnaest [devetna-est]
20 dvadeset
21 dvadeset jedan [yedan]
22 dvadeset dva
23 dvadeset tri [tree]
30 trideset [treedeset]
31 trideset jedan [yedan]
40 četrdeset [cheterdeset]
50 pedeset
60 šezdeset [shezdeset]
70 sedamdeset
80 osamdeset
90 devedeset
100 sto

120 sto dvadeset
200 dvijesto [dveeyesto]
300 tristo [treesto]
400 četiristo [cheteereesto]
500 petsto
600 šesto [shesto]
700 sedamsto
800 osamsto
900 devetsto
1,000 tisuća [teesoocha]
2,000 dvije tisuće [dveeyeh teesoocheh]
5,000 pet tisuća [teesoocha]
10,000 deset tisuća
1,000,000 milijun [meeleeyoon]

Ordinals

1st prvi [pervee]
2nd drugi [droogee]
3rd treći [trechee]
4th četvrti [chetvertee]
5th peti [petee]
6th šesti [shestee]
7th sedmi [sedmee]
8th osmi [osmee]
9th deveti [devetee]
10th deseti [desetee]

Conversion Tables

1 centimetre = 0.39 inches	1 inch = 2.54 cm
1 metre = 39.37 inches = 1.09 yards	1 foot = 30.48 cm
1 kilometre = 0.62 miles = 5/8 mile	1 yard = 0.91 m
	1 mile = 1.61 km

km	1	2	3	4	5	10	20	30	40	50	100
miles	0.6	1.2	1.9	2.5	3.1	6.2	12.4	18.6	24.8	31.0	62.1

miles	1	2	3	4	5	10	20	30	40	50	100
km	1.6	3.2	4.8	6.4	8.0	16.1	32.2	48.3	64.4	80.5	161

1 gram = 0.035 ounces	1 kilo = 1000 g = 2.2 pounds

g	100	250	500
oz	3.5	8.75	17.5

1 oz = 28.35 g
1 lb = 0.45 kg

kg	0.5	1	2	3	4	5	6	7	8	9	10
lb	1.1	2.2	4.4	6.6	8.8	11.0	13.2	15.4	17.6	19.8	22.0

kg	20	30	40	50	60	70	80	90	100
lb	44	66	88	110	132	154	176	198	220

lb	0.5	1	2	3	4	5	6	7	8	9	10	20
kg	0.2	0.5	0.9	1.4	1.8	2.3	2.7	3.2	3.6	4.1	4.5	9.0

1 litre = 1.75 UK pints / 2.13 US pints

1 UK pint = 0.57 l	1 UK gallon = 4.55 l
1 US pint = 0.47 l	1 US gallon = 3.79 l

centigrade / Celsius   °C = (°F - 32) x 5/9

°C	-5	0	5	10	15	18	20	25	30	36.8	38
°F	23	32	41	50	59	64	68	77	86	98.4	100.4

Fahrenheit   °F = (°C x 9/5) + 32

°F	23	32	40	50	60	65	70	80	85	98.4	101
°C	-5	0	4	10	16	18	21	27	29	36.8	38.3

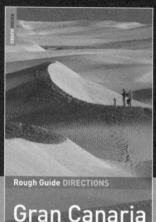